DEX

hitecture

INDEX
Architecture

Edited by Bernard Tschumi and Matthew Berman
Assisted by Jane Kim

The MIT Press
Cambridge, Massachusetts
London, England

A COLUMBIA BOOK OF ARCHITECTURE

INDEX Architecture, A Columbia Book of Architecture

First MIT Press edition, 2003

This book was printed and bound in Canada.

Library of Congress Cataloging-in-Publication Data

INDEX architecture : a Columbia architecture book / edited by Bernard
Tschumi, Matthew Berman ; assisted by Jane Kim.
    p. cm.
ISBN 0-262-70095-6 (pbk : alk. paper)
1. Columbia University. Graduate School of Architecture, Planning and
Preservation. 2. Architecture—Study and teaching—New York (State)—
New York. 3. Architecture, Modern—Sources. I. Tschumi, Bernard, 1944–
II. Berman, Matthew, 1972– III. Columbia University.

NA2300.C65 I53 2003
724'.6—dc21

2002038672

10 9 8 7 6 5 4 3 2 1

Editors: Bernard Tschumi, Matthew Berman
Assistant Editor: Jane Kim; Designer: 2x4, New York City; Copy Editor:
Stephanie Salomon; Interview Transcription: Edward Gunn; Editorial
Assistants: Irene Cheng, Tarry Chung, Steven Clarke, Lucy Creagh

INDEX includes work produced in the Columbia Graduate School of
Architecture, Planning and Preservation (GSAP) Master of Architecture and
Advanced Architectural Design programs between 1988 and 2003, with
an emphasis on the mid-1990s. All interviews were conducted by Matthew
Berman at GSAP between 1999 and 2002. The definitions included in INDEX
are excerpted from Merriam-Webster's Collegiate Dictionary, 10th ed.
(Springfield, Mass.: Merriam-Webster, Incorporated, 1993).

D: Columbia Documents of Architecture and Theory
Volumes 7/8/9 (triple volume)
INDEX Architecture is part of the D: Columbia Documents of Architecture
and Theory series, published with sponsorship from Shinryo Corporation.

The Editors would like to thank David Hinkle and Sonya Marshall for
their help.

pp 10a–11a: Brigit Schonbrodt and Alexandra Ultsch, Advanced Studio V,
Jesse Reiser and Nanako Umemoto, critics, Fall 1999

Contents

Stan Allen

Asymptote–Hani Rashid
and Lise Anne Couture

Karen Bausman

Kathryn Dean

Evan Douglis

Kenneth Frampton

Leslie Gill

Hanrahan + Meyers

Laurie Hawkinson

Steven Holl

Jeffrey Kipnis

Kolatan/MacDonald

Greg Lynn

Reinhold Martin

Mary McLeod

Reiser + Umemoto

Bernard Tschumi

Mark Wigley

At the end of the 20th century, the international architectural scene began to undergo an important change. A new culture, reflecting the contemporary age and its networks of information and mass media images, emerged in opposition to the contextualist and historicist morphologies prevalent during the 1980s. Within the context of this developing culture was an architectural school embarking on a particular experiment. The question asked in the architecture programs of the Columbia University Graduate School of Architecture, Planning and Preservation was: Could a school, by definition an institution in which knowledge is transmitted, become a place for generating new forms of architectural thought? Instead of being influenced by the world of practice, in the way that architectural academies traditionally have followed the teachings of masters from the Beaux Arts to Le Corbusier and others, could a school directly address the culture of its time and influence practice itself?

As a school, we were fascinated by the precedents of the early-19th-century Beaux Arts treatises on architectural theory, the rigorous 20th-century Bauhaus pedagogy, and, different but equally remarkable, the examples of the Cooper Union under John Hejduk and the Architectural Association under Alvin Boyarsky. We nevertheless felt that it was time to consider a new model. After all, we were entering the 21st century; we were part of a world city, New York; and we were at the dawn of the age of the Internet and inextricably linked with global technology and culture.

We also asked another question: How could the School generate an architecture culture that would not be reductive, representing the stylistic or intellectual approach of a single interest group or perspective, but instead reflect and thrive on differences of opinion and conflicting points of view? How could the university—one of the last havens of freedom of thought and expression, with relative autonomy from market constraints and media clichés—be used as a site to develop a serious discourse on the definition of architecture? Our model became the city—the big city, where multiplicity and difference foster complexity and invention.

Architecture and the making of cities include provoking new programs, social practices, spatial configurations, construction techniques, and political priorities. Could these aims, we asked, similarly inspire the organization of the School as a creative epicenter? We decided to try. We invited young architects whose relatively limited practical experience was counterbalanced by boundless talent and energy. We asked them to teach what they knew or wanted to know about. By encouraging the faculty to develop their interests with the help of students, the School quickly became a laboratory for ideas, concepts, and material constructions. Each studio critic was

given sufficient authority and means to pursue his or her ambitions, so
that a multi-culture of competing ideas, discussions, and polemics would
result. The process was accelerated by an unprecedented integration
of new computer tools into design studios, where digital technology was
conceptualized as a mode of thinking about architecture rather than as
a simple drafting machine. Prominent thinkers of a new generation were
invited as visiting theorists to provide a critical framework for these
architectural and design explorations. Finally, the School's production
was disseminated widely, particularly through *Abstract*, an annual
publication of design work.

The School encouraged a way of teaching in which students and
faculty collaborated at the forefront of architecture. For many faculty members, teaching, research, and practice merged into an integrated process
that additionally permitted them to develop their own work in a creative
manner. Inspired by advanced technologies, the studios became a breeding
ground for ideas. They also became a place for polemical discourse in which
conventional definitions of architecture were challenged. Importantly, the
School also tried to encompass a growing dimension of urban experience—
one increasingly located at the boundary between the real and the virtual,
the material and the immaterial, as the digital world assumed an enlarged
role in contemporary city life.

Instead of attempting to translate the School's contribution to this
developing culture into a chronology or a treatise on education, we decided
to document these conversations, topics, and polemics in the form of an
index. Like an index, this book does not summarize or inclusively represent,
but rather points to or "indicates" a cross-fertilization of ideas between
theory and practice and between education and the world of making.

How was *INDEX* assembled? We began by reading the studio briefs
from the early 1990s onward. Subsequently, the studio briefs were examined and edited down to their central ideas. Matthew Berman, then a
student, began a series of interviews with selected faculty members and
studio critics. The result was a document encapsulating each critic's teaching and practice. Recurring words or phrases became the key terms around
which the writings, interviews, and images selected by the critics as repre-
sentative of their studios were organized. We did not aim for ideological
coherence. On the contrary, reflecting the richness of metropolitan diversity,
there are the differences of opinion and multiple points of view that characterize the vitality of the School. A cross-referencing of terms encourages a
multivalent reading of the concepts discussed. It is our hope that, as conceived, *INDEX* will point to the dynamics of architectural discourse today.

Bernard Tschumi, Dean

trend

*On the one hand, Columbia sets trends, yet on the other, many trends are
accepted without question by the students. Is that a concern?*
I am a big fan of trends. People coalesce around certain strategies and
ideas for a period of time, and they spread very rapidly throughout the
School. You can exhaust an entire topic and move on, whereas professional practice moves slower.

THOMAS HANRAHAN

It cannot be underestimated how fashionable Columbia is as a school, and
how important it is that it remains a fashionable school. Oscar Wilde's
dictum that if fashion were not so terrible we would not have to change it
four times a year holds true for architecture right now. I am interested
in the ability of architecture to think through changeability as a conceptual
design provocation rather than as an obstacle to timelessness and good
taste. You can either try to change yourself and your teaching every year,
or you can just build a machine that changes it for you while keeping the
work fashionable. Most other design fields have found ways to build variation and change into their discourse. They think, conceptualize, and theorize change and evolution in a way that architects have yet to do. Being in
such a fashionable place forced me start to thinking about branding, variation, and all of these market issues. The fact that it is a fashionable, global
school, located in New York City, forces the issue even more. You cannot
underestimate the culture of the School and the need for it to stay fresh.
It is a very particular school in a particular place with a culture of
novelty just swarming around it.

GREG LYNN

*There is a tendency within architecture to want to codify one's work as
one is making it, to justify it, to make it a bigger event.*
There is a conversation that goes on at Columbia that can be trendy. I do
not often participate in it because I think architecture only comes from
individuals who lead lives that revolve around a meditation about space; if
your work does not spring from that source, it can be thin. I have a desire
to communicate with the world on my own terms and therefore I want to
set out what those terms are. I am interested in Tadao Ando's and Alvaro
Siza's work and in work that expresses unique positions in the world.
  There is a tendency in the United States to create stars and to follow
trends, and every ten years there is a whole group of buildings that are constructed to represent those fashions. Curves, for example, are very fashionable right now; yet, in a few years that group of buildings will most likely
look dated. They are usually built by contractors who do not quite know
why they are doing what they are doing, but they are doing their best to
simulate the architect's design. We designed a gym for the New York City
Housing Authority called "Wave Line," in which we designed a slightly
curved roof. It took months for us to calibrate the alignments of the various
pieces so that we could get roofing contractors to bid on it.
  I met with a client recently who, after talking to me and reviewing my
work said, "It seems what you are really interested in is to create things
that are timeless, undatable." I responded, "You are absolutely correct."
I feel incredible angst over anything that has a time frame associated with

VICTORIA MEYERS

cross-reference
Directs reader to
related terms

trend · type

it. The trendiness that flies through architecture can be very datable. I prefer to exist outside of it. I am much more interested in the way that an
artist exists in the world in relation to the history of the human race. I am
less interested in whether or not the thing that I do is the most current
thing that would make the cover of a glossy publication.

I also try to bring that out in my students. If I see someone producing
something that mimics what is around them or is fashionable, I push them
to investigate their own unique thoughts and rethink what they are doing.
That is the only way that you can really be in the world as an artist, and
that is what I have always looked for in my students.

see PEDAGOGY, COLUMBIA

guide words
Indicate entries that
fall alphabetically
between the guide
words on the spread

PLATES 4.22–4.23

plate reference
Directs reader to one of
four color plate sections

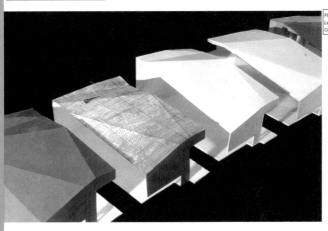

FIG. 149 Hanrahan + Meyers,
*Latimer Gardens Community
Center:* "Wave-Line," 2002.

figure
Identifies author and
project name of
illustration

critic guide
Indicates inclusion of
a particular critic on a
spread. See page 7a
(Contents) for list of
critics. Biographies of
all contributors can
be found at the end
of the book.

type

"The studio attempted a different apprehension of type by multiplying its
conventional limits; or, put another way, by encouraging a fundamental
shift from type understood as the essential, static geometric lineament
underlying building to type as a performative condition. A convergence of
flows; of graduated scales and limits—to which an inscription of type in
the conventional sense represents but an artifact in a field of flux. Complexity theory provides a compelling model and term for this shift. We will
use the theoretical physicist Murray Gell-Mann's theories on complex adaptive systems and his concept of the 'schema' as a structure that exceeds
type."[14]

REISER/UMEMOTO
14. *From Type to Schema:
Westchester County Center,*
Advanced Studio V, Fall 1995

footnote
Gives bibliographical
information for text

type
  1. (a) a person or thing believed to foreshadow another; (b) one having
  qualities of a higher category; (c) a lower taxonomic category selected as
  a standard of reference for a higher category; also: a specimen or series
  of specimens on which a taxonomic species or subspecies is actually
  based
  2. a distinctive mark or sign

Merriam Webster's Dictionary

definition term
Is excerpted from
*Merriam-Webster's
Dictionary*

letter guide

T

A

abstract/abstraction

"Introduction to architecture must be abstract in nature. The site is given only as a generic volumetric boundary, and the student is asked to define space by means of lines and surfaces, working most often in large-scale models. As a consequence of this abstraction, the emphasis is placed on the development of an architectural idea as a spatial and sectional construct and on the placement and passage of the individual subject through these spaces."[1]

THOMAS HANRAHAN
1. Core Architecture Studios, Fall 1994.

"[The studio process] involved a decontextualization, a removing or 'bracketing' of an experience relative to its own temporal context, which in turn initiated the first abstract constructions involving time and space. These constructions made it possible for students to approach the actual site with the beginnings of a spatial and constructional strategy."[2]

THOMAS HANRAHAN
2. Core Studio II, Spring 1996.

abstract

1. (a) disassociated from any specific instance; (b) difficult to understand; (c) insufficiently factual
2. expressing a quality apart from an object
3. dealing with a subject in its abstract aspects
4. having only intrinsic form with little or no attempt at pictorial representation or narrative content

Merriam Webster's Dictionary

see DIAGRAM; DRAWING; IDEA/CONCEPT; MODERN/MODERNISM; PHENOMENON/
PHENOMENOLOGY; STUDIOS, CORE; TEACHING

**aesthetics/
appearance**

Is the aesthetic an a priori condition of formal development?
Form might not always be the first question, but it always has to be the last question. The question of form should never be postponed, avoided, or denied. *Bernard Tschumi often says that it doesn't matter what "it" looks like, and at the "Anymore" conference in Paris in 1999, Peter Eisenman surprisingly reiterated this point by saying, "I don't really care what it looks like. It doesn't need to be photographed."*
It does matter what it looks like. If you are not explicit about form, aesthetics will operate by subterfuge. The blob started as a computer technique that provoked many questions about geometric multiplicity. Not coincidentally, blobs look like something: they are voluptuous; they reflect light iridescently; they are nonuniform. You can see all those qualities in them, and clearly these are the material, formal, and aesthetic consequences of using that tool. Discovering these consequences takes practice, time, accidents, mistakes, and variation.

GREG LYNN

GREG LYNN

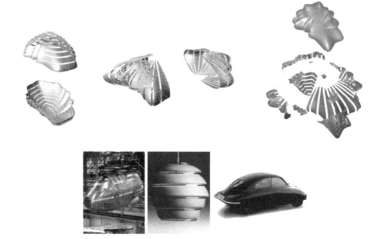

FIG.1 Greg Lynn, *PGLife Showroom*, 2000.

You have said that you do not care what architecture looks like and you have written about the fetishization of aesthetics. What do you mean by that?

I have no aesthetic morality, but the project has to do something. What it looks like has to be embedded in what it does. The visual appearance is there to support the concept and may be quite different from project to project. If you look beneath the surface you will see a number of processes or conceptual strategies that tend to recur in different projects.

BERNARD TSCHUMI

In the early stages of computer design at Columbia there was a fascination with the production of beautiful computer imagery. Did the introduction of computers into the curriculum foster a disproportionate emphasis on aesthetics?

Computers are primarily anti-conceptual. They quickly anesthetize your critical sense, and take over with predictable and seductive imagery. At the same time, if you unleash their hidden conceptual potential and become a tough editor, they are incredible accelerators both in making things and in sharpening concepts.

BERNARD TSCHUMI

If the work has rigor, the questions that it raises are valid questions regardless of whether or not it addresses content or context. Not only do you respect the work, but you encourage it, even if it may not address the questions that you would ask yourself. The intent is always to accelerate the production of ideas. I am against curriculum committees that protect academic disciplines from challenges or questions.

see BLOB; COMPUTER

America

"The belief, more prevalent perhaps in the United States than elsewhere, that every intractable condition can be resolved through a technological fix is surely a delusion. The seemingly endless American commodification of the environment through continuous land speculation and suburban subdivision has all the makings of a long-term ecological and cultural disaster, particularly in view of our automobile dependency, the continual consumption of gasoline and corresponding generation of excessive carbon

KENNETH FRAMPTON
3. Sara Hart, "Technology, Place, and Architecture" (interview), *Architecture* 88, no. 7 (July 1999): 116.

dioxide, among other pollutants. The sticking point is obvious, namely, that to make low-rise, high-density land settlement mandatory while introducing high-speed rail would entail restricting the ideologically sacrosanct freedom of the individual; the corporate establishment enforces excessive levels of energy and land consumption, whether we like it or not. I am not referring to the fate of the traditional city, which is sealed in more ways than one (hence, the urban preeminence of historic preservation), but rather to the need to maintain and redeem in some way the apocalypse of the infinite megalopolis."[3]

From material culture, it is possible to discern certain popular nineteenth-century mythologies that fueled the formation of an American national identity. First developed in visual icons—paintings and postcards—these depictions of place were seminal in formulating conceptions about manifest destiny, individualism, democracy, industrialism, and natural landscape. These images not only propagated a national ideology, but were instrumentalized by the highway system in the strategic placement of overlooks, rest stops, and truck stops. It is ironic that as clearly as these vistas define and unify a national self-image, they defy placement in specific local environments."[4]

see LANDSCAPE; NATURE; STRUCTURE; SUBURB

LESLIE GILL
4. *Scenic Overlook(s): Interstate I-90, Butte, Montana, Brooklyn-Queens Expressway, Brooklyn, NY*, Advanced Studio VI, Spring 1997.

FIG.2 Catherine Jones, *The Evening Redness in the West or the Metallic Frontier, Butte, Montana*, Advanced Studio VI, Leslie Gill, critic, Spring 1995.

architectonic

"The architectonic element is considered as more than an abstract mark characterizing space, but subjected to issues of site, structure, and enclosure. The architectural idea is contextualized and objectified, suggesting that architectural space stands both inside and outside of time, in the realm of both experience and construct."[5]

THOMAS HANRAHAN
5. Core Studio II, Spring 1993.

architectonic
1. of, relating to, or according with the principles of architecture
2. having an organized and unified structure that suggests an architectural design

see PEDAGOGY, COLUMBIA

Merriam Webster's Dictionary

architecture culture

Recently there seems to be a conscious move away from linguistic rhetorical models and toward something that emanates from within the discipline of architecture itself.
Our generation is finally becoming active and getting out from under the shadow of the older generations. The embrace of digital technology, for example, has been experienced firsthand by our generation and that cannot

HANI RASHID

A

be acquired or theorized by an older generation. This has influenced the way we think and work. We all disdain the notion of the architect parading under the cape of Alvar Aalto or propped up by the cane of Frank Lloyd Wright. I am deeply respectful of the preceding generation in terms of the sheer amount of dismantling that was necessary, particularly Rem Koolhaas and Bernard Tschumi. When I see certain other architects lecture, I am too aware of those proverbial oversized round black glasses that are fused onto the architect's face. They may not all be wearing them—instead, it might be a bow tie or suspenders—but it is always indicative of a certain self-absorption and the belief in the heroic nature of the "architect." Today the interesting groups are hybrids, many of them couples and small groups like FAT, Muff, NOX, OCEAN, dECOi, and so on. These groups are systematically getting rid of the older model of modern architect as hero. We cannot walk into meetings with clients or city officials today and seriously contend that because we are architects we wield authority and can produce utopia—nobody buys that. The up side is that we are much freer as a discipline with many more possibilities than those of previous generations.

"Architecture, which historically mirrors the cultural ethos of its time, now confronts an insurgence of desire for the negation of borders, whether delineated by the emergence and proliferation of new information technologies, the flow of capital, or the turbulent geopolitical realignments witnessed since the Cold War."[6]

EVAN DOUGLIS
6. *An Architecture of Waiting*, Core Studio II, Spring 1997.

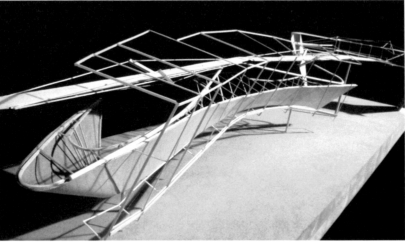

FIG. 3 Jonathan Chace, Core Studio II, Evan Douglis, critic, Spring 1997.

Rafael Moneo has suggested that thirty years ago, students looked to the masters for ideas, whereas today the masters are turning to the students. What would you say as we begin the 21st century?
The studios and schools have changed—everything is computerized and almost no one uses a drawing board anymore. In our office we have 18 people doing what would have taken 25 people to do. The machines are playing an increasingly larger role and therefore you have to think differently. I do not think that machines can ever conceive, so the soul and

STEVEN HOLL

spirit of architecture are still part of an analog process. The conceptual condition that transpires between the brain and the hand begins what later might become a digital process. My watercolor concepts are instantly scanned into and become part of large digital drawings. Now, I am drawing more than ever to keep up with the computer process.

What are architects talking about on the West Coast?
The architects talk about the same things, only with different people in a different milieu. As architecture becomes more global and what Bernard Tschumi terms "deregulated," the place where you work becomes more important for the cultural atmosphere and less important for building a practice. I think this is why New York has so many good architects and so little good architecture.

GREG LYNN

An architect's work, no matter how small, has the possibility of transforming the way we see the world. Strong work makes things a little less certain, opening our minds to different possibilities. A good school simply teaches people to think and produces work that demands thought. And thinking is the product of uncertainty.

MARK WIGLEY

Architecture itself is nothing but a particular way of thinking. We are so quick to read philosophers from outside architecture because we are somewhat nervous and afraid of the truly radical thoughts that are possible through architecture's own operations. The moment you legitimize a design with a ready-made theory, you have taken away much of its strangeness. The sense that you need to quote the latest philosophy to legitimately discuss your architecture is based on the mistaken idea that objects are not interesting. A school should take pride in what architects have learned about objects over the last two thousand years, while simultaneously embracing the idea that we still have never figured it out.

Every good teacher always thinks that the next day, the next student, the next drawing, might add to this long history. The dependence on outside authorities will inevitably remove this sense of mystery. It is paradoxical that we bring in people who find our world mysterious in order to kill off the mystery. Maybe the problem is that we are ultimately afraid of this radical mystery at the heart of our discipline. Or we are simply afraid to communicate to the world how deeply puzzled we are by architecture.

art/artist

"The studio will be a simultaneous study of the physical and optical dimensions of space and its expression through structure. The computer study will be initiated through investigations of light in the work and writings of Robert Irwin, James Turrell, and Dan Graham. Working backward from the particular to the general, a series of vessels will be developed to understand the passage of time in one day. These vessels are then linked to create a sequence, space, landscape, or relationship, which will become the conceptual framework for the museum space."[7]

KATHRYN DEAN
7. Museum for Contemporary Sculpture, Advanced Studio IV, Spring 2000.

PLATE 1.01

As an architect you are attuned to abstract art and you have a public that is not educated about that art. Unfortunately, our culture does not support

VICTORIA MEYERS

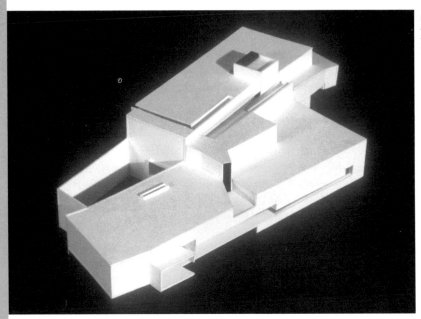

FIG. 4 Mike Yung, *Day Space: Museum for Contemporary Sculpture*, Advanced Studio IV, Kathryn Dean, critic, Spring 1997.

the kinds of investigations that go on in the studios at Columbia, for example. There is no connection between the life that the students will lead postgraduation and the life that the School establishes for them in the studio. I chose to pursue a creative life and paid a price for that pursuit. Most people will not want to pay that price. Students often have this sense of, "I am devoting my life to this. I am giving it my all." I always say to them, "No, I devoted my life to it. I gave it my all and you are a student and you are looking into the window of my life, but I do not know that you are going to stay with it because this life," as Steven Holl has said many times, "is like choosing the life of a monk." If you do not want that life and you are not willing to invest that sort of energy, you have to leave it or it will elude you. To be an artist requires that you have a vision and you have to recognize that you might go through your life without anyone ever recognizing the validity of that vision. Vincent van Gogh, for example, had a vision about life that he expressed in his paintings. He never made money from the paintings when he was alive yet they are probably the most valued paintings in the Western world today. You are dealing with ideas that are placed into the world through the visual medium of space, which is even more complex than painting. If you are going to do work of any value, it has to spring from a unique and determined path and that can be a very lonely experience.

see LIGHT; MUSEUM; TREND

artifice

"A depleted postindustrial center, Butte [Montana] remains an ideological testament to the schism between artifice and nature. The ever-expanding need for minerals has scarred the surrounding grounds, forcing mine tailings and run-off down toward I-90, a constant contaminated zone. Heroic, expansive, and deadly, it is the impermeable threshold between city and highway."[8]

LESLIE GILL
8. *Scenic Overlook(s): Interstate I-90, Butte, Montana, Brooklyn-Queens Expressway, Brooklyn, NY*, Advanced Studio VI, Spring 1997.

artifice

Merriam Webster's Dictionary

1. (a) clever or artful skill; (b) an ingenious device or expedient
2. (a) an artful stratagem; (b) false or insincere behavior

author

How has the role of the author changed over time? Do buildings still point back to their author?

Peter Eisenman may set up an apparently objective series of transformational operations, but he knows exactly the result he desires, so he is functioning as much as an author as Frank Gehry is. Eisenman may be designing the process instead of designing the object, but he is designing the process in order to achieve a certain result. We have moved beyond those questions and discussions, which in part has to do with an awareness of the potential complexity of those issues. The hand of the author can be visible, but there are other effects that are at work as well.

STAN ALLEN

Can we look at an Asymptote project and say, "That is an Asymptote project"?

I am thinking back to a very important subway ride I had from Columbia University when I first started teaching. I was twenty-nine years old and I happened to be with a more established architect who also once was a twenty-nine year-old upstart at the School. He turned to me and said, "Hani, if you want to make it in this field, you have to do what Rem told me to do—you need to imitate yourself." I remember sitting there thinking, "Okay, impossible." I realized my response was critical in thinking about a trajectory for both our practice and my teaching methodology, which were only beginning to form.

HANI RASHID

One of the effects of the fetishization of the computer as author has been to reinforce a bubble around the discipline. The further internalization of the discipline displaces the author as a point of contact between the object and the world. Because the author is both a designer, a producer, and a political agent, the attempt to project that subjectivity onto the computer is very important.

REINHOLD MARTIN

The author clearly did not die with the death of the author. For example, signature architects, many of whom have been identified with the project of killing off the author, turn out to be just one more brand.

The younger generation is very deliberate about refusing authorship.

Right, the computer made me do it. Anybody who understands computing knows that computing is full of authorship, we just have to know what software is. Software is a code that is written by authors. You displace the authorship onto the software, which itself is authored.

REINHOLD MARTIN

The idea of washing one's hands of the failures of modernism is still playing itself out, and there have been naive attempts to discard the sense of authorship that came with it.

There is a historical discussion about the advent of the author as an individual who develops work, and then there is the question of whether the author ever existed at all. I do not believe he or she ever existed,

JESSE REISER

A

which gives an openness to the architecture and to the discourse. The author was constituted as a monolithic entity and soul, and it became solipsistic, where no one could recognize anything in common. It was personalized and closed. Now, it is about a commonality and participation in the growth of projects, and the author is not always important in that respect. Ego, will, and desire are still there.

see CITY; COLLAGE; INDEX; PROCESS

authority

see ARCHITECTURE CULTURE; COMPUTER

autoscape

"Quixotic in its vision for the future, [the network of highways] is understood today through the clarity of its formal and programmatic continuity. The implied benefits of leisure, tourism, and suburban expansion, so important to its implementation, have diminished. The autoscape has become a relic, generally used and understood for only a portion of its potential. As the aging infrastructure is rebuilt and maintained, the interstitial space of the roadside de/attraction presents a potential for invention, the meeting place of the known and the unknown, the tourist and the resident."[9]

LESLIE GILL
9. *Scenic Overlook(s): Interstate I-90, Butte, Montana, Brooklyn-Queens Expressway, Brooklyn, NY*, Advanced Studio VI, Spring 1997.

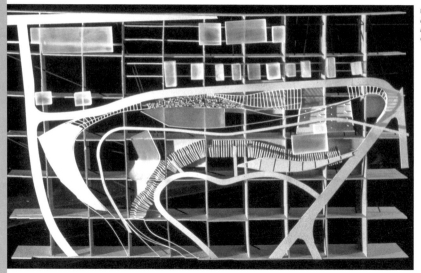

FIG. 5 John Kim, *Anaconda Research, Hastings-on-Hudson, NY*, Advanced Studio VI, Leslie Gill, critic, Spring 1998.

B

biology

"Biology and photography are both concerned with relaying information. Biology is the study of successive changes in genetic information and matter over time. Biotechnology allows for the investigation and manipulation of genetic material, sometimes resulting in the creation of new species. Photography is a traditional technique for cataloguing information with the aid of a chemical process. Given that a new animal species car be 'created' with the manipulation of genetic matter, we will seek to reorganize biological information using procedures of photographic manipulation. A geneticist's model is 'operative' insofar as it enables man to deliberately interfere and work toward desirable 'natural' organic mutations. How can the geneticist's model of information organization be used to design morphological structures that effect a realignment of borders, territories, and habitation for animals and man?"[1]

KAREN BAUSMAN
1. *Zoo*, Advanced Studio V, Fall 1997.

"By examining the anatomical behavior of a series of flying species, each student set out to identify clues to the mysterious nature of flight. Biological models served as paradigmatic structures for the creation of a new architecture."[2]

EVAN DOUGLIS
2. *Foreign/Domestic*, Core Studio II, Spring 1995.

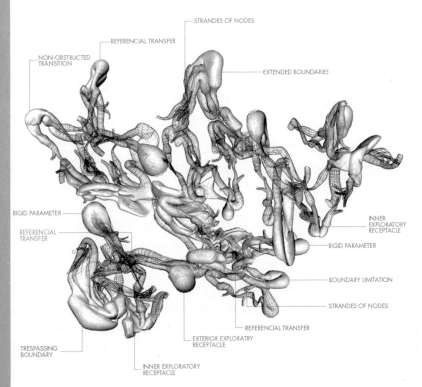

FIG. 6 Jun Kumazawa, *Autogenic Structures: Center for Contemporary Arts, Rome*, Advanced Studio VI, Evan Douglis, critic, Spring 2000.

STRANDES OF NODES

REFERENCIAL TRANSFER

NON-OBSTRUCTED TRANSITION

EXTENDED BOUNDARIES

RIGID PARAMETER

REFERENCIAL TRANSFER

INNER EXPLORATORY RECEPTACLE

RIGID PARAMETER

BOUNDARY LIMITATION

STRANDES OF NODES

REFERENCIAL TRANSFER

TRESPASSING BOUNDARY

EXTERIOR EXPLORATORY RECEPTACLE

INNER EXPLORATORY RECEPTACLE

biology

Merriam Webster's Dictionary

1. a branch of knowledge that deals with living organisms and vital processes
2. (a) the plant and animal life of a region or environment; (b) the life processes, especially of an organism or group

see COMPUTER; ORGANIC/ORGANICISM

blob

"With few exceptions, the recent projects that make use of topological surfaces do so for the development of complex roof forms, and roofs, however programmatically complex, are still in the end just roofs. [The roof projects have sometimes invited overly hasty responses by critics.] Isn't this just the 1960s all over again? Isn't this more or less Buckminster Fuller redux? Until blob organizations develop beyond the prototype of the shed, they will remain open to such accusations."[3]

GREG LYNN
3. "Blobs (or Why Tectonics Is Square and Topology Is Groovy)," *ANY* 14 (1996): 60.

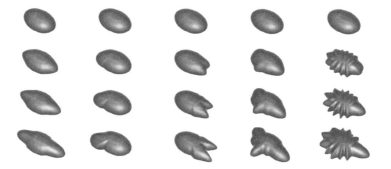

FIG. 7 Greg Lynn, *PGLife Showroom*, 2000.

"Blobs constitute a formal intervention in contemporary discussions of tectonics. That is, blobs intervene on the level of form, but they promise to seep into those gaps in representation where the particular and the general have been forced to reconcile—not to suture those gaps with their sticky surfaces but to call attention to the necessary existence of gaps in representation. Blobs suggest alternative strategies of structural organization and construction that provide intricate and complex new ways of relating the homogeneous or general to the heterogeneous or particular.... [A] blob is a gelatinous surface with no depth; its interior and exterior are continuous.... The term *blob* connotes a thing which is neither singular nor multiple but an intelligence that behaves as if it were singular and networked but in its form can become virtually infinitely multiplied and distributed."[4]

4. Ibid., 58–59.

"[I]n blob modeling, objects are defined by monad-like primitives with internal forces of attraction and mass. Unlike a conventional geometric primitive such as a sphere, which has its own autonomous organization, a meta-ball is defined in relation to other objects. Its center, surface area, mass, and organization are determined by other fields of influence.... The surfaces are surrounded by two halos of relational influence, one defining a zone of fusion, the other defining a zone of inflection. When two or more meta-balls are related to one another, given the proximity of their halos, they can either mutually redefine their respective surfaces based on their particular gravitational properties or they can fuse into one contiguous surface defined not

5. Ibid., 59–60.

by the summation or average of their surfaces and gravities but instead by the interactions of their respective centers and zones of inflection and fusion. A meta-ball aggregate is defined as a single surface whose contours result from the interaction and assemblage of the multiple internal fields defining it."[5]

"Blob" architecture has been criticized by the architectural media for being nothing more than a novel aesthetic.
First, I am happy to have things debased and popularized these days, as the disdain for the popular is one quality of architects that I am eager to shed. I understand the aesthetics of surfaces. Architecture works at several levels, one of which is the aesthetic. I would never deny that blob architecture has distinct shapes, mostly due to geometry. The medium that I use to design and teach is curved. Even a cube is made of curves, just straight curves, and once it is inflected these curves are expressed.
see AESTHETICS/APPEARANCE; COMPLEXITY

GREG LYNN

body

"The semester will be divided into three sections, each concentrating on a condition of enclosure. The first two investigations will be short problems that focus on escalating scale and the human body. During the remainder of the semester, individual students will formulate programs that address the nature of discipline as an architectural space of production. Prisons, hospitals, schools, monasteries, convents, and military barracks are institutions of discipline, enforcing methods that enable the meticulous control of the operations of the body, both collectively and individually."[6]

KAREN BAUSMAN
6. *Eastern State Penitentiary: Discipline and the Architectural Space of Production,* Advanced Studio V, Fall 1994.

"Aimed at a natural ground of discovery, the studio encouraged speculation in the following issues:
–Re-examination of 'program' as primary structure of thought
–Phenomenological analysis as strategy to recover the 'body's recollection of being.'"[7]

EVAN DOUGLIS
7. Core Studio II, Spring 1993.

"The program questions the nature of interaction between built space and orderly/disorderly sensory perception of the body while offering an opportunity to understand and subvert established sensory codes. The therapy will involve the body, architectural space/form, and perceptual mediators."[8]

SULAN KOLATAN
8. *Rehabilitative Institute for the Study of Perceptual Disorders,* Advanced Studio IV, Spring 1992.

"The body will figure as a locus . . . The literal body—its weight, its impress, its mobility, its multiplicitous affects—is less a definition than an extended and infinitely extensible set of potentialities."[9]

REISER/UMEMOTO
9. *Architecture "One to One,"* Advanced Studio, Summer 1996.

body
    1. (a) the main part of a plant or animal body especially as distinguished from limbs and head; (b) the main, central, or principal part
    2. the organized physical substance of an animal or plant either living or dead
    3. (a) a mass of matter distinct from other masses; (b) something that embodies or gives concrete reality to a thing
see CONFINEMENT; EXCAVATION; IMPURITY; LIGHT

Merriam Webster's Dictionary

B

boundary

"Area Rule: rather than follow the strict linearity of the given system and string together a series of isolated, discrete architectural objects, we have developed the interventions on the basis of existing property lines, articulated surfaces, and contiguous areas. Surfaces fold up and form structures, blurring the strict division of architecture and landscape."[10]

STAN ALLEN
REISER/UMEMOTO
10. "RAAUm: Croton
Aqueduct," *Architectural Design*
63, no. 3–4 (March/April 1993):
86–89.

"The ubiquitous presence of electronic surveillance technologies obliterates the necessity of a spatially fixed relation between the 'observation center' and the observed. The observation center is 'central' only in that it is the place of confluence of communication networks. Similarly, the electronic monitor transgresses the physical boundaries of the building by screening interior and exterior side by side, rendering them apparently equal and interchangeable."[11]

SULAN KOLATAN
11. *NYPD Police Station:
Avenue of the Finest*, Advanced
Studio V, Fall 1995.

see ABSTRACT/ABSTRACTION; FRONTIER/EDGE/MARGIN; STUDIO/PRACTICE

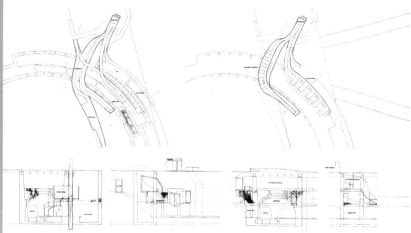

FIG. 8 Terry Surjan, *Police Headquarters, Avenue of the Finest*, Advanced Studio V, Sulan Kolatan, critic, Spring 1993.

building/ construction

I would like to think of building in a more abstract sense, as a state of "evolving." In other words, how have the questions I have set out to pursue as an educator and a maker offered me insights into the complexity of architecture as a discipline? Since there is obviously a symbiotic relationship between my activities within the academic studios and my own architectural production, it is inevitable that the notion of building resides somewhere between the material and immaterial state. The challenge is to find a balance so that they are able to inform one another continually.

    My role as director of the architecture galleries at Columbia has afforded me a unique opportunity to extend some of my interests within the arena of exhibition design. Although some projects have more explicitly demonstrated my own ideological interests related to unpredictable systems of growth—*Liquid Assets*, for example—in every case the programmatic intentions of the exhibition material demanded the reevaluation of accepted exhibition protocol.

EVAN DOUGLIS

What does building mean to you?
I want to build spaces that take people outside of the world of architecture. Building is like war. You can have an idea but you have to convince people

STEVEN HOLL

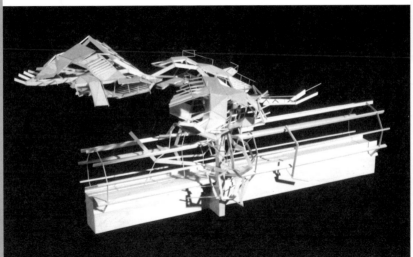

FIG. 9 Robert Holton, *An
Architecture of Waiting*, Core
Studio II, Evan Douglis, critic,
Spring 1997.

to follow you and you have to get the material and proportions correct. Whenever a good building goes up, we should all go and praise the hell out of it because it is so hard to put up a good building! Look at Manhattan— there are hardly any good buildings done in the very recent past. All these talented people here and we have to return to Roche Dinkeloo's 1967 Ford Foundation, Saarinen's 1963 CBS Building, or Wright's 1959 Guggenheim Museum. It is a sad state of affairs for a city like New York, a supposed cultural capital. I have one built project in Manhattan. It's the Storefront for Art and Architecture, where the inside becomes the outside. It was built for $55,000. Vito Acconci and I did it for free because we wanted to build something in New York.

When we first started working on the O.K. Apartment, most of the reactions were, "You can't build that," and the funny part is even after it was built, people still said you can't build it. When we present it in lectures, we go through the computer renderings and process work and show the built work, and quite often the first question is, "So when will it go under construction?" Model making and construction methods are radically different now.

WILLIAM MACDONALD

You have said that you are no longer dealing with the technology of construction but the construction of technology. At the dawn of the Internet age this seemed to be true. Do you still think this is true now?
We deal not only with the construction of technology but also with the construction of thinking processes. You must generate the question and see where it takes you, rather than taking the answer as a starting point. In an educational context, you are always dealing with dynamic forces, not only with the weight of past practices.

BERNARD TSCHUMI

   Historically, schools of architecture had a professor of structure, who was an engineer, and a professor of construction, who was often an architect who would teach how the building industry puts buildings together. This method taught a set of answers rather than how to investigate the question.

At Columbia, we wanted to challenge that separation between structure and construction. We started something called the Building Technology Sequence, and invited engineers and architects to teach. We have the best person dealing with membranes, the best person dealing with mechanical systems, and the best person dealing with steel structures involved with the various exercises in the sequence. You have to make sure that architecture is not only about concepts but also about their materialization.

If you did not have to answer to accreditation organizations, how would you collapse the various divisions of architectural education?

I am, on the one hand, enormously critical of registration boards, but I agree with their requirement that design and construction at large be integrated, which is what we all do in an architectural office. I wish we could do it more at the School, but time is too short and you get a better result from the students by keeping design and the nitty-gritty of construction apart as separate courses.

In my own work I always bring the structural engineers and HVAC consultants in during the early weeks of conceptual development, before the shape has been finalized. The architectural process is relatively slow and requires an enormous amount of experience to correlate all of the ingredients. It is important for students to understand all the different parts when they are at school, but it might take them two or three years after they graduate to put them together. In other words, we give them the knowledge while they are in school, knowing that education in architecture does not stop the day you graduate.

As an architect, I have now started to understand certain things, but after nearly 20 years I am still learning. The understanding that the learning process will go on and on is totally different from what occurs in most other disciplines.

BERNARD TSCHUMI

The architect is first and foremost an intellectual. Architects have to talk a lot to make a building, and they only make a building in order to talk about it. There is no such thing as a building without mountains of words. The architect is not a practical person but a person who thinks and speculates about building. We cannot simply contrast the work that goes on inside a school and the work that goes on outside because in both cases it is highly speculative, theoretical work.

What happens if you take the words away?

Architecture completely disappears. Why do you point at a building? Because you think that it is talking—about itself, the economy, or us. The very word "architecture" as distinct from "building" marks this moment. Architecture is simply building that has become articulate.

MARK WIGLEY

see DRAWING; GEOMETRY; METHODOLOGY; PEDAGOGY, COLUMBIA; SERIALITY/MASS PRODUCTION; STUDIO/PRACTICE

C

capital/capitalism	see ARCHITECTURE CULTURE; TIME

catastrophe

"Despite potential protestations to the contrary, it is likely that [Réne] Thom's catastrophe nets were first introduced into architecture as a mere formal technique more or less simultaneously by Carsten Jule-Christiansen in Die Anhalter Faltung project, Eisenman in the Rebstock Park, Kipnis in the Unité de Habitation at Briey installation, and Bahram Shirdel in the Nara Convention Hall. Inevitably, architects and philosophers alike would mistakenly find this in itself a catastrophe for all concerned.... The kind of complexity engendered by this alliance with Thom is substantially different than the complexity provided by either Venturi's decorated shed or the more recent conflicting forms of Deconstructivism. Topological geometry in general, and the catastrophe diagrams in particular, deploy disparate forces on a continuous surface within which more or less open systems of connection are possible. This diagram is catastrophic because it can represent abrupt transformation across a continuous surface."[1]

GREG LYNN
1. "The Folded, the Pliant, and the Supple," in *Folds, Bodies, and Blobs* (Brussels: La Lettre Volée, 1998), 125.

"[W]here one would expect that an architect looking at catastrophes would be interested in conflicts, architects are finding new forms of dynamic stability in [Réne Thom's catastrophe] diagrams. The mutual interest in Thom's diagrams points to a desire to be involved with events which they cannot predict. The primary innovation made by those diagrams is the geometric modeling of a multiplicity of possible co-present events at any moment. Thom's morphogenesis engages seemingly random events with mathematical probability."[2]

2. Ibid., 126.

CATIA system	see TECHNOLOGY
change	see ECOLOGY; HOUSE/HOME; INFRASTRUCTURE; PEDAGOGY, COLUMBIA; STRUCTURE; STUDIOS, CORE; STYLE; TREND

chimera

"The chimerical system produces cross-categorical couplings in which the initial systems are inextricably merged, that is, transformed into a system or systems with entirely new identities. Employing a 'chimerical mode,' the studio looked at ways of coupling categorically different systems by identifying and exploiting compatibilities and affinities between them."[3]

SULAN KOLATAN
3. *Chimera 3: Mongrel Structures*, Advanced Studio V, Fall 1997.

PLATE 1.02

"The chimerical differs in crucial ways from other forms of hybrid systems, such as collage, montage, or the prosthetic. While the latter are also systems in which the diverse parts operate together, these parts never lose their individual identities. In fact, the individual identity of each part, specifically the (categorical) difference, is more pronounced in systems based on strategies of juxtaposition or superimposition. And because each

KOLATAN/MACDONALD
4. "William MacDonald and Sulan Kolatan: Recent Work," *Columbia Documents of Architecture and Theory*, vol. 6 (1997): 123.

part exists as a discrete entity linked to other discrete entities, the whole can be taken apart. The idea of irreversible, irreducible hybridity, both as concept and product, would not have been thinkable within the paradigm of mechanics to which the techniques of collage and montage are linked. In a chimera, the relationship between the constituent parts is not one of interconnection or adjacency. At least, not simply. The limits of the parts, the exact delineations of the thresholds between parts, are not clearly identifiable. Rather, like the result of a successful graft, the border disappears."[4]

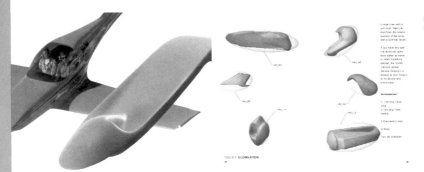

FIG. 10 Kolatan/MacDonald Studio, *Vehicles*, 1996.

In our design for the Raybould house, the issue of chimera is addressed in terms of the relationship between the landscape, the existing house, and the new addition. The roofscape of the existing house is registered onto similar conditions found in the landscape regardless of scale or category, for example, ridge to ridge, valley to valley, etc. This conceptual material is worked out using particular blending techniques, which transform the original relationships. These new relationships are then cast back into

WILLIAM MACDONALD

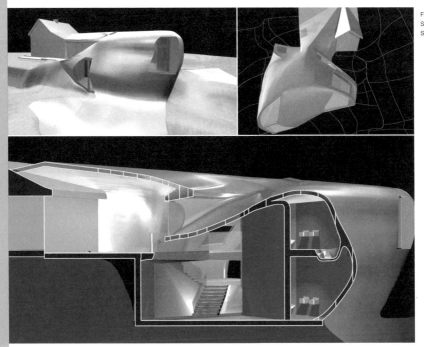

FIG. 11 Kolatan/MacDonald Studio, *Raybould House*, Sherman, Connecticut, 1998.

the landscape according to their previous mappings and transformed again, formulating new structures, such as pool cabanas, entry bridge pavilions, barn additions, and terraces. This procedure is reversed and cast back into the house, in order to develop particular refined scales of built-in furnishings, such as seating alcoves.

One of the new discoveries that came from our work on the O.K. Apartment deals with issues of feedback. There are some built-in furniture pieces in the house that are conceptually and literally part of the structure's overall network. Developing smaller interior aspects of the house is very different from the hierarchical top-down process that relates everything by scale. Through the feedback relationships you can influence the larger shell and envelope of the building while tying in smaller-scale furniture and interior pieces that affect the larger structure.

SULAN KOLATAN

PLATE 1.03

FIG. 12 Kolatan/MacDonald Studio, *Resi-Rise*, 2000.

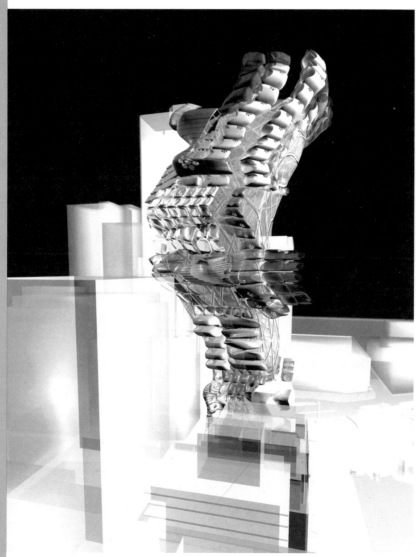

C

chimera

Merriam Webster's Dictionary

1. (a) capitalized: a fire-breathing she-monster in Greek mythology having a lion's head, a goat's body, and a serpent's tail; (b) an imaginary monster compounded of incongruous parts

2. an illusion or fabrication of the mind; especially: an unrealizable dream

3. an individual, organ, or part consisting of tissues of diverse genetic constitution

city

"There is no doubt that the form of the city is undergoing a mutation; and further, that new configurations and urban effects are emerging more rapidly than the ability of the disciplines of architecture or planning to theorize and understand them, much less exercise any kind of rational control. . . . Much recent theory of the city has focused on mapping the effects of these ineffable factors, understanding the city as an interconnected network of circuits and exchanges, mirroring power relations and political spaces."[5]

STAN ALLEN
5. *Colossal Urbanism*, Advanced Studio V, Fall 1993.

"Infrastructural work recognizes the collective nature of the city and allows for the participation of multiple authors. Infrastructures give direction to the future work of the city not by establishment of rules or codes (top-down), but by fixing points of service, access, and structure (bottom-up)."[6]

6. *Event/Infra/Structure*, Advanced Studio VI, Spring 1998.

"What could a 'small city' imply today? Among other things, a 'small city' could mean a suburb, a city neighborhood, a shopping mall, a small town or an enclave within an 'edge city.' Mies's project (Museum for a Small City) anticipates the decentralization of the postwar American city; today we can use this project as a basis to comment critically on an ongoing process and to redirect the development of the periphery."[7]

7. *Museum in the Suburbs*, Advanced Studio VI, Spring 1997.

FIG. 13 Field Operations, Stan Allen and James Corner, *French Embassy Garden*, New York, New York, 2001.

"The city, understood as a field and a concept in flux, is seen here as the locus not only of today's most urgent social and political issues but also as society's most concentrated creative and critical endeavor."[8]

8. *VOID SITE: Museum of the City of New York*, Advanced Studio, Summer 1994.

"Today we maneuver about revised social strata that are without discernible limits, manufacturers of the so called I-bahn (the Autobahn meeting information space). Here newfound liberations from the office, desk, car, home, and, by extension, vectors of consensus, autonomy, and privacy are leaving in their wake a reconstituted notion of city-space. Even the once steadfast urbanisms of public and sacred place, the space of commerce, and

HANI RASHID
9. *Ibahnia*, Advanced Studio, Summer 1994.

notions of privacy and event are being systematically redefined by yet to be manufactured cyber-counterparts: markets, libraries, museums, cinemas, parks, kiosks, brothels, and schools, all inevitably promising to be strewn across the globe."[9]

"Both projects this semester began with an examination of the dynamic and temporal aspects of music and cinema, asking the students to relate the indeterminate and momentary to the physical presence of the city. The working method in the studio formed the basis for continuing discussions concerning the stability and instability of the city and the potential for the 'moment of program' to provide degrees of indeterminacy and architectonic precision."[10]

THOMAS HANRAHAN
10. Core Studio II, Spring 1996.

"The significance of the horizon and the de-mapped city shifted the emphasis from section to plan and from site to map. Architecture was studied as an aspect of infrastructure, as the development of a particular structure relative to an experience that is governed by an understanding of the city as a regional field."[11]

11. Core Studio II, Spring 1994.

see CONTEXT; DIAGRAM; ENTROPY; FRAME; IMAGE; KYOZONE; LOCAL/GLOBAL; MODERN/ MODERNISM; NETWORK; STUDIOS, CORE; URBAN

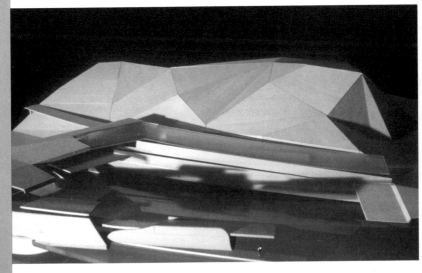

FIG. 14 Woong Yang, Core Studio II, Thomas Hanrahan, critic, Spring 1995.

clients   see PRACTICE/CLIENTS

co-citation   "As an index, [co-citation] functions according to a principle similar to that used in any keyword-based library search. Listing all works related to the same keyword, it thus reveals nonapparent conceptual connections across categories such as humanities and sciences. Interestingly, the next level of organization is constructed as a map, a geographic description of relational knowledge. In this kind of map, groups of co-cited papers are organized in clusters, each cluster representing a network of interrelated, co-cited publications. . . . Their spatial organization is based on continually evolving hierarchies that are contingent upon frequency of citation and thus subject to change over time."[12]

KOLATAN/MACDONALD
12. "William MacDonald and Sulan Kolatan: Recent Work," *Columbia Documents of Architecture and Theory*, vol. 6 (1997): 122.

"The term 'co-citational' is defined here as a chart of network hierarchy established less by location and more by convenience of access. Actual spatial distance is rendered irrelevant (non-adjacent space) in favor of a series of variables such as frequency, availability, and accessibility."[13]

WILLIAM MACDONALD
13. William MacDonald, *Co-Citational Cities*, Advanced Studio, Summer 1994.

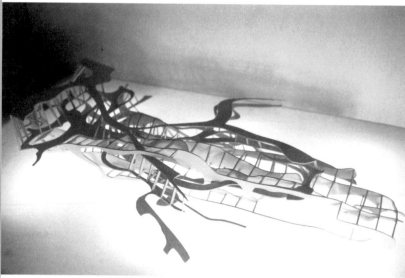

FIG. 15 Maia Small, Core Studio II, William MacDonald, critic, Spring 1997.

Co-citation is interesting to me because it is by definition continually changing according to multiple influences. It takes on a non-hierarchical structure as a field because it is about the frequency and intensity of citations. Therefore, the feedback structure is shaped simultaneously by external influences and internal relations. We would like to think of our work as methodologically rigorous in terms of those ideas, but not as formulaic. People often confuse work done on a computer with a kind of formulaic, prescriptive, or deterministic way of working, yet we try to use the computer to inform new conditions that might arise.

WILLIAM MACDONALD

One of our interests in the Angelika project was to understand the many different kinds of publicness and the effect that they have on each other. Another key concept in the project is "co-citation," which is an archiving technique that comes from the archiving of legal precedents. What's conceptually interesting about the notion of co-citation is that it makes connections across categories based on quotations and citations of texts and thereby allows you to read systems for their differences as well as their similarities. By understanding correspondences and affinities in categorically different systems, you can begin to construct new systems that operate between both.

SULAN KOLATAN

PLATE 1.04

co-

1. with: together: joint: jointly
2. in or to the same degree

Merriam Webster's Dictionary

citation
1. an official summons to appear
2. an act of quoting; especially: the citing of a previously settled case at law
3. mention: as (a) a formal statement of the achievements of a person receiving an academic honor; (b) specific reference in a military dispatch to meritorious performance of duty

collaboration

What interests you about the collaborative process?

I am not interested in collaboration as a way of blurring the result. Collaboration asks everyone to be even more precise about who they are and what they do and thereby allow new information to come into practice. For the North Carolina Museum of Art we were trying to deal with form and how to insert Barbara Kruger's Helvetica Extrabold Italic type into the landscape. The computer became a very powerful tool for us and facilitated the process. I was interested in working with text and I learned about working in a landscape.

see INTERDISCIPLINARY; STUDIO/PRACTICE

LAURIE HAWKINSON

collage

What is the purpose of your analysis of botanical specimens?

This particular process allows for the testing of what I call "collaged space." Specimen and site can each be read in terms of the other. Nevertheless, and regardless of the pedagogical tool being employed at any one time, the goal for myself and for my students is the same—to reach for the unknown in one's work. This is critical in the development of any author's voice.

KAREN BAUSMAN

PLATE 1.05

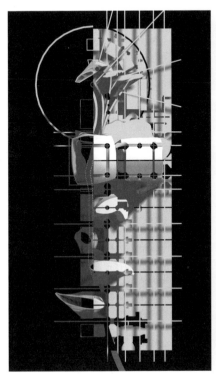

FIG. 16 Stephen Shwe, *Gotham Gothic: Unpacking the Cathedral, Desire and Technique*, Advanced Studio V, Karen Bausman, critic, Fall 1996.

C

collage   *Merriam Webster's Dictionary*

     1. an artistic composition made of various materials (as paper, cloth, or wood) glued on a surface

     2. the art of making collages

     3. an assembly of diverse fragments

     4. a work (as a film) having disparate scenes in rapid succession without transitions

see CHIMERA

colossal

"'Colossal urbanism' refers to much more than the size of recent urban interventions. While taking into account the unprecedented scale of new development, it introduces specific questions of dimension, scale, and figuration into the consideration of urban experience. Jean-Pierre Vernant notes for example, that the original Greek sense of the word kolossos had 'no implication of size.' What is specific to the colossal is a disproportion of both size and shape: a condition where architecture displaces sculpture through scale, and sculpture disturbs architecture through the introduction of a figuration that resists clear description. The colossal is excessive with regard to the codes of both sculpture and architecture. Edmund Burke devised the aesthetic category of the sublime to describe works of art at a scale so large that they began to compete with nature in their evocation of terror and beauty; Immanuel Kant understood the colossal as 'almost too large for any presentation'; Jacques Derrida has noted that the colossal is an 'unframable,' and therefore indeterminate concept. Like the experience of the contemporary city, the colossal object is so vast that it can no longer be perceived completely at any moment. It resists consideration as a unity."[14]

STAN ALLEN
14. *Colossal Urbanism*,
Advanced Studio V, Fall 1993.

"It is anticipated that the thematic of the colossal may serve to reintroduce into architecture such critically suspect, but nonetheless necessary, concepts as beauty, nostalgia, and emotion."[15]

15. Ibid.

colossal   *Merriam Webster's Dictionary*

     1. of, relating to, or resembling a colossus

     2. of a bulk, extent, power, or effect approaching or suggesting the stupendous or incredible

     3. of an exceptional or astonishing degree

see SCALE

communication

Politics, persuasion, and propaganda play a role in architecture and have always done so. There is a disparity between what those outside of a project would consider specialized and esoteric ideas, and the popularization and legitimization of those ideas to the public. I do not think it is corrupt; it is just the reality. You present a project, a park for example, according to the interests of the audience. You tell people you are going to connect their neighborhood to a wider park along the water's edge, but they are not interested in knowing the precise geometrical models you are using. They are interested in the effect and what it is going to do for them.

JESSE REISER

see POTENTIAL; PRACTICE/CLIENTS

competition

It is probably more effective if a dean, chair, or director acts as a coach rather than as a player who competes with the faculty. Teaching is a competitive activity: you compete for the interests of your students and demonstrate the results through the students' work. But the dean needs to know the game inside out, outside in, and should be a player in the arena beyond the school.

BERNARD TSCHUMI

complexity

"Complexity involves the fusion of multiple and different systems into an assemblage that behaves as a singularity while remaining irreducible to any single simple organization.... A rigorous theorization of diversity and difference within the discipline of architecture requires an alternative system of complexity in form—a complex formalism that is in essence freely differentiated. Recently, a typology of topological geometries for modeling complex aggregates has been developed. The most interesting example is the development of 'isomorphic polysurfaces' or what in the special-effects and animation industry is referred to as 'meta-clay,' 'meta-ball,' or 'blob' models."[16]

GREG LYNN
16. "Blobs (or Why Tectonics Is Square and Topology Is Groovy)," *ANY* 14 (1996): 59.

"Within science, complexity is a watchword for a new way of thinking about the *collective* behavior of many basic but interacting units, be they atoms, molecules, neurons, or bits within a computer.... *[C]omplexity is the study of the behavior of macroscopic collections of such units that are endowed with the potential to evolve in time.* Their interactions lead to coherent collective phenomena, so-called emergent properties that can be described only at higher levels than those of the individual units. In this sense, the whole is more than the sum of its components."[17]

see COMPUTER; CYBERNETICS; TYPE

17. Peter Coveney and Roger Highfield, *Frontiers of Complexity* (New York: Fawcett Columbine, 1995), 7.

component

"In this studio, urbanism was considered in terms of components and strategies of assembly. The studio emphasized the development of uniform yet heterogeneous surfacing strategies for the horizontal plinth of Columbia's Morningside campus. The initiative of the studio was to invent a component system of construction that is flexible and variegated in its implementation and construction."[18]

GREG LYNN
18. *Plinth: Options Studio,* Advanced Studio V, Fall 1996.

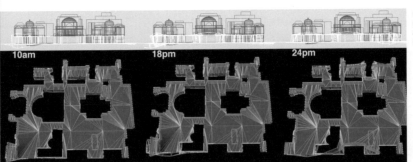

FIG. 17 Jan Loeken and Kristina Loock, *Plinth: Options Studio,* Advanced Studio V, Greg Lynn, critic, Fall 1996.

component
  1. a constituent part

Merriam Webster's Dictionary

2. (a) any one of the vector terms added to form a vector sum or resultant;
(b) a coordinate of a vector; also: either member of an ordered pair
of numbers

computer

"I took the notion of 'paperless' very seriously in the sense of it being a complete, radical experiment—to actually rid ourselves of not the paper so much, but what the paper implies as an authority."[19]

HANI RASHID
19. Quoted in Matthew Barhydt, "Paperless Studio," *Oculus* 57, no. 10 (June 1995): 15.

I came back to Columbia because I was interested in trying to understand how to use the computer differently than how others had used it. The computer is great at understanding and processing complexity in a way that modernism never did. It allows you to look at things simultaneously. I became interested in how you could understand something changing in time, like light or perception—qualities that exist in time naturally.

KATHRYN DEAN

When computers were introduced in the early 1990s, things shifted radically and the quality of work initially suffered. The fervor has subsided and it is now being used more as an operative device, which I really respect. For example, Greg Lynn and Lise Anne Couture's studios use it as a unique instrument within the studio environment. There was an initial panic to absorb it because you were seen as being nonconformist if you did not, and that has changed. One needs to find a balance, because many people are realizing that there are limitations as well as benefits and they are beginning to change their studios.
Do you use the computer as a design tool in your practice?
We use Microstation, but I try to find people with diverse strengths. We also use metal, glass, wood, and paper; it ranges from project to project.

LESLIE GILL

How has the introduction of computer technology affected the studio sequence?
The computer is another tool. Although the emphasis on physical models in the first-year studio provides grounding, the students intuitively digest the computer imagery that they see in the advanced studios and try to make it concrete. The translation back and forth between the digital and physical media enriches the School.

THOMAS HANRAHAN

"[We are] trying to use the computer less as a renderer and more as a form and pattern generator [to] generate organizations and study them in very conventional ways. . . . Everything gets deformed. Design shifts a little bit— you're kind of breeding design rather designing."[20]

GREG LYNN
20. Quoted in Matthew Barhydt, "Paperless Studio," *Oculus* 57, no. 10 (June 1995): 15.

With respect to the relationship between research at the university and my personal practice, I owe a great debt to Columbia. It was the intersection of my interest in the history and theory of geometry with the experiment in digital pedagogy called the "paperless studio" that launched my recent design work and writing. The computers were introduced into the School both conventionally, in their niche in the basement, and unconventionally, in the studio environment. The decision to have faculty rotate through

GREG LYNN

the paperless studios revolutionized the way that designers used the digital media. It also changed the forms of practice of both the faculty and the students. In both respects that experiment catapulted a lot of people into what they are presently doing. Of course, as in all experiments, there were liabilities. At Columbia this shift into a fertile but young medium caused an overinvestment in procedural thinking.

PLATES 1.06–1.07

"The computer was conceptualized and thematized in two ways. First, in its ability to be used in the conceptual process of design by setting particular parameters and allowing the computer to participate fully in its computational and instrumental capacities. Second, by investigating the impact of electronic space on the physical environment and vice-versa; issues that arise are accessibility, availability, speed, etc."[21]

WILLIAM MACDONALD
21. *citiLOOP*, Advanced Studio, Summer 1995.

The computer is a tool with its own logic; you can participate with it, but ultimately you are responsible for setting up the way in which it performs. You are responsible for its conceptual grounding, for its critical response, and ultimately for your results and self-assessment: deciding whether to start again, where to start again, or where to continue. That aspect can be lost because the computer is very efficient in terms of production. Ultimately there is another set of concerns with regard to the step following production that is a matter of experience.

WILLIAM MACDONALD

It deceives to a certain degree; it appears to be more architecture, more complete, and more complex than it actually is. Unless you are aware of those levels of deception and appearance, it's very easy to get seduced.

SULAN KOLATAN

The computer is not a natural thing. It is a historical artifact, a material thing. The materialism of computing has to take into account the history of computing as well as the institutional and aesthetic and cultural context out of which computing emerges. For example, one reason that during the '90s we got buildings that look like dinosaurs was because the software was designed to produce dinosaurs. We saw that in the movies. We do not have furry buildings yet, because Maya fur just appeared on the scene. Maybe we will get furry buildings soon—I am using that example because the software refers to the representation and modeling of biological entities. It is as if the representation of biological form is seen to be more advanced and more complex than mechanical form, or the form of collage and montage, as if it is a natural step in this linear evolution.

REINHOLD MARTIN

"The development of models constructed of computational material... attempt to utilize the computational potentials inherent within material behaviors in order to produce a richer milieu in which architecture might be developed. [In spite of the extensive use of the computer,] it will not be the sole determinant for the production of organizational models. The computer will be recognized for its reductive capacities and will be useful in taming the fecund efflorescence of material logics."[22]

REISER/UMEMOTO
22. *Convergent Structures*, Advanced Studio V, Fall 1998.

see AESTHETICS/APPEARANCE; ARCHITECTURE CULTURE; AUTHOR; CO-CITATION; COLLABORATION; DESIGN; GEOMETRY; MATERIAL/MATERIALITY; METHODOLOGY; PEDAGOGY, COLUMBIA; PERFORMANCE; PROCESS; REAL; STUDIOS, ADVANCED; TEACHING; TECHNOLOGY; VIRTUAL/ACTUAL

concept   see IDEA/CONCEPT

confinement

"This course is based on the premise that one can create architecture utilizing the concept of confinement as a basis for invention. Three concepts will define a point for departure: the collapsing scale of confinement and the resulting imprint of compression on the human body; the obligatory insulation from society required by confinement; and finally, the definition of an architectural language within the boundary of that interior realm. Confinement, whether voluntary or imposed (i.e. hospitals, monasteries, harems, think tanks, prisons, etc.), implies segregation from society that is at once inbred and hermetic, while mimicking in microcosm society at large. The balance between the desires of the individual and the needs of the collective are fraught with tension—one that demands flexibility for the former and ritual for the latter."[23]

KAREN BAUSMAN
LESLIE GILL
23. *Confinement: A Study of Architectural Space Within*, Advanced Studio VI, Spring 1992.

construction   see BUILDING/CONSTRUCTION

context

"The logistics of context suggests a way out of the polarized debate (between the contextualism of Leon Krier or the so called 'New Urbanists,' and deconstruction and related stylistic manifestations) by recognizing the limits to architecture's ability to order the city, and at the same time, to learn from the complex self-regulating orders already present in the city. Attention is shifted to systems of service and supply, a logics of flow and vectors. This implies close attention to existing conditions, carefully defined rules for intensive linkages at the local scale, and a relatively indifferent

STAN ALLEN
24. *Library, Archive, Atlas*, Advanced Studio V, Fall 1995.

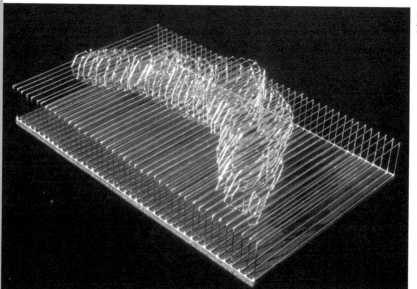

FIG. 18 Ken Takahashi, *Library, Archive, Atlas*, Advanced Studio V, Stan Allen, critic, Fall 1995.

attitude toward the overall configuration. Architecture needs to learn to manage the complexity of context, which paradoxically, it can only do by giving up some measure of control."[24]

context

Merriam Webster's Dictionary

1. the parts of a discourse that surround a word or passage and can throw light on its meaning
3. the interrelated conditions in which something exists or occurs

see HISTORY; LOCAL/GLOBAL

convergence

"The primary aim of this studio was to stake out a terrain for architectural speculation and experimentation based on the convergence of two major cultural, technological, and discursive vectors: the so-called 'posturban' and 'posthuman.' This is a convergence marked by a dispersed territoriality no longer centered on the density, sensory stimulation, or dynamism of the twentieth-century city, and a denaturalized, technologically mediated sub-jectivity adrift in an alien, entropic landscape."[25]

REINHOLD MARTIN
25. *Technopolis: Post-urban/Post-human*, Advanced Studio VI, Fall 1998.

FIG. 19 Martin/Baxi Architects, *Entropia: Homeoffice*, 2001.

crisis

"The crisis of the architectural academy is at least in some measure a reflection of the crisis facing the profession. In this context we may posit the thesis that the more the practice of architecture becomes removed from the needs of the society as a whole, the more it tends to become an overly aes-theticised discourse that addresses itself exclusively to the spectacular pre-occupations of an *arriviste* class. Inside architectural schools this discourse is often served by a mystifying theoretical eclecticism, drawn largely from other disciplines, and removed from the basic conditions and needs of environmental design."[26]

KENNETH FRAMPTON
26. "Seven Points for the Millennium: An Untimely Manifesto," *Journal of Architecture* 5, no. 1 (Spring 2000): 23.

cybernetics

Cybernetic theory was a way of understanding that we were doing multi-variate calculations and generating forms out of multivariate relationships, which is merely calculus. We need to understand how these calculus-based forms operate. Part of the process involves waiting to observe results, but after you have seen it happen 15 times and notice the patterns, you have to intervene in the system.

GREG LYNN

c

We are hearing words like "function" and "real" again after a 30-year hiatus, and we are experimenting with the idea of feedback that was popularized by cyberneticists in the mid-20th century. How is what you are doing different?

Christopher Alexander and Jane Jacobs were the first cybernetics-influenced architects. Alexander had a grammar and syntax organized within a cybernetic paradigm. If you are asking if Columbia has a grammar and syntax, the answer would be yes. Is it different than Christopher Alexander's? Yes. Complexity theory and all of the terminology that came with it was a way of coming to grips with the fact that, because of the computer, calculus had taken over our design tools. What is great about Columbia is that these issues have been investigated critically from baroque architecture to cybernetics. They have been analyzed and there have been diverse positions within the faculty. Keller Easterling was very critical of generating form and wanted a pure cybernetics of information transfer, whereas Stan Allen was pushing more toward urbanism, and Jesse Reiser and I were more interested in form. There were a lot of competing strategies and a lot of debates took place.

see MATERIAL/MATERIALITY

GREG LYNN

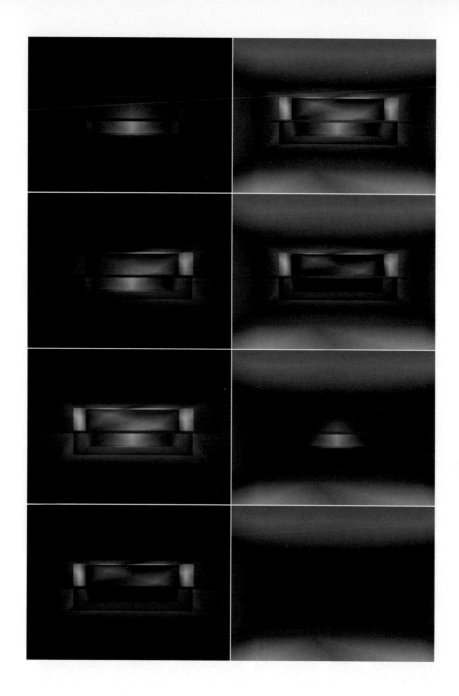

art/artist

1.01

Joseph Lee

*Museum for Contem-
porary Sculpture*

Advanced Studio IV

Kathryn Dean, critic

Spring 2000

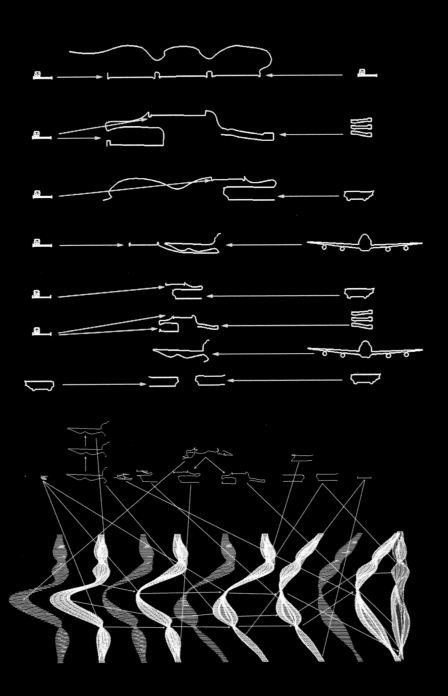

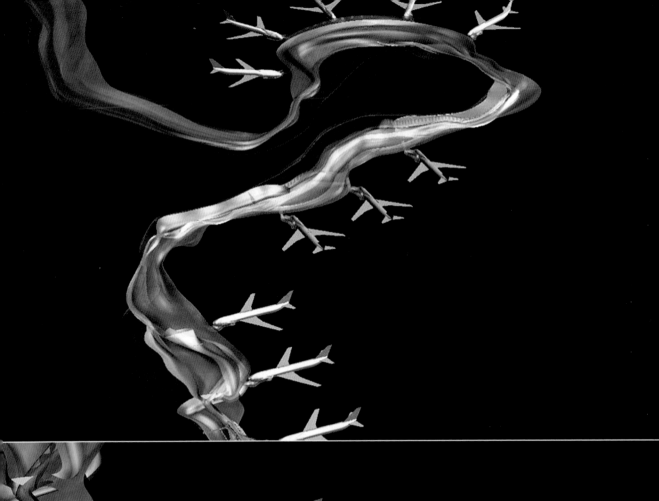
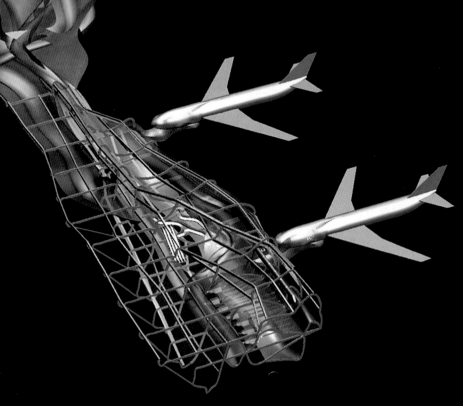

chimera

1.02

Roger Hom

Chimera 3: Mongrel Structures

Advanced Studio V

Sulan Kolatan, critic

Fall 1997

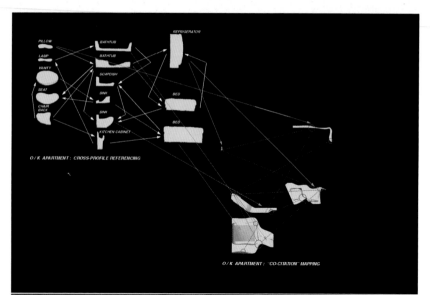

O / K APARTMENT : CROSS-PROFILE REFERENCING

O / K APARTMENT : "CO-CITATION" MAPPING

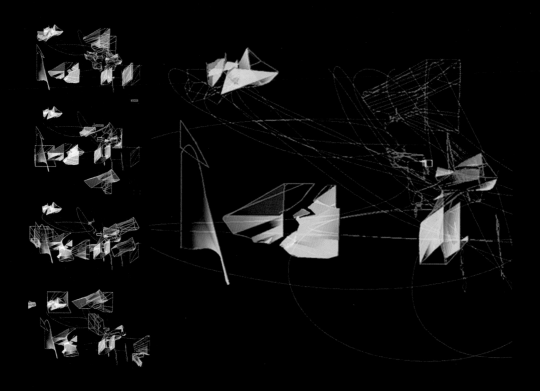

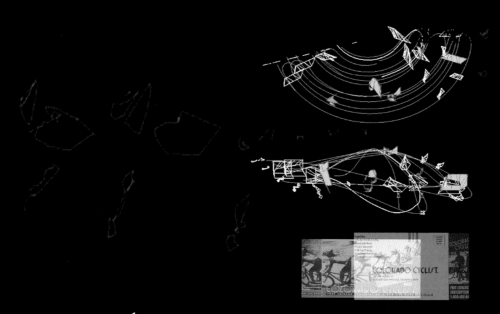

chimera

1.03 (left)

Kolatan/MacDonald
Studio

O.K. Apartment

New York, New York

1997

co-citation

1.04 (right)

Jia Lin Le

*Composited
Architectures for the
Port Authority Bus
Terminal*

Advanced Studio

William MacDonald,
critic

Summer 1997

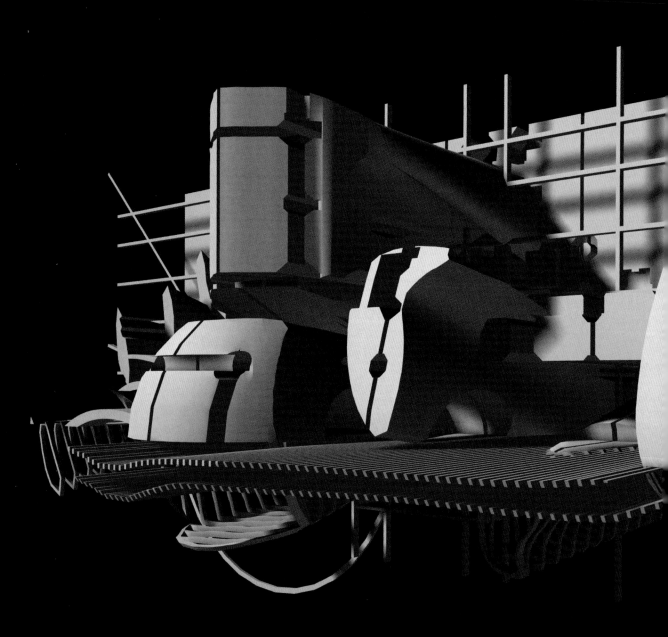

collage
1.05
Stephen Shwe
Gotham Gothic
Advanced Studio V
Karen Bausman, critic
Fall 1996

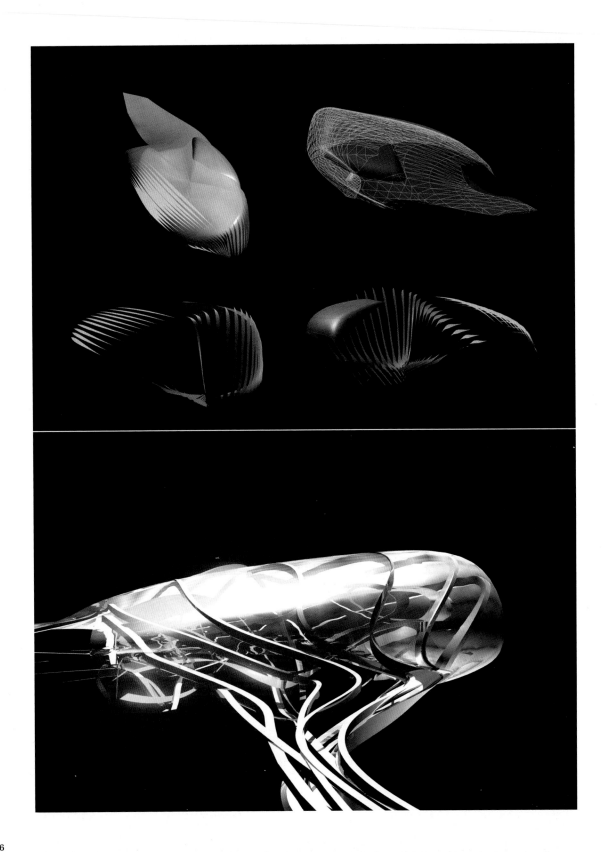

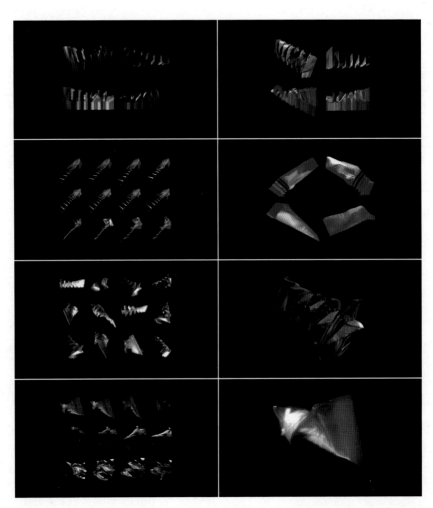

computer

1.06 (left)

Matthias Blass, Tsu-Ying Chiang, Gin-Shung Chester Huang, and Astrid Piber

Advanced Studio VI

Greg Lynn and Jeffrey Kipnis, critics

Spring 1999

1.07 (right)

Greg Lynn

OMV H2 House

1999

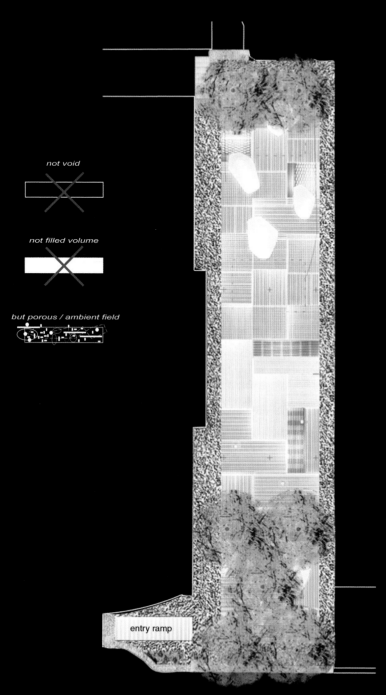

not void

not filled volume

but porous / ambient field

STRANGE ZONE
 planting
 lanterns

PERFORMANCE ZONE
 service outlets
 movable seating
 program surfaces

MEDIA GROVE
 programmed lighting
 speakers
 media installations

entry ramp

FIFTH AVENUE SIDEWALK

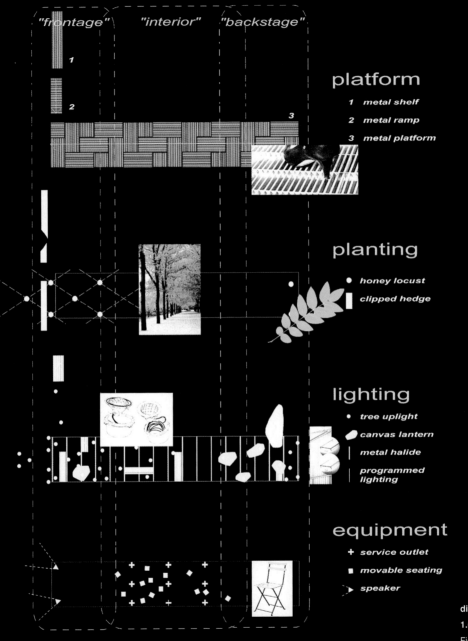

"frontage"   "interior"   "backstage"

platform

1 metal shelf
2 metal ramp
3 metal platform

planting

● honey locust
▮ clipped hedge

lighting

● tree uplight
◗ canvas lantern
❙ metal halide
❘ programmed
  lighting

equipment

✚ service outlet
▪ movable seating
➤ speaker

diagram

1.08

Field Operations,
Stan Allen and
James Corner

*French Embassy
Garden*

New York, New York

2001

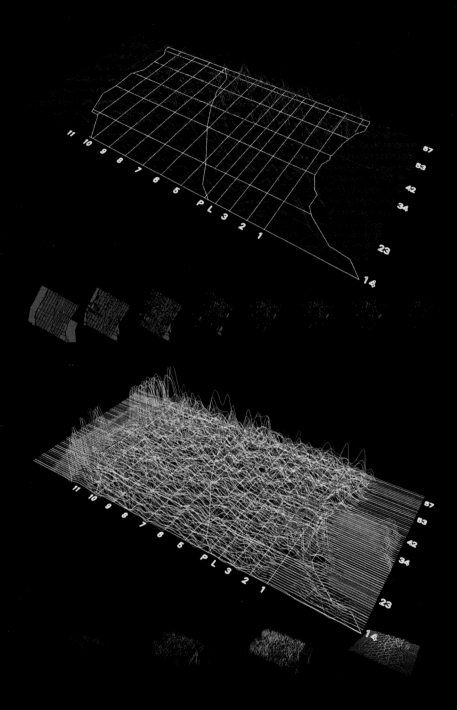

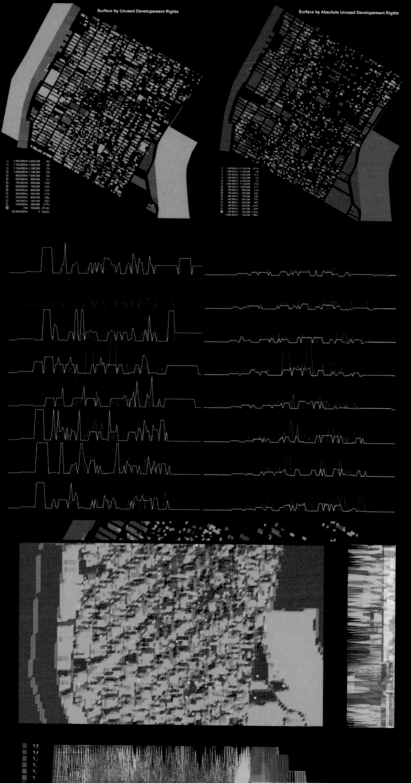

Surface by Unused Developement Rights

Surface by Absolute Unused Developement Rights

diagram

1.09

Axel Friedman

*Datascapes New York:
Artificial Ecologies*

Advanced Studio V

Stan Allen, critic

Fall 1998

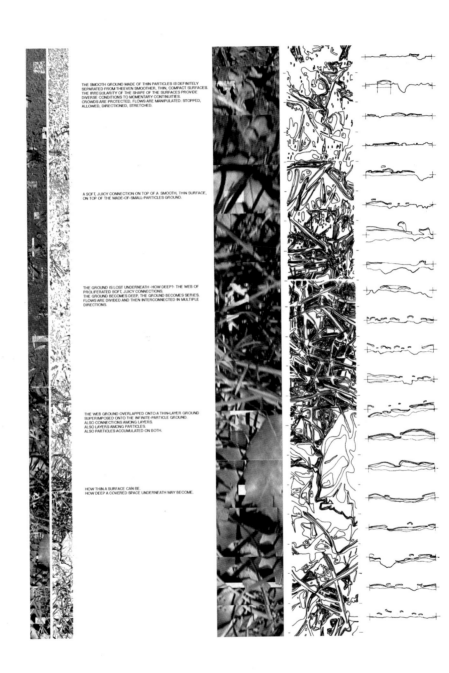

THE SMOOTH GROUND MADE OF THIN PARTICLES IS DEFINITELY
SEPARATED FROM THE EVEN SMOOTHER, THIN, COMPACT SURFACES.
THE IRREGULARITY OF THE SHAPE OF THE SURFACES PROVIDE
DIVERSE CONDITIONS TO MOMENTARY CONTINUITIES.
CROWDS ARE PROTECTED, FLOWS ARE MANIPULATED: STOPPED,
ALLOWED, DIRECTIONED, STRETCHED.

A SOFT, JUICY CONNECTION ON TOP OF A SMOOTH, THIN SURFACE,
ON TOP OF THE MADE-OF-SMALL-PARTICLES GROUND.

THE GROUND IS LOST UNDERNEATH -HOW DEEP?- THE WEB OF
PROLIFERATED SOFT, JUICY CONNECTIONS.
THE GROUND BECOMES DEEP, THE GROUND BECOMES SERIES.
FLOWS ARE DIVIDED AND THEN INTERCONNECTED IN MULTIPLE
DIRECTIONS.

THE WEB GROUND OVERLAPPED ONTO A THIN-LAYER GROUND
SUPERIMPOSED ONTO THE INFINITE-PARTICLE GROUND.
ALSO CONNECTIONS AMONG LAYERS.
ALSO LAYERS AMONG PARTICLES.
ALSO PARTICLES ACCUMULATED ON BOTH.

HOW THIN A SURFACE CAN BE.
HOW DEEP A COVERED SPACE UNDERNEATH MAY BECOME.

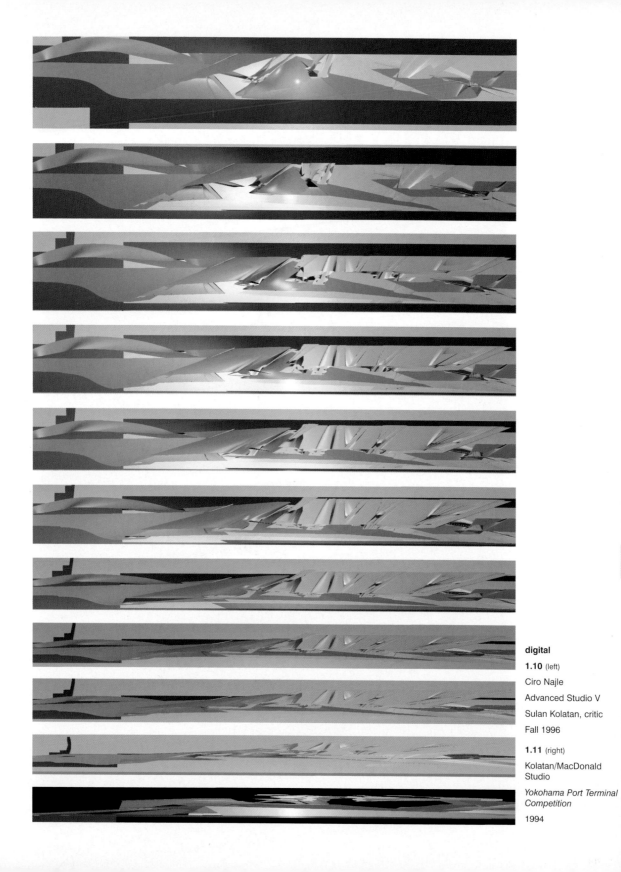

digital

1.10 (left)

Ciro Najle

Advanced Studio V

Sulan Kolatan, critic

Fall 1996

1.11 (right)

Kolatan/MacDonald
Studio

*Yokohama Port Terminal
Competition*

1994

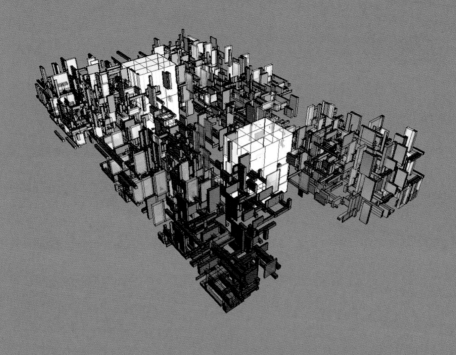

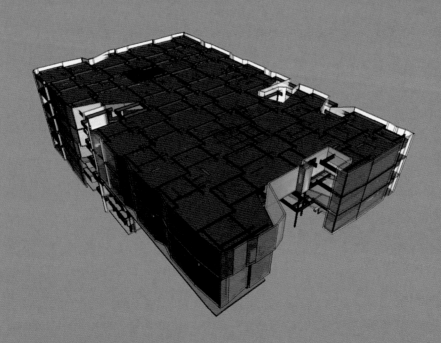

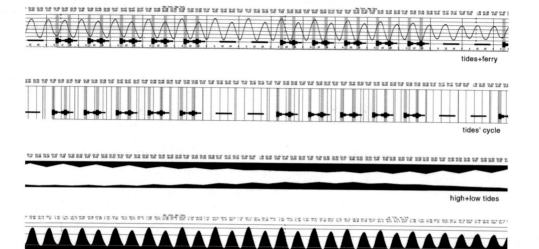

tides+ferry

tides' cycle

high+low tides

tidal movement

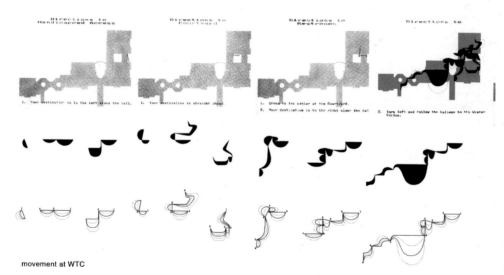

movement at WTC

entropy

1.12 (left)
Tim Nichols
Entropy Lab
Advanced Studio V
Reinhold Martin, critic
Fall 1999

1.13 (right)
Kaori Sato
*Variable Rates:
Movement and
Difference*
Core Studio II
Reinhold Martin, critic
Spring 1998

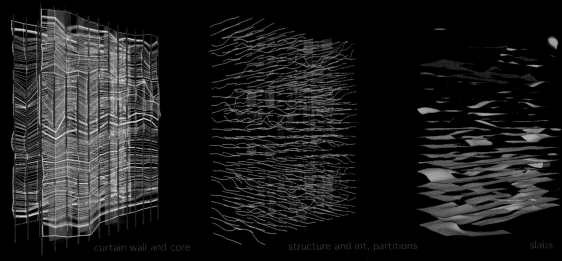

curtain wall and core

structure and int. partitions

slabs

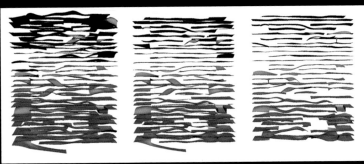

perspective sections

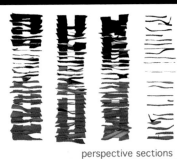

meeting point

hybrid

1.16 (left)

Stephane Kervyn de Lettenhove

Advanced Studio V

Jesse Reiser and Nanako Umemoto, critics

Fall 1999

1.17 (right)

Karen Seong and Megumi Tamanaha

Advanced Studio V

Jesse Reiser and Nanako Umemoto, critics

Fall 1999

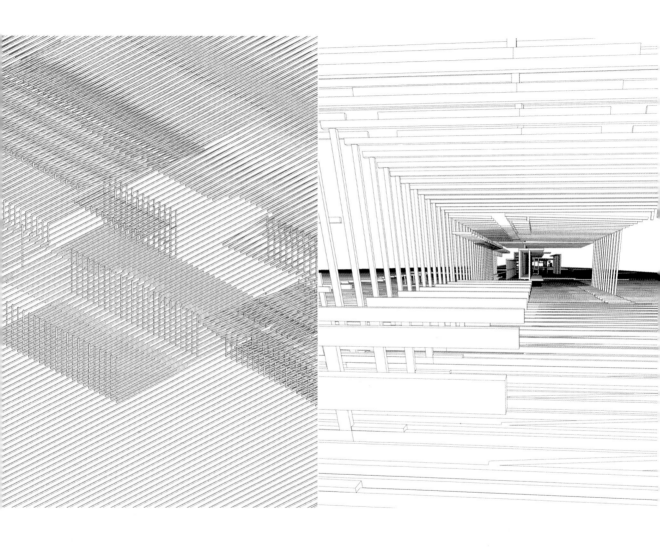

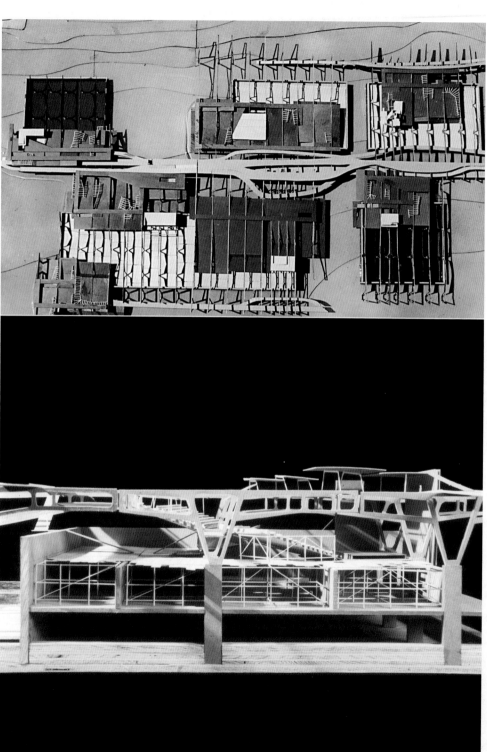

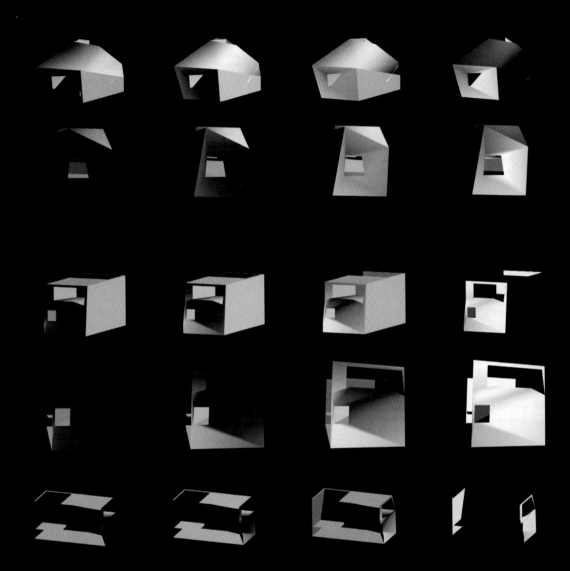

intuition

1.20 (left)

Asako Akazawa

*Museum for Contem-
porary Sculpture*

Advanced Studio IV

Kathryn Dean, critic

Spring 2001

1.21 (right)

Dean Wolf Architects

Spiral House

Armonk, New York

1998

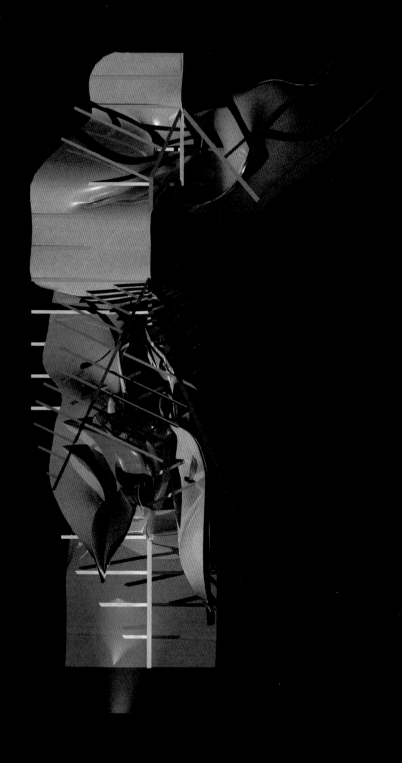

intuition

1.22 (left)

Marcelo Spina

*E-Z Architecture:
Counterfeit Paradigms
of Dwelling in the Mail
Order House*

Advanced Studio

Evan Douglis, critic

Summer 1996

1.23 (right)

Evan Douglis

The Oblique Function
(exhibition)

1997

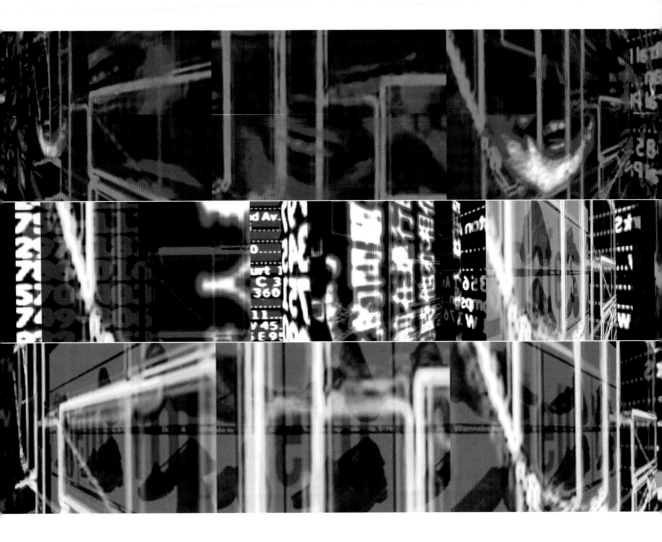

kyozone

1.24

Ridzwa Fathan

Tokyo Extreme

Advanced Studio VI

Hani Rashid, critic

Spring 1995

D

design

"Training in building design is a tripartite procedure involving three different media at the same time; that is to say (i) the hand drafting of initial concepts before passing to other modes of representation, (ii) the continual building of models at all scales in order to assess the concepts under consideration and (iii) computer-aided design to be used for drafting and modelling in relation to the other two modes. Obviously one needs to oscillate constantly between all three modes in the generation of a design."[1]

KENNETH FRAMPTON
1. "Seven Points for the Millennium: An Untimely Manifesto," *Journal of Architecture* 5, no. 1 (Spring 2000): 22–23.

diagram

"Although diagrams can serve an explanatory function, clarifying form, structure, or program to the designer and to others, and notations map program in time and space, the primary utility of the diagram is as an abstract means of thinking about *organization*. The variables in an organizational diagram include both formal and programmatic configurations: space and event, force and resistance, density, distribution, and direction. In an architectural context, organization implies both program and its distribution in space, bypassing conventional dichotomies of function versus form or form versus content. Multiple functions and action over time are implicit in the diagram. The configurations it develops are momentary clusters of matter in space, subject to continual modification. A diagram is therefore not a thing in itself but a description of potential relationships among elements, not only an abstract model of the way things behave in the world but a map of possible worlds."[2]

STAN ALLEN
2. "Diagrams Matter," *ANY* 23 (1998): 16.

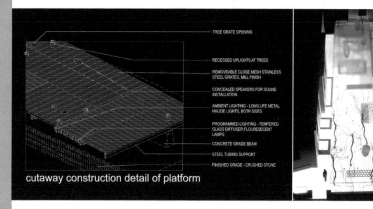

cutaway construction detail of platform

FIG. 20 Field Operations, Stan Allen and James Corner, *French Embassy Garden*, New York, New York, 2001.

There is an uncanny similarity between Alexander's discussion of the diagram as an organizational tool and the algorithmic design processes that are used today.

In principle, Alexander's theory is tremendously interesting, but the images and projects that have been produced in practice just do not interest me. What is important about the way this stuff has been played out at Columbia is that it is not a purely academic or theoretical discussion. People

STAN ALLEN

who are practitioners—Greg Lynn, Jesse Reiser, and myself, for example—were using these studios to try out ideas. We identify ourselves as practitioners first and theorists only consequent to that. In other words, we are not so interested in getting the theory right. The mistake that so many people make is to think that the answer is already there in the theory. The test is to see what it gives you architecturally. What is interesting about Alexander for me is part of a more general link back to issues of the 1960s. For example, many of the images that I use in the diagram discussion come from a book entitled *RSVP Cycles: Creative Processes in the Human Environment* by Lawrence Halprin. You can refer to some of the principles of Alexander's and Halprin's work, but that does not necessarily lead you to the same conclusions. I would question the idea that any theory will inevitably lead to a particular result.

Halprin is actually a more interesting person to me. His work as a landscape architect is more interesting than Alexander's as an architect. His wife is a choreographer, and many questions about notation and ideas about event spaces were all played out both in his theory and in his practice. I would say at one level that it is just a difference in sensibility. You can work with similar material, but because of a different sensibility you get different results. Mine is an architectural sensibility that is different than Alexander's or Halprin's.

PLATES 1.08–1.09

When we talk about a truly innovative architecture, we are not talking only about new formal approaches. The diagram figures nicely into a theory of form because the diagram itself can easily be translated into a formal structure, and that captivates architects. It is this one-to-one correspondence that is effectively just another form of legitimization. Through the diagram certain architects have propped up their ideas by suggesting that if their work is derived from science, biology, or a particular theorem then it substantiates the formal object. I do not think that innovation is rooted in such thinking.

HANI RASHID

One of the reasons that we find the works of Fluxus or the Situationists interesting is because these groups embraced the city and space as open ended, at the level of what could potentially happen, and that incompleteness and ambiguity is a very compelling place for the architect to work. One cannot transfer the work of Fluxus directly into architectural form. Instead we interrogate architecture as a set of circumstances, such as interiority, the way certain phenomena affect architecture, the way the contemporary idea of body is being redefined vis-à-vis new spatialities, and so on.

If the word "diagram" does apply to us, it is in a much more expansive way. A diagram does not have to be a set of two-dimensional lines that are then somehow extruded or transformed into three-dimensional form. A diagram could be the image of somebody sitting on an airplane with a laptop and wireless modem connecting him or her to one country while the transatlantic journey is being mapped on the airplane's video screen, so that he or she is in three time zones simultaneously.

LISE ANNE COUTURE

*In your design studios, do you encourage students to make use of informa-
tion that is specifically nonrepresentational and nonarchitectural?*
Our studio research is less about the content of information space than
about a particular complexity model. Students use the nonlinear behavior
of weather patterns as if they were external to architecture, which leads
to an argument about the diagram. If you understand the constraints of
dynamics and the way that structures behave, then the diagrams derived
from weather are actually universal. They appear to have origins in weather
but they relate to several different kinds of material organizations—
weather is one and architecture could possibly be another. There is a perception that you are evaluating models from outside the discipline, but
you eventually realize that they can operate from within.
see DRAWING; IMAGE; PROCESS; TIME

JESSE REISER

difference

see COMPLEXITY; INFORMATION; LOCAL/GLOBAL; OTHER

differentiation

"Rather than use differences to destabilize urban organizations, this studio
attempted to produce new urban organizations and stabilities through
processes of differentiation, i.e., attempts to engender differentiated urban
organizations without arresting those differences in the formal conflict of
heterogeneous fragments. The models of smooth mixture are *continuous*,
yet within their local intrications *heterogeneou*s elements are maintained.
Such a logic of intricate connections begins with a system of local provisional connections between dissimilar elements from which new urban
networks emerge."[3]

GREG LYNN
3. *Smooth Urbanism*, Advanced
Studio VI, Spring 1993.

"Regularity in architecture should not be a fully discredited notion in our
time. The diversity that is witnessed in complex systems, whether it be in
nature or architecture, is dependent not on a perfect irregularity or regularity, but upon a sophisticated expression of forces in matter. Further, the elements of these interactions, however indifferent to the accidents of form,
are productive of complex organizations at larger scales. We are intrigued
by the idea that projects could exhibit regularity at the macro and micro
scales, while incorporating high capacities of differentiation and variability
at the middle scales."[4]
see SERIALITY/MASS PRODUCTION

REISER/UMEMOTO
4. *Housing on the River Plate,
Argentina*, Advanced Studio VI,
Spring 1999.

digital

"I am thinking about the histogrammatic constitution of the digital image,
the information that shapes the particular appearances on its surface. . . .
It is worth noting that this process is based on an inextricable link between
quantitative and qualitative attributes. That is to say, the presence of more
or less of certain tonal values in particular places produces categorical
difference. An 'architectural mosaicism' is thus a histogram invested with
spatial and/or programmatic values."[5]

SULAN KOLATAN
5. *Chimera Formation on
Morningside Heights*, Advanced
Studio V, Fall 1996.

One of the causes of alliances within the Columbia faculty is the newness
of the digital medium. When artists initially began working with video,
everybody was lumped together as "video artists," as if that meant only one
thing. With the computer we frequently run up against the preconceptions

SULAN KOLATAN

formed outside of Columbia about the work going on here and, because of this, we continually have to differentiate and describe what we are doing. There are certain overlapping interests at the School but there are also very specific interests of ours that are not always apparent.

Video, as a medium, is a good example because it also provided for both technological and conceptual breakthroughs in the production of art. The potential of digital design and digital manufacture in the production of architecture today may, in fact, be a more fundamentally radical transformation than that of video to art at that time. The common interest, among some of the faculty, in exploring digital design and its implications and consequences on architectural/cultural production has afforded an accelerated, intensive environment of debate and discourse that is cultivating unique trajectories of design research.

WILLIAM MACDONALD

PLATES 1.10–1.11

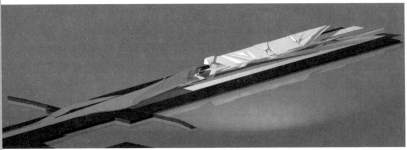

FIG. 21 Kolatan/MacDonald Studio, *Yokohama Port Terminal Competition*, 1994.

digital

Merriam Webster's Dictionary

1. of or relating to the fingers or toes
2. done with a finger
3. of, relating to, or using calculation by numerical methods or by discrete units
4. of or relating to data in the form of numerical digits
5. providing a readout in numerical digits
6. relating to an audio recording method in which sound waves are represented digitally (as on magnetic tape) so that in the recording wow and flutter are eliminated and background noise is reduced

see ARCHITECTURE CULTURE; COMPUTER; PERFORMANCE; REAL; VIRTUAL/ACTUAL

drawing

What are your thoughts on the dichotomy between drawing and building in architecture?

That is only a problem if you begin with the idea that drawings and diagrams are abstract and unreal, and buildings are real and concrete. For example, I have written about a recent shift in the critical understanding of Mies. He has often been discussed in terms of what Beatriz Colomina has called the "son of the stonemason school": bricks and mortar, steel and glass, materiality and presence. But that is completely counterintuitive to the experience of Mies's buildings, which are all about ephemeral effects— light, shadow, reflection, expanding and contracting space. Over the past fifteen years people like Michael Hays, Josep Quetglas, and Robin Evans

STAN ALLEN

FIG. 22 Mabel Wilson, *Single Family House*, Advanced Studio VI, Stan Allen, critic, Spring 1991.

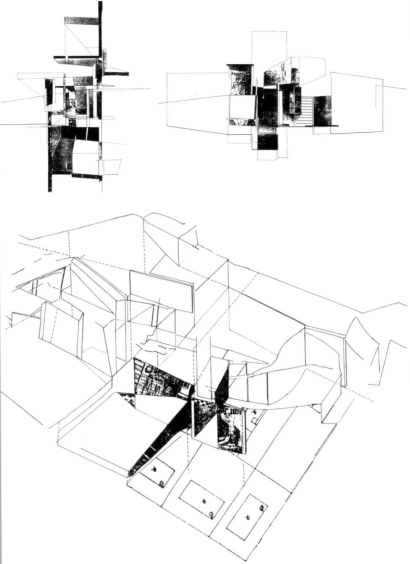

have written about Mies in terms of these ephemeral, virtual effects. This is an interesting test case because the architect who is most frequently identified with essentialist tectonics, with material presence, is currently being understood in terms of ephemeral effects and virtuality. John Hejduk once said that the painter by the nature of his work begins with the real world and works toward abstraction, whereas the architect by virtue of his work begins with abstraction and works toward reality. But, he says that the significant work of architecture, when it reaches that condition of reality, is that which retains something of its original abstraction. So the split between drawing and building is only a problem if you insist on enforcing that dichotomy between drawing and building. At the end of the day, building is in some ways a much more abstract activity than design. Daniel

Libeskind made a very funny remark in the early 1990s during the initial stages of construction of the Jewish Museum. He said something like: "I spend my days meeting with consultants and with the money people; I'm looking at all these charts, graphs, critical paths, and budget summaries, and I am perfectly comfortable with that. My work has always been about graphics." Architects like MVRDV are interesting because they suggest that the process of construction may be all about graphics, but it is no less real for that. This is a notion of reality that is much more peculiar and abstract than what we do in the studio.

drawing

Merriam Webster's Dictionary

1. an act or instance of drawing; especially: the process of deciding something by drawing lots
2. the art or technique of representing an object or outlining a figure, plan, or sketch by means of lines
3. something drawn or subject to drawing: as (a) an amount drawn from a fund; (b) a representation formed by drawing

see ARCHITECTURE CULTURE; INDEX; METHODOLOGY; PEDAGOGY, COLUMBIA; PROCESS; WATERCOLOR

durability

"Normally, we associate durability with traditional heavy materials such as marble and granite; hence, there is an unavoidable association between the monumental and durable. It is conceivable, however, that one can build out of high-quality industrial materials and also attain considerable durability. Under certain conditions very well-made wooden buildings are also durable, particularly if they are maintained. Today there is an ecological aspect to durability; hence the ethic that one should not design and realize buildings that are disposable. To this one may add the spiritual and cultural dimension of tradition, as something that is indispensable to sustaining the continuity of a place and its sense of identity. The tectonic plays a role in terms of determining the quality through the way in which it is built."[6]

KENNETH FRAMPTON
6. "An Interview with Kenneth Frampton," *Oz 20* (1998): 78.

ecology

"The orientation of the studio marks a shift toward a procedural architecture. Specifically, I propose to use the idea of an artificial ecology as
the organizing basis for the work of the studio. However, ecology and landscape are not so much models for the form as for the process of work.
We will pursue an expanded architectural agenda that might give equal
importance to structure (spatial and territorial organization), functioning
(the day-to-day events and activities taking place on a site), and change
(the evolution of sites over time)."[1]

STAN ALLEN
1. *Datascapes New York:
Artificial Ecologies*, Advanced
Studio V, Fall 1998.

CIRCUIT ECOLOGIES

A SERIES OF INTERLOCKING RIBBONS AND SURFACES PROVIDE WELL SERVICED SPACES FOR
ALL ACTIVE PROGRAMS, EVENTS, AND CIRCULATION DEMANDS TO COLONIZE THE SITE IN TIME

FIG. 23 Field Operations, Stan
Allen and James Corner,
Downsview Park Competition,
2000.

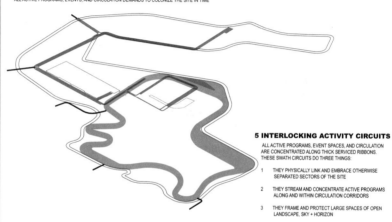

5 INTERLOCKING ACTIVITY CIRCUITS

ALL ACTIVE PROGRAMS, EVENT SPACES, AND CIRCULATION
ARE CONCENTRATED ALONG THICK SERVICED RIBBONS.
THESE SWATH CIRCUITS DO THREE THINGS:

1   THEY PHYSICALLY LINK AND EMBRACE OTHERWISE
SEPARATED SECTORS OF THE SITE

2   THEY STREAM AND CONCENTRATE ACTIVE PROGRAMS
ALONG AND WITHIN CIRCULATION CORRIDORS

3   THEY FRAME AND PROTECT LARGE SPACES OF OPEN
LANDSCAPE, SKY + HORIZON

THROUGH FLOW ECOLOGIES

A CONTINUOUS MATRIX OF DRIFT AND GRADIENT FIELDS ALLOWS FOR THE MOVEMENT AND ORGANIZATION
OF DRAINAGE AND WILDLIFE FLOWS, HABITATS AND PLANTINGS, TOGETHER WITH SITE FURNISHINGS, LIGHTING, AND INFORMATIONAL MARKERS

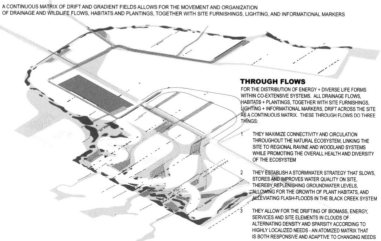

THROUGH FLOWS

FOR THE DISTRIBUTION OF ENERGY + DIVERSE LIFE FORMS
WITHIN CO-EXTENSIVE SYSTEMS. ALL DRAINAGE FLOWS,
HABITATS + PLANTINGS, TOGETHER WITH SITE FURNISHINGS,
LIGHTING + INFORMATIONAL MARKERS, DRIFT ACROSS THE SITE
AS A CONTINUOUS MATRIX. THESE THROUGH FLOWS DO THREE
THINGS:

1   THEY MAXIMIZE CONNECTIVITY AND CIRCULATION
THROUGHOUT THE NATURAL ECOSYSTEM, LINKING THE
SITE TO REGIONAL RAVINE AND WOODLAND SYSTEMS
WHILE PROMOTING THE OVERALL HEALTH AND DIVERSITY
OF THE ECOSYSTEM

2   THEY ESTABLISH A STORMWATER STRATEGY THAT SLOWS,
STORES AND IMPROVES WATER QUALITY ON SITE,
THEREBY REPLENISHING GROUNDWATER LEVELS,
ALLOWING FOR THE GROWTH OF PLANT HABITATS, AND
ALLEVIATING FLASH-FLOODS IN THE BLACK CREEK SYSTEM

3   THEY ALLOW FOR THE DRIFTING OF BIOMASS, ENERGY,
SERVICES AND SITE ELEMENTS IN CLOUDS OF
ALTERNATING DENSITY AND SPARSITY ACCORDING TO
HIGHLY LOCALIZED NEEDS - AN ATOMIZED MATRIX THAT
IS BOTH RESPONSIVE AND ADAPTIVE TO CHANGING NEEDS

ecology

    1. a branch of science concerned with the interrelationship of organisms and their environments

    2. the totality or pattern of relations between organisms and their environment

see TECHNOLOGY

Merriam Webster's Dictionary

---

edge

see FRONTIER/EDGE/MARGIN

---

edutainment

". . . My point is that do not concentrate
on what I state, create, or debate
I might be great, and you might admire
But what I say is to take you MUCH higher
MORE higher than the physical plane
to the plane of forces in the astral plane
The mental plane, and the final three
They're all around you, yet you can't see
So grab the sphere of life and aim it
and you'll be guided by Edutainment."[2]

see E-GORA

2. KRS-One, *Edutainment*, Edutainment, Boogie Down Productions, Jive 1368, 1990.

E-gora

"The E-gora is a globally accessible non-place where a virtual public is increasingly present. It is not only the 'net' space and its substrata of e-mail, chat, and VRML worlds that form it, but also those other 'familiar' territories such as public access television, C-Span, Court TV, or the voyeuristic spectacles of 'caught on tape' programming that are equally powerful entities within the vastness of the electro-sphere. Other players include the ubiquitous 'theme mall'—an offspring of the Las Vegas Strip—which has further been transformed into the simulacra of the new Universal Studios, Disney World, and other 'escape environments.' These places where 'real' events are contained by virtual spectacles have spawned a new Edutainment industry. The domestic scale spaces of the theme-restaurant, interactive game arcade, brand boutique such as Nike World, or even urban-scale sites like Times Square are all effectively technological spaces where hypertextual iconography flows and circulates endlessly, making for a marketplace that is electronically inflected and imagistically saturated. These locations as 'first reality' manifestations are effectively the glimpses of the emergence of the E-gora. Where the E-gora continues its transformation toward a global entity within the ether of networks and band-width real estate, the local conditions of architecture and urbanism seek a new spatiality capable of forming entirely new assemblies from these vectors of meaning and artifact."[3]

HANI RASHID
3. *E-GORA*, Advanced Studio, Summer 1997.

---

electronic marketplace

"Propelled by an ideology of progress, the delirium for consumption has disturbed the balance of an already tenuous distinction between the individual and the collective in modern mass societies. The electronic marketplace now reconfigures the traditional boundary between appearances and commonplace values in western culture pertaining to inner and spiritual truths."[4]

EVAN DOUGLIS
4. *E-Z Architecture: Counterfeit Paradigms of Dwelling in the Mail Order House*, Advanced Studio, Summer 1996.

electro-sphere

"The appropriation and celebration of the transmittability and dispensing
of three-dimensional entities across the electro-sphere is a fundamental
extension of Marshall McLuhan's notion that global village will be formed
symptomatically of and by 'retribalization.' The presence and proliferation
of VRML throughout the Internet, for example, marks a moment in history
where communication technology is meeting spatial manufacture head
on. Information and space are now fusing as disembodied circumstances
that are mutable, transformational, temporal, and mnemonic."[5]

HANI RASHID
5. *Informing Interiorities:
Prototypical Investigations in
VRML*, Advanced Studio V, Fall
1997.

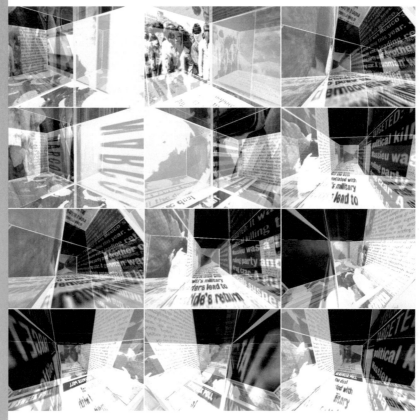

FIG. 24 Xavier Calderon, *Media
City: Architecture at the Interval*,
Advanced Studio V, Hani
Rashid, critic, Fall 1994.

entropy

"This studio proposes the recognition of entropy as a positive architectural
term, as a counter-strategy to the often camouflaged organicist tendency
toward order in contemporary architectural speculation. Entropy is the
shadow of all organization; it is the background noise from which all
dynamic patterns emerge.

  Formal techniques, programmatic strategies, and site-specific responses
must be converted into weapons against themselves, becoming only so
much raw material to be reformatted according to entropic principles. This
is therefore not about 'inventing' new forms, new programs, or new sites
as such. It is about reinventing them, again and again, by submitting them
to a process of continuous sampling, splicing, mixing, and distortion that
renders the original unrecognizable, in an eternal return toward infinity
(or zero)—the white noise of positive feedback.

REINHOLD MARTIN
6. *Entropy Lab*, Advanced
Studio V, Fall 1999.

This research located itself at a convergence of forces that marks a dispersed territoriality no longer centered on the density, sensory stimulation,
or dynamism of the 20th-century city—a zone occupied by a denaturalized,
technologically mediated, and structurally alienated subjectivity, adrift.
For just as the suppression of entropy is the hallmark of the signal-to-noise
ratios that underlie every naive technological utopianism conjured up by
the information age, so must all counter-architectures look upon the
urbanity-degree-zero of already existing future cities as an opportunity
to maximize alienation and accelerate entropy, in recognition of their
critical and even utopian value."[6]

PLATES 1.12–1.13

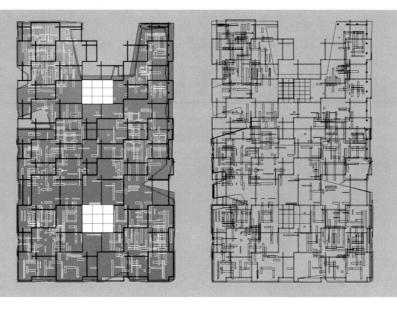

FIG. 25 Tim Nichols, *Entropy
Lab,* Advanced Studio V,
Reinhold Martin, critic, Fall
1999.

epiphany

I have had very strong epiphanies in my career, and each time everything
shifts. One of them occurred when I turned 40 and decided that I was
never again going to work for a client whom I did not like, who was not
going to build my work.

Have you worked with clients who didn't support your work?

When we first started practicing in New York, we had two bodies of work:
bad neoclassical apartment renovations and a published body of very
modernist work that won awards. It got us into trouble because we had
no interest in the other stuff. When the recession hit we put our practice
into storage and I took a full-time teaching job at Cornell. We started
interviewing clients instead of having them interview us. Ever since
then our practice has changed. We build projects that we like, and we work
with people who we like, and it is a much better situation for everyone.

My other epiphany, if you could call it that, was my decision to start
writing. I have files and files of things that I have written about that I am
finally revising and editing. There is a strong and valid intellectual basis
for the body of work that we have produced, yet I believe it is not one that
is publicly discussed. I think that is problematic, yet as an artist you do

VICTORIA MEYERS

VICTORIA MEYERS

not put yourself into a public realm with something you are working on until it is ready to be in that public realm. I have always felt an incredible shame for people who solidify themselves too early.

evolution

"The studio sought to illuminate the critical role of conceptual thought in the evolutionary process of all tectonic proposals. Intensive studies into the syntactical nature of architecture and its capacity to incite the imaginary became the basis of invention."[7]

EVAN DOUGLIS
7. *Foreign/Domestic*, Core Studio I, Fall 1995.

excavation

"How does one erase something and then re-create that which is erased through a trace? Find a body. Erase the body. Represent the body (new body) which is traced through a process of excavation."[8]

VICTORIA MEYERS
8. *Chapel of the Innocents*, Advanced Studio IV, Spring 1996.

exhibition

see BUILDING/CONSTRUCTION

expansion, lateral

"Most developer-driven applications (of air-right and zoning laws) result in vertical accumulations only. The studio will test alternative and opportunistic interpretations that would incorporate but not be limited to strategies of lateral expansion, interconnection, annexation, fragmentation, and dispersal."[9]

SULAN KOLATAN
9. *Malltown Manhattan*, Advanced Studio V, Fall 1994.

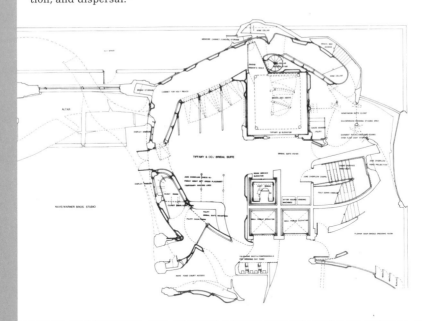

FIG. 26 Bruce Johnson, *Malltown Manhattan*, Advanced Studio V, Sulan Kolatan, critic, Fall 1994.

lateral

1. of or relating to the side
2. situated on, directed toward, or coming from the side
3. extending from side to side
4. produced with passage of breath around the side of a constriction formed with the tongue

Merriam Webster's Dictionary

expansion

1. expanse
2. the act or process of expanding
3. the quality or state of being expanded
4. (a) an expanded part; (b) something that results from an act of expanding
5. the result of carrying out an indicated mathematical operation: the expression of a function in the form of a series

experience   see ART/ARTIST; IDEA/CONCEPT; PHENOMENON/PHENOMENOLOGY; REAL

experimentation   see COMPUTER; MATERIAL/MATERIALITY; NORMATIVE; PEDAGOGY, COLUMBIA; STUDIOS, CORE; TEACHING

F

feedback

"In an architectural 'machine' such as this, the technical desire to integrate each system—mechanical systems, laboratory spaces, support spaces, office spaces, etc.—into a functional whole (however flexible and open) will be confronted with the possibility of dissolving these entities into one another, and introducing a new notion of functionality based not on performative efficiency but mutual interference. In other words, the aim will not be to 'generate' new forms of laboratory and office space based on external factors, but to confront this machine with its own convention and norms—to induce it to interfere with itself, to turn in on itself, and to infiltrate itself with its own determinacies."[1]

REINHOLD MARTIN
1. *Technopolis: Post-urban/ Post-human*, Advanced Studio V, Fall 1998.

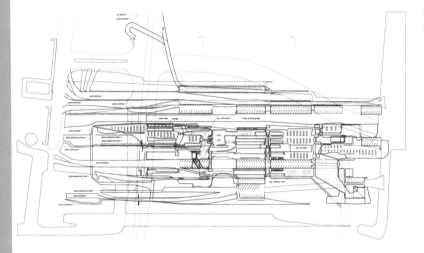

FIG. 27 Maia Small, *Technopolis: Post-urban/ Post-human*, Advanced Studio V, Reinhold Martin, critic, Fall 1998.

In what ways are we looking at the question of feedback more critically now than the architects who were influenced by the same theories in the 1950s and 1960s?

It is not a question to which I think there is a self-evident or easy answer. You could substitute a feedback model for a linear model of history for example. One of the classic critiques of feedback is the closed loop, which a lot of the theory of today has already anticipated. Self-organizing systems tend to refer themselves to open systems, which are still organisms. And the impression is that one overcomes the totalizing dimensions of the feedback loop systems theory by opening the system out to its environment and through taking in "forces" from the external environment and processing them in order to get a form. It is attempting to stage a spatial and temporal indeterminacy. It is not just that spatial indeterminacy is the latest thing along the line; it is that the line itself is thought at an indeter-

REINHOLD MARTIN

minate level. It is history itself as not fully indeterminate, because history is determinate.

see CHIMERA; CO-CITATION; ENTROPY; NONLINEAR; ORGANIZATION; PARTICLES; STUDIO/PRACTICE; TECHNOLOGY

field

"A field condition is any formal or spatial matrix capable of unifying diverse elements while respecting the identity of each. Field configurations are loosely bounded aggregates characterized by porosity and local interconnectivity. The internal regulations of the parts are decisive; overall shape and extent are highly fluid. Field conditions imply a shift from the one toward the many, from individuals to collectives, from objects to fields. Field conditions are bottom-up phenomena, defined not by overarching geometrical schemas but by intricate local connections. Interval, repetition, and seriality are key concepts: a shift from demarcating lines to unifying surfaces. Program and event can unfold freely across the given field. Form matters, but not so much the form of things as the forms between things."[2]

STAN ALLEN
2. *Field Conditions*, Advanced Studio VI, Spring 1995.

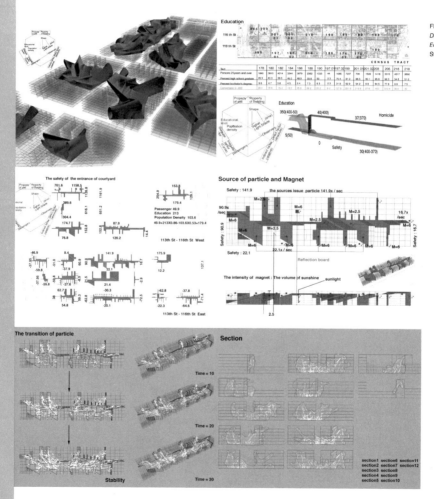

FIG. 28 Masatoshi Naito, *Datascapes New York: Artificial Ecologies*, Advanced Studio V, Stan Allen, critic, Fall 1998.

You have talked about the disappearance of the frame and the introduction of the field. On the one hand, this suggests a lack of determinacy, yet on the other hand, when discussing the field, you talk about the forces that are at play within the field, and about a precise accumulation and analysis of data, which, if played out, could be construed as ultra-deterministic.

What is interesting about field conditions and datascapes is that while the data may be highly deterministic, the effects can never be predicted in advance. A strict definition of field is not about material; it is about immaterial forces. When you run an electrical field through a plate that has metal filings on it, those filings will align but the filings are not the field, they just register the invisible forces of the field. This is a dilemma for architects: we are interested in those invisible forces, but we know that we can never work directly with them, only with the graphic or the material registration of those forces. Architecture can be a registration of immaterial forces, but architecture itself is material; it is concrete; it is object-like. To deny that is to paralyze yourself as an architect. As an architect, you do not write the script, you build the theater and construct the surfaces on which events play out. The information that you embed in those surfaces is going to have an impact on those events, but you do not design the events. This returns to the sense of working concretely within the limits of the discipline. For me it is more interesting to ask what you can do within these limits than to try desperately to escape them.

STAN ALLEN

"The field upon which architecture is deployed in our 'post-information age' is broader and less well defined. The singular point of view or experience is replaced by a 'non-perfectionist' architecture that deliberately builds on notions of the unpredictable, the unplanned, and remains open-ended with respect to future possibilities.... The ever increasing rate of change creates a constantly fluctuating condition which demands not a space of stability and false certitude but one that offers multiple readings and infinite possibilities. This opens up the field of architecture for pioneering reinvention within the misalignments, thus a 'non-perfectionist' architecture."[3]

ASYMPTOTE
3. Georgi Stanishev,"Designing the Unpredictable" (interview), *World Architecture* 54 (March 1997): 75.

"A generic tenement flat serves as the territorial field for future intervention. Inflective patterns of daily routine found inscribed within the domestic offer evidence toward the creation of new programs of dwelling."[4]

EVAN DOUGLIS
4. *The Building in Pain: Disagreeable Beauty in the Domestic Realm*, Advanced Studio, Summer 1994.

"Using animation-based software, urbanism can be investigated as a network of interacting fields and forces rather than as a tableau of inert objects that can be exchanged and replaced.... During the term, the studio experimented with the ways in which fields and forces can shape and engender discrete, concrete forms of organization. Rather than beginning with buildings or objects, we began with urban flow conditions. However, this studio invested heavily in architectural objects and the aim of the experiment was the proposal of architectural spaces and organizations that are engendered from forces and fields."[5]

GREG LYNN
5. *Tokyo Experiment IV: Tokyo Das Kapital*, Advanced Studio VI, Spring 1996.

FIG. 29 Kolatan/MacDonald Studio, *Berlin Spreebogen Competition*, 1993.

field   *Merriam Webster's Dictionary*

    1. (a) an open land area free of woods and buildings; (b) an area of cleared enclosed land used for cultivation or pasture; (c) the place where a battle is fought; (d) a large unbroken expanse

    2. (a) an area or division of an activity; (b) the sphere of practical operation outside a base (as a laboratory, office, or factory); (c) an area constructed, equipped, or marked for sports

    4. the individuals that make up all or part of the participants in a sports activity; especially: all participants with the exception of the favorite or the winner in a contest where more than two are entered

    5. the area visible through the lens of an optical instrument

    6. (a) a region or space in which a given effect (as magnetism) exists; (b) a region of embryonic tissue capable of a particular type of differentiation

    7. a set of mathematical elements that is subject to two binary operations the second of which is distributive relative to the first and that constitutes a commutative group under the first operation and also under the second if the zero or unit element under the first is omitted

see ORGANIZATION; PERFORMANCE; TECHNOLOGY

film

I have always been interested in the inverse pedagogical methods of Joseph Beuys and Jean-Luc Godard. Godard systematically dismantles film on every level from structure to assembly and yet the outcome is indisputably film. You ask certain questions regarding making, reading, and experience when you view a Godard film, and these same questions should be put to architecture.   HANI RASHID

How did your interest in the films of Alfred Hitchcock influence the research in your studio?
Hitchcock uses spatial techniques to describe narrative in a unique way. I try to understand and build this interesting space between the urban   LESLIE GILL

environment, its perimeter, and the extreme. He is someone who uses that very clearly and instrumentalizes it within the medium of film.

Architecture and criticism use a lot of references. I try to build in an understanding of at least one of these other pieces by studying the original reference rather than the criticism of it.

see IMAGE; MONTAGE

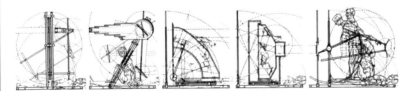

FIG. 30 Stephen Wang, *North by Northwest: A Study of the Mystery/Spy Genre,* Advanced Studio VI, Karen Bausman and Leslie Gill, critics, Spring 1991.

form

KATHRYN DEAN

Certain ideas about time and force that lead to the generation of form are being taken apart. Time and force are being understood as ideas of duration and change rather than as generators of images of time. In the early explorations of animation in architecture, there was a formal rigor and that was limiting. How that form was related to the conditions in the world was not always so obvious.

There has been a shift across the board in terms of questioning whether generating a formal result is really going to do anything for anyone beyond a few architects. Michael Bell and Mark Wigley have shifted the tone of the School in this regard by asking questions about the importance of these results. This regrounds the School and in many of the classes there is a discussion of real-life practice issues.

F

This project was concerned with developing structures generated from the close tracking of material logics as they undergo physical change. We began with a given dynamic, such as ink mixing with water, to establish an initial morphology: an index of structural development. This form/structure was then analyzed in terms of force, the lines of which were rigorously translated into another material system, one of virtual or actual string."[6]
see AESTHETICS/APPEARANCE; DIAGRAM; FIELD

REISER/UMEMOTO
6. *Convergent Structures*, Advanced Studio V, Fall 1998.

frame

In your Spring 1994 studio brief, you applied the concept of the frame to the city of Las Vegas, implying that the city itself is an object to be consumed.

I "framed" for the purposes of studying an aspect of the city—the Strip—and proposed that the material outside of that "frame" was to specifically inform the Strip. Las Vegas is horrifying, ugly, and fascinating; it is about issues of density, sprawl, exaggeration, consumption, blankness, and dryness—it is a view into a version of our future. Many of the third-year and AAD students had never been to the West, often having focused on New York and the East. By focusing on Las Vegas, they had an opportunity to observe many things first-hand, including the rampant development and suburban sprawl, which in Las Vegas is particularly gruesome and exaggerated. Las Vegas is also about the desert. I have taken the students to Michael Heizer's *Double Negative* as well as the Hoover Dam, both of which exist outside the "frame" of the city and are often ignored. We also use the research and analysis from *Learning from Las Vegas* because, even though it is dated, as a process it is very interesting. The city has changed radically since then; there are traffic jams and you can no longer move at 40 miles an hour. That incredible document exists as a model but it is now inaccurate and we need to reframe it.

LAURIE HAWKINSON

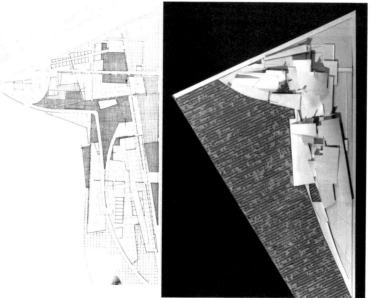

FIG. 31 Kirsten Mercer, *Studio Las Vegas*, Advanced Studio VI, Laurie Hawkinson, critic, Spring 1994.

How do you frame a city that is growing faster than any other city in this country?

This, of course, is an impossible task. We narrowed our focus by looking at different subjects. In 1994, we looked at programs that engaged the people who live in Las Vegas: the "unknown" residential population. Everything in Las Vegas is geared toward the visitor but there is a huge population that makes this thing work. For instance, the amount of food that must be brought in, processed, delivered, prepared, and removed is mind-boggling. One student, Kirsten Mercer, proposed an old-age home for a day visitor. It was a great program and an interesting project.

In 1995, there was a competition for a federal courthouse, which we took as a program for another studio. We tested how this building typology works within the city, changes it, or how it is modified because of it; Las Vegas is a real moving target.

In 1997, I used a competition for David's Island, New York, as a studio program and the students wanted to go to Las Vegas and see the variety of landscapes and programs out there. We used Las Vegas as a lens through which we could view David's Island.

see FIELD; IDEA/CONCEPT; STUDIOS, CORE

LAURIE HAWKINSON

PLATES 1.14–1.15

FIG. 32 Ferda Kolatan, *Courthouse, Las Vegas, Nevada*, Advanced Studio VI, Laurie Hawkinson, critic, Spring 1995.

Plan view underneath freeway overpass

Areas of court-related programs merged into existing downtown fabric such as freeway, parking structure, sidewalk, and bus stop.

Plan view of sidewalk

frontier/edge/margin

"We are focusing on 'links' rather than 'divisions.' The struggle is not to explore the borders or limits that architecture has with other disciplines but rather to recognize and understand ways in which architecture is influenced and in turn exerts influence. The presupposition that there is a separation between architecture and other fields of cultural influence is problematic for us. We seek to blur that distinction."[7]

ASYMPTOTE
7. Georgi Stanishev, "Designing the Unpredictable" (interview), *World Architecture* 54 (March 1997): 1.

What constitutes the margin?
Perhaps it can be defined by looking at other disciplines, such as modern painting, sculpture, and film, where certain groups stood in defiance to accepted styles and tastes. I suppose in architecture the margin exists in areas that are not considered legitimate to the practice as it is currently defined. In some ways virtual reality as an architecture, not as entertainment, is marginal, as is the use of certain types of technology to make buildings liquid, breathe, fluctuate, and so on, through the incorporation of computer systems. These two areas interest us and they are both perceived as "radical." Their marginality is only a function of the slowness and reticence of architects to understand their irreversible and profound impact.

HANI RASHID

You seem to be interested in the redefinition of boundaries—Las Vegas, for example.
I am interested in how edges, boundaries, and lines can be dissolved. I am interested in engaging architecture on all fronts, wherever it can be found and worked. One cannot engage the potential complexities of site and program by working exclusively with form.
see BOUNDARY; LOCAL/GLOBAL; MODERN/MODERNISM; REAL

LAURIE HAWKINSON

function

see MODERN/MODERNISM; PERFORMANCE; REAL

G

generation

Many of the discussions I have had with the faculty suggest that the divide between the younger and older generation came as a result of the latter's condemnation of the architectural signature.

I am going to disagree with all of the mental constructs that are implied in what you just said—the concept of generation, the category of signature, the category of fashion.

  The notion of category or generation is a very useful classification system, but it is only a system. I would never encourage the freezing of categories into generations. I think it is very important to keep it moving even though there are some people who have been longer at it than others.

see ARCHITECTURE CULTURE; PERFORMANCE

BERNARD TSCHUMI

geometry

"To the extent that geometry is the preferred language for architectural communication, its interrogation has become the dominant form of writing in architecture. More precisely, the majority of both spatial and theoretical innovations in architecture have become increasingly dependent on geometric conflicts.... [A]ny writing in architecture must begin with a geometry that does not reduce matter to ideal forms. Geometries that not only maintain but measure amorphousness in some form resist the definition of writing against architecture."[1]

GREG LYNN
1. "Probable Geometries: The Architecture of Writing in Bodies," *ANY* 0 (May–June 1993): 44–45.

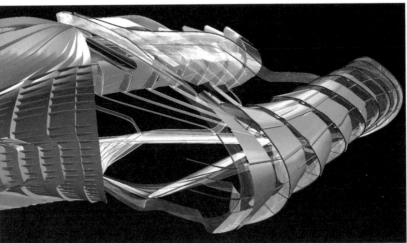

FIG. 33 Rosalinda Malibiran, Aspassia Papazaharia, Annie Shu, and Alexandra Ultsch, *The Symbiote (Predator Germ Cell Project)*, Advanced Studio VI, Greg Lynn, critic, Spring 2000.

"At the outset, each student was asked to select one of a series of examples of topologically complex figures documented in a mathematical handbook, and to produce a scaleless model and a full graphic description of the object. These objects and the subsequent transformations to which they were subjected became a collective resource on which the work undertaken was able to draw for the remainder of the term. The radical contingency

REINHOLD MARTIN
2. *Topological Thought: House*, Core Studio II, Spring 1999.

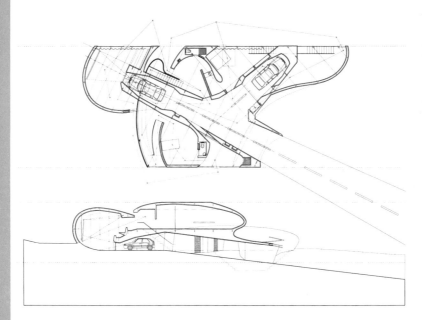

FIG. 34 Keith Kaseman,
Topological Thought: House,
Core Studio II, Reinhold Martin,
critic, Spring 1999.

of formal techniques was thus confronted directly, through the recognition that complex topological manipulations (such as those studies) could be carried out in a variety of geometric systems. In all cases, however, the question of the 'house' was reformulated as a question of unstable and contingent relations inside and outside, activated at a number of scales."[2]

"I have always been fascinated by geometry and its relationship to life through built form. It is often said that architecture is 'frozen music.' More precisely stated, architecture is really frozen form. In contrast, the world is in a state of constant movement, placing architecture in an intermediary role. It is in fact part of the language of architecture to create a dialogue between the geometrical and the constructional precision of the building and the transitory, impermanent sensations of space.... Geometry is a mathematical construct. It is drawn, fixed on a surface, and looked at from a distance. Experience is comprehended. It is sequential, related to space, topological, and looked at from inside. The projects in the studio should provide a means for inhabiting both realms."[3]

VICTORIA MEYERS
3. *Line*, Advanced Studio V,
Fall 1998.

We first developed a model for the Graz Music Theater competition that hinges on the relationship between the way we utilized the computer in the office and in the studio. It helped us to understand how to resolve the use of complex geometry toward a material definition in structure and building. An engineer named Ysrael Seinuk, with whom we collaborated in our structures class at Cooper Union, initially suggested the model. We showed him an Alias drawing of the vault for the theater and he said that it was not applicable in a one-to-one translation with the structural design, so we had to find a way of modeling it with materials. He suggested a catenary system similar to the one used by Antoni Gaudí but, in our case, forces act in several different directions and locations within this environment. We had

JESSE REISER

to build an augmented system where gravity, lateral, and transverse forces would modify the structural array of the catenary.

There were a series of arguments that developed at the School with affiliated people like Sanford Kwinter and Jeff Kipnis, regarding computation and calculations. Although I do not use those words, they appear to clarify the similarities and differences between what one would find in the computational stage of the computer and the computational space of materials. One could argue that computer modeling is reductive because it models itself on material behavior first, but has difficulty incorporating a variety of behaviors.

geometry   *Merriam Webster's Dictionary*

   1. (a) a branch of mathematics that deals with the measurement, properties, and relationships of points, lines, angles, surfaces, and solids; broadly: the study of properties of given elements that remain invariant under specified transformations; (b) a particular type or system of geometry

   2. (a) configuration; (b) surface shape

   3. an arrangement of objects or parts that suggests geometric figures

see COMPLEXITY; COMPUTER

global

see LOCAL/GLOBAL

history

"[I]deally architectural history should be taught as cultural history, which is a challenge since architects and architectural historians are not generally trained to approach the topic in this way. It is important that curricula be developed to include within their overview three important subsets; the history of landscape, technology, and industrial design. It is certain that different subsets will have to be emphasized in different cultural situations, depending on the part of the world in which the architect is being trained."[1]

KENNETH FRAMPTON
1. "Seven Points for the Millennium: An Untimely Manifesto," *Journal of Architecture* 5, no. 1 (Spring 2000): 22.

"If the simple reconstitution of historic building types is frustrated by modern urban complexities, the interrelational properties of these complexities may be a way of rethinking urban form and program. Correlations draw attention toward interdependent characteristics in an urban field. Diverse building sections and program relations are a kind of prepositional chart suggesting the intrinsic intersection of programs as a bond, fastening, or disjunctive force."[2]

STEVEN HOLL
2. "Within the City: Phenomena of Relations," *Design Quarterly* 139 (1988): 13.

FIG. 35 Steven Holl, *MIT Residence*, Cambridge, Massachusetts, anticipated completion 2003.

When you discussed the MIT project, you spoke about a very specific analysis of context, site, and history. How do you begin to reconcile these issues in the design process?

Rudolph Steiner said, "Every site on Earth has a history." That's very important to me. It does not need to be engaged directly, but to do something without knowing anything about it is completely insensitive as an architect. I applaud radical building, but I have no tolerance for stupidity and lack of awareness. It's like a surgeon performing an operation without knowing anything about the patient. A minimum amount of knowledge about a situation is important. I don't see that as historicism; it's common sense. The site of our MIT project, for example, was part of the Charles River until the river was filled in. The soil alone couldn't hold up the buildings, so we had to build a giant mat of concrete six or eight feet thick and

STEVEN HOLL

the whole building floats on it, like a ship. The building is like a sponge, with porosity functioning as a programmatic concept. This mat foundation goes back to the geological history of the site. The more you know about the situation when you are making something, the more exciting it is, but I don't think it has to do with postmodernism or modernism per se. It has to do with a depth rather than a shallowness. We have more information now than ever. You can get any kind of information on the Internet, but that doesn't necessarily yield more wisdom. Spending a couple of days doing a little research about a site or a situation is minimal when you end up spending five years between the beginning of a project and when it's occupied. Students don't understand that 13 weeks in the studio is nothing compared to the time it takes to realize a work of architecture.

see MATERIAL/MATERIALITY; MODERN/MODERNISM; PEDAGOGY, COLUMBIA; REAL; TEACHING; TREND

house/home

"The house, often posited as a paradigm of beauty in popular culture, is on the contrary a concealed site for conflicting social practices. Inflective patterns of daily routine found within the domestic offer evidence toward the creation of new programs of dwelling."[3]

EVAN DOUGLIS
3. *The Building in Pain: Disagreeable Beauty in the Domestic Realm*, Advanced Studio, Summer 1994.

"Behind the curtain of apparent normalcy flow rapid exchanges of desire, information, and power moving back and forth through the surface of material possession. It is here we find a highly sophisticated arena of control. This general method of domination resonates in the program of the Mail-Order House. A service industry offers to the consumer-at-large an entire menu of suburban home plans in the form of paper documents. Masquerading as the architect's counterfeit, the system endlessly recycles flat parodies of postmodernism in the promise of delivering the buyer's ideal 'dream house': a seamless exploitation of fantasy where the recombinant caricatures of architecture are sold as the ultimate utopian accessory."[4]

4. *E-Z Architecture: Counterfeit Paradigms of Dwelling in the Mail-Order House*, Advanced Studio, Summer 1996.

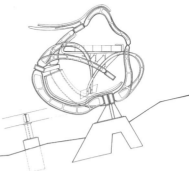

FIG. 36 Adam Dayem, Core Studio II, Evan Douglis, critic, Spring 1999.

"The single-family house has been and remains an exemplary subject for formal and programmatic innovation. It was expected that an unusual degree of specificity and detail would be attained in these projects, inasmuch as many issues of domesticity would not be brought out solely through conventional architectural description. Furthermore the so-called 'fitting out' of the house necessitated consideration of issues that, in

REISER/UMEMOTO
5. *Sub-Urbanity*, Advanced Studio VI, Spring 1996.

projects of larger scope, would be termed trivial or not within the architect's purview. The house, therefore, was to be understood as a complex field of resistances where the conventions of architecture (or architects) would confront the manifold conventions of everyday life. A conservative theater of operations—yet one not immune to change. In the worlds of Rilke, 'One is never so close to change as when life seems unbearable even in the smallest and most everyday things.'"[5]

house   *Merriam Webster's Dictionary*

   1. a building that serves as living quarters for one or a few families

   2. (a) a shelter or refuge (as a nest or den) of a wild animal; (b) a building in which something is housed

   3. a family including ancestors, descendants, and kindred

   4. (a) a legislative, deliberative, or consultative assembly; especially: one constituting a division of a bicameral body; (b) the building or chamber where such an assembly meets; (c) a quorum of such an assembly

   5. (a) a place of business or entertainment; (b) (1): a business organization; (2): a gambling establishment; (c) the audience in a theater or concert hall

   6. a type of dance music mixed by a disc jockey that features overdubbing with a heavy repetitive drumbeat and repeated electronic melody lines.

see CHIMERA; GEOMETRY; MEMORY; MODERN/MODERNISM; NORMATIVE; OTHER

hybrid

"This studio focused on the search for a new type of urbanism in the form of what we will call a hybrid interchange. The purpose of this formation is twofold. First to enable the precise mixing of what are presently distinct stratified urban domains: fabric, green space, elevated highway, primary streets, secondary streets, etc. Second, beyond simply combining the known, to foster the development of new and perhaps unanticipated programs and organizations as an inherent property of the hybrid."[6]

REISER/UMEMOTO
6. *125th Street Interchange,*
Advanced Studio V, Fall 1996.

PLATES 1.16–1.17

hybrid   *Merriam Webster's Dictionary*

   1. an offspring of two animals or plants of different races, breeds, varieties, species, or genera

   2. a person whose background is a blend of two diverse cultures or traditions

   3. (a) something heterogeneous in origin or composition; (b) something (as a power plant, vehicle, or electronic circuit) that has two different types of components performing essentially the same function

see CHIMERA; ORGANIC/ORGANICISM; REAL; SURFACE

I

idea/concept

"The studio stressed the procedural and operational character of architecture—its capacity to initiate and support a complex series of events in the world, rather than to refer hermetically to its own history, or to the process of design."[1]

STAN ALLEN
1. *Event/Infra/Structure*, Advanced Studio VI, Spring 1998.

You ask your students to ask a lot of questions. How do you define the parameters within which those questions are asked?
There are boundaries, but the boundaries are synonymous with particular goals and aspirations that we have for the students and their work. It has to do with the level of investment in the concept and in the technical representational tools that can frame and support that concept. They need to understand the power of a map or a plan; they need to understand which section to draw and why; they need to understand the power of the model and the power of bringing related material as references. Abstract ideas from other disciplines can be brought to architecture just as they can be employed to make a painting or a film. We need to learn how to take an idea and move it through the material of architecture. It is important that the students understand how to work with certain conventions because what they do will have a relationship to building. Whether the project gets built or not, architecture is always the frame.

LAURIE HAWKINSON

"By 1980 I had begun to read philosophers like Henri Bergson and Maurice Merleau-Ponty, who talked about the difference between time, which is an abstract idea, and duration, which is how we experience time. Some events seem like weeks, when they're only moments, while others are over before they begin. Space is like that, too. I learned that *how* we experience something, not some abstract idea, is primary to the meaning of our existence, and that is what my architecture had to address."[2]

STEVEN HOLL
2. Quoted in Aaron Betsky, "Steven Holl" (interview), *Metropolitan Home* 30, no. 6 (November/December 1998): 66.

"This studio will employ neither the hermetic *Gesamtkunstwerk* of the Wagnerian theater nor attempt to 'democratize' the values of the *ancien régime*. Rather than despairing at the loss of a presumably coherent public realm we will consider ways of establishing 'transversal' alliances that would trace 'diagonal lines' of possibility in the social, political, and ultimately architectural fabric. The competition program (contrary to the impulse to either negate or synthesize) will be of immense value in this undertaking. Nothing in the program is to be discarded—rather it is to be reapportioned and proportioned according to the imperatives of continuity. This is as much a formal model as a social one. What should be sought are the paradigms that would attenuate the liminal conditions of architecture: those moments engendered classically by thresholds. Desired are morphologies that would suspend the well-known dialectics of inside/outside, structure/ornamentation,

REISER/UMEMOTO
3. *Cardiff Bay Opera House*, Advanced Studio, Summer 1994.

public/private, etc., while at the same time, addressing the requirements of the competition brief."[3]

see FRAME; PEDAGOGY, COLUMBIA; STUDIOS, CORE

identity

see CHIMERA; NOSTALGIA

image

There is an intense production of imagery at Columbia, which has led some people to view the School's program as singular. Do you see a rigor to this production of imagery?

The media is still in its infancy both in the School and in a larger context. We are moving toward a refinement where the work is beginning to challenge the bias of the software. The origination of information, however, is unique to the faculty and students, all of whom are committed to the investigative process.

KAREN BAUSMAN

FIG. 37 Tamara Iwaselzko, *Fantastic Manhattan: Dissecting the Table, the Umbrella, the Sewing Machine*, Advanced Studio V, Karen Bausman, critic, Fall 1995.

Why is the process of photographing an object important to you?

It is not about the image; it is the transference of information. Photography is a traditional technique for cataloging information, realized only with the aid of a chemical process. Today that process of organizing information has, to a large degree, been digitized and the resulting images can be manipulated with various software applications. As we seek to reorganize biological information utilizing photographic procedures, does this mean these "specimens" exist in two dimensions only? Are these "specimens" symbols or are they models? Are they real? You're separating performance from material conditions.

KAREN BAUSMAN

"The studio looked at the pleasure of the city and its intrinsic relationship to the density of image. Image carries with it association, memory, content,

KATHRYN DEAN

4. *Institute for Contemporary Photography, New York City,* Advanced Studio IV, Spring 1998.

and desire. These pleasures are intrinsic to multiple art forms and make up much of the interest in modern life in the city."[4]

In a time when we are so saturated and co-opted by the sensual imagery of the culture industry, how do you avoid falling into the production of those same images?

I am not as interested in the image as a surface as much as I am interested in the structure or the instrument that forms the image. In terms of my work, I go either with the program or with the structure of the image and an understanding of the inherent canon that forms it. Through this unmaking, I can interpret it from my vantage point at the beginning of the 21st century.

LESLIE GILL

One great thing that comes out of the design studios is that students imagine great projects. They have no idea whether they can be done or not. They only know how to let the process of developing the project augment the project. They know how to illustrate a great idea and carry it to a certain level of representation, where the building or the project always represents the idea.

JEFFREY KIPNIS

The projects are diagrammatic and are developed to the level of a caricature, but students are not very good at seeing. They are so easily seduced by completely boring shiny objects. They have developed too much conceptual technique and far too little visual understanding of the consequences of that technique. There is a really great distinction in contemporary painting, for example, between image and picture painting.

The notion of the image comes from film studies, in which the picture has no material basis of any significance, or the materiality does not divert the image into another effect. Painting, which is everything in the painting including any image, avoids the discourse of the materiality of itself, like abstract expressionism. The really beautiful thing in the middle is a picture where the two come together. The picture is no longer about the phenomenology of materials nor an envy of film, but something quite different. Architecture is best when all of its effects are specific to material conditions without being anything like a phenomenology of materiality. You ask yourself what effects architecture can produce that no other discipline can. Those are rarely going to be instances that are open to paraphrase. If you have an idea for a project, that means it has already begun, it is merely languishing in the world of a diagram. The diagram is a machine to move materiality around, and all you need to do is move the material to represent the idea. Nothing irreducible occurs until the virus of an idea inhabits the body and produces a new kind of organism.

see AESTHETICS/APPEARANCE; COMPUTER; LANDSCAPE; PEDAGOGY, COLUMBIA; TEACHING

impurity

"Activities are defined as 'impure' when they threaten prohibitions on cleanliness, sexuality, and gender relations. Traces of this domestic order reveal the cultural anxiety attached to social constructions of the body."[5]

EVAN DOUGLIS
5. *The Building in Pain: Disagreeable Beauty in the Domestic Realm*, Advanced Studio, Summer 1994.

indeterminacy	see FEEDBACK; MOVEMENT; STUDIOS, CORE	

index	"[A]rchitects do not make buildings, they make drawings for buildings. In architecture the index points back not to a moment of physical contact but to the implied movements (cuts, displacements, grid shifts, shears, inversions, rotations, and folds) carried out within the abstract materials of drawing itself. Drawing may function as an index of a complex and sometimes dynamic process, but the building is an index of the fixed form of the drawing (which is necessarily complete—frozen—before the process of construction begins). Even the more radical operations of process (invoking chance, nonlinear geometries, or the readymade) are forced at a certain moment to hypostasize the complexities of process into a 'snapshot' to which the building then stands in mimetic relation: a conventional representation of perhaps unconventional materials. The reading of such a work inevitably evokes the deductive/divinatory paradigm of the index as a series of clues pointing back to the event of design and the hand of the author. This is a fundamentally modernist practice, reflecting a belief in the object's capacity to carry traces of its origin and making a corresponding belief in interpretation as unmasking a self-referential play of meaning."[6]	STAN ALLEN 6. "Tracks, Trace, Tricks," *ANY* 0 (May/June 1993): 10. PLATE 1.18

index
1. (a) a device that serves to indicate a value or quantity; (b) something that leads one to a particular fact or conclusion
2. a list arranged usually in alphabetical order of some specified datum: as (a) a list of items treated in a printed work that gives for each item the page number where it may be found; (b) a bibliographical analysis of groups of publications that is usually published periodically

see CO-CITATION; TRACE

Merriam Webster's Dictionary

individual/ individualism	*Where does the individual fit within the collective?* Increasingly we live in a global monoculture where work-play, sport-art, and politics are indistinguishable. The challenge is to establish a strategic position whereby ideas are not immediately consumed as "style," but allowed to develop to the full complexity needed to answer specific requirements of a larger cultural context. see AMERICA; CONFINEMENT	KAREN BAUSMAN

information	"[The Steel Cloud] is an episodic architecture inspired by optical machinery, flight simulation, surveillance technologies, and the omnipotence of telecommunications networks; an architecture configured from the instantaneous and forged out of the ever-revised structures of speed and information that now completely engulf our notion of a city."[7] "The 'post-Information age' refers to the ubiquitous and excessive contemporary condition of media culture, one that has proliferated to the extent that there is no longer any 'information' to be had from Information. The infinite possibilities for navigating have made any search for 'information' an infinite pursuit."[8]	ASYMPTOTE 7. "Analog Space to Digital Field," *Assemblage* 21 (August 1993): 30. 8. Georgi Stanishev, "Designing the Unpredictable" (interview), *World Architecture* 54 (March 1997): 74.

"The space of interactivity coupled with the prospects of multimedia are inevitably opening the way for architects to operate within the folds of information space developing and devising as of yet unforeseen territories for human interaction and dwelling."[9]

HANI RASHID
9. http://www.interactive.archi-tecture.com, Advanced Studio VI, Spring 1996.

"[According to Bateson's Rule,] a loss of information is accompanied by an increase in symmetry.... The terms 'information' and 'difference' are almost interchangeable. Homogeneity is understood as sameness or lack of difference. And disorganization is associated with an absence of differ-ence (information) and therefore, symmetry. Thus are difference, informa-tion, and organization related."[10]

GREG LYNN
10. "The Renewed Novelty of Symmetry," Arch Plus 128 (1995): 82.

information

1. the communication or reception of knowledge or intelligence
2. (a) knowledge obtained from investigation, study, or instruction; (b) the attribute inherent in and communicated by one of two or more alterna-tive sequences or arrangements of something; (c) (1): a signal or character representing data; (2): something which justifies change in a construct that represents physical or mental experience or another construct; (d) a quantitative measure of the content of information; specifically: a numer-ical quantity that measures the uncertainty in the outcome of an experi-ment to be performed

see IMAGE; NORMATIVE; SPACE; SYMMETRY; VIRTUAL/ACTUAL

Merriam Webster's Dictionary

infrastructure

"Infrastructures are flexible and anticipatory. They work with time and are open to change. By specifying what must be fixed and what is subject to change, they can be precise and indeterminate at the same time. They work through management and cultivation, changing slowly to adjust to shifting conditions. They do not progress toward a predetermined state (as with master planning strategies), but are always evolving within a loose envelope of constraints.... Infrastructure creates a directed field, where different architects and designers can contribute, but it sets technical and instru-mental limits to their work. Infrastructure itself works strategically, but it encourages tactical improvisation.

Infrastructures accommodate local contingency while maintaining over-all continuity. In the design of highways, bridges, canals, or aqueducts, for example, an extensive catalogue of strategies exist to accommodate irregu-larities in the terrain (doglegs, viaducts, cloverleafs, switchbacks, etc.), which are creatively employed to accommodate existing conditions while maintaining functional continuity. Infrastructure's default condition is reg-ularity—in the desert, the highway runs straight. Infrastructures are above all pragmatic. Because it operates instrumentally, infrastructural design is indifferent to formal debates. Invested neither in (ideal) regularity or in (disjunctive) irregularity, the designer is free to employ whatever works in particular conditions."[11]

STAN ALLEN
11. *Event/Infra/Structure*, Advanced Studio VI, Spring 1998.

PLATE 1.19

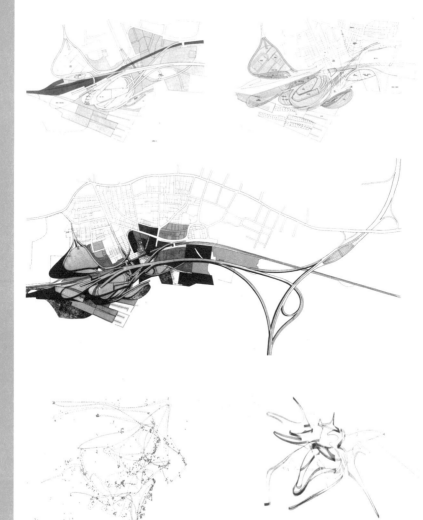

FIG. 38 Tony Owen, *Colossal Urbanism*, Advanced Studio V, Stan Allen, critic, Fall 1993.

FIG. 39 Maha Arakji, *Tokyo Studio: Mollusk City*, Advanced Studio VI, Stan Allen, critic, Spring 1994.

"The relationship between global systems of transport and exchange and specific or local architectural proposals have been understood (within modernism) as being mutually exclusive or in some dialectical relationship with one another.... The success of the proposal [of a proposed high-speed vehicular loop and the contexts it crosses] hinges on the capacity of the morphologies to actively mediate between global systems of transport and exchange and a specific site in the city. The morphologies must therefore, necessarily, derive from and be affiliated with the global (highway) system, yet be responsive to the context. In this sense they are globally rather than contextually driven."[12]

REISER/UMEMOTO
12. "Jesse Reiser and Nanako Umemoto: Recent Work," *Columbia Documents of Architecture and Theory*, vol. 6 (1997): 158, 166.

infrastructure

Merriam Webster's Dictionary

1. the underlying foundation or basic framework (as of a system or organization)
2. the permanent installations required for military purposes

3. the system of public works of a country, state, or region; also: the resources (as personnel, buildings, or equipment) required for an activity

see AMERICA; AUTOSCAPE; CITY; LINK/LINKAGE; NETWORK; STRUCTURE

instrumental

"This studio focused on the aggregate/compound processes and their conceptual and operational instrumentality in architectural design. In particular, it was premised on the notion of mosaicism or chimera. Both of these terms are descriptions of a 'pathological' condition, which occurs either spontaneously or is produced of diverse genetic parts."[13]

SULAN KOLATAN
13. *Chimera Formation in Morningside Heights*, Advanced Studio V, Fall 1996

FIG. 40 Katrin Kloetzer, Core Studio II, William MacDonald, critic, Spring 1998.

instrumental
1. (a) serving as a means, agent, or tool; (b) of, relating to, or done with an instrument or tool
2. relating to, composed for, or performed on a musical instrument
3. of, relating to, or being a grammatical case or form expressing means or agency
4. of or relating to instrumentalism

see MODERN/MODERNISM

Merriam Webster's Dictionary

interdisciplinary

My studios are very interdisciplinary. I did a sampling studio in which I collaborated with DJ Loop, I have brought in my artist friend Bruce Pearson, and I have brought in a professor from the mathematics department when I did the fourth-dimension studio. I have been in contact with a female physicist, Dr. Lene Hau, at Harvard who was in the *New York Times* recently because she discovered a way of slowing light down to 38 miles per hour. I have always wanted to find some way of having a studio in which the students could create buildings in which one can compare the speed of light and the speed of sound. Waves fascinate me because they are a basic component of matter, and the current discussion about computer-generated wave forms doesn't interest me the way that the basic phenomena of nature and light do.

see COLLABORATION; FRONTIER/EDGE/MARGIN; MUSIC; TEACHING; THEORY

VICTORIA MEYERS

interface

"One way that we began to reconsider architecture was in its role as 'interface.' This architecture has been regarded as a mediating structure not only between physically adjacent conditions but between diverse sites, separate or simultaneous events, as well as between divergent and irreconcilable cultural forces."[14]

ASYMPTOTE
14. Georgi Stanishev, "Designing the Unpredictable" (interview), *World Architecture* 54 (March 1997): 75.

"The project aims to create a public interface with Rockefeller University. The interface will allow the public to understand the human body in relationship to the theoretical work of the scientists at the university. The interface will reveal the implications of nonlinear dynamics on the physical world, for example, including the biological sciences. Research currently taking place at the university centers on the problem of patterns, growth, and form, and their dynamics in space and time. These studies attempt to create an interface between pure science, mathematics, and the biological world. The new public interface attempts to communicate that erudite research into a visceral registration through the creation of spatial models."[15]

VICTORIA MEYERS
15. *Architecture and the Body: Visceral Interface*, Advanced Studio, Summer 1996.

interface
1. a surface forming a common boundary of two bodies, spaces, or phases
2. (a) the place at which independent and often unrelated systems meet and act on or communicate with each other; (b) the means by which interaction or communication is achieved at an interface

Merriam Webster's Dictionary

intuition

If you rely on a certain definitive process as a way to make work, you will never discuss anything new. By understanding what belongs and what does not belong within a process, you learn how to self-edit. This intuition enables you to discover new complexities.

KATHRYN DEAN

FIG. 41 Dean Wolf Architects, *Earth Sky Knot*, 1998.

How do you teach that?

I teach students to trust their instincts and try out many options until they find one that works. For example, the idea that you start with an understanding of the private realm and then move out to the public realm is backward from what most architects would do. I am not interested in making a statement in the world if it is going to affect people in a negative way. My partner, Chuck Wolf, and I started working with small things, like a tiny studio and a tiny apartment, and then gradually moved outward. It prejudices space. It prejudices occupation. It is not backward in prejudicing those, but what is naturally prejudiced out of that is space, occupation, existence, life—different kinds of connections.

KATHRYN DEAN

PLATES 1.20–1.21

There is always something called intuition. Students find inspiration at three in the morning after two cups of coffee and a chocolate bar and the critic is not necessarily there, and the student is not necessarily sitting behind Adorno or Deleuze. You have to allow those kinds of openings to emerge. Only then are you able to reevaluate them in relation to the intentions that were set up or to accommodations that would have to be put into place. It may not have been exactly like what you had expected, so you either revise the conceptual position slightly or keep it and revise the model you just made.

   I would not give an exercise unless I wanted to do it myself. The more curious thing is when something happens in the Columbia studio that forces me to revise my own position. There is an assumption that everything emerges from my office studio into my academic studio, and that is not the case.

see PROCESS; STUDIO/PRACTICE

EVAN DOUGLIS

PLATES 1.22–1.23

investigation   see MODERN/MODERNISM; PEDAGOGY, COLUMBIA; PROGRAM; REAL; TEACHING

J

jury

MARK WIGLEY

At the heart of architectural education is the design jury, which requires multiple voices, all of whom will argue about what an object may or may not mean. First, there is a student trembling beside a model, then there is a ring of well-dressed experts, none of whom agree about anything, then a ring of students, and then witnesses. Everybody is crowded around as if maybe, late in the afternoon, after a full day of talking, something new will emerge in the discussion. No one is sure what is in front of them, or what exactly to say, but when all of those unsure people interact with the outside world, suddenly they have total confidence in what they are doing.

How do you teach people to maintain this sense of awe and mystery about what they are doing even after they move into an office where they are working on practical projects? How do we give architects the confidence to communicate that they do not know all the answers? A school of architecture should cultivate in its students a love of the discipline and the belief that architects—like filmmakers, painters, philosophers, and mathematicians—have the capacity to offer intelligent reflections on the world.

The responsibility of a school might simply be to allow the architect's personality, which is at once overly optimistic and full of doubt, to survive.

landscape

2.01

Dean Wolf Architects

Earth Sky Knot

1998

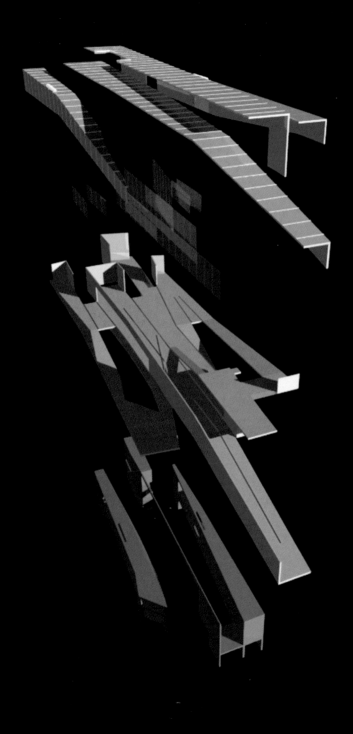

light
2.02
Adam Dayem
*Museum for
Contemporary Sculpture*
Advanced Studio IV
Kathryn Dean, critic
Spring 2000

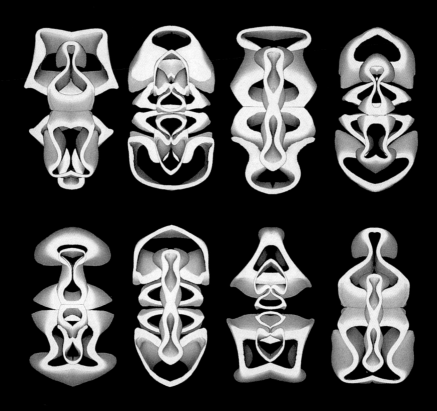

material/materiality

2.03 (left)

Evan Douglis

*The Presence of
Objects* (exhibition)

1999

2.04 (right)

Seungki Min

Core Studio II

Evan Douglis, critic

Spring 1999

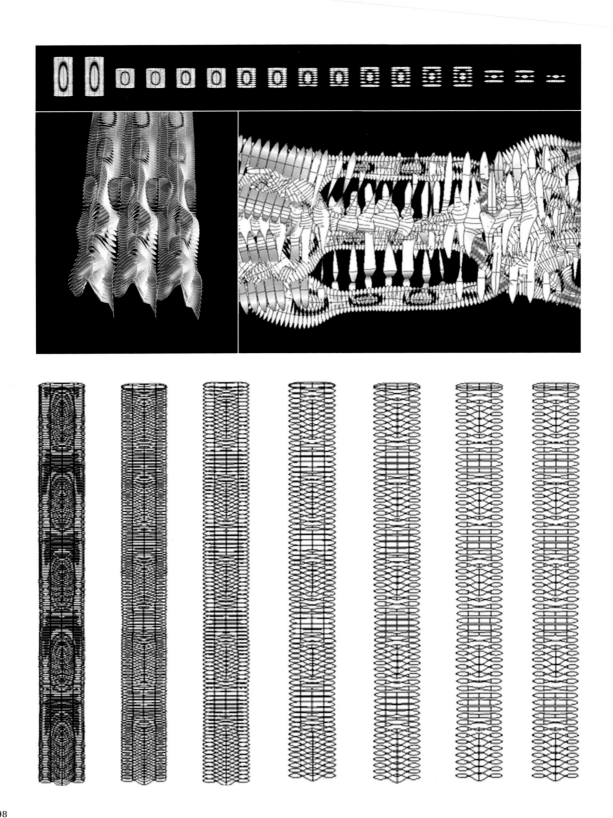

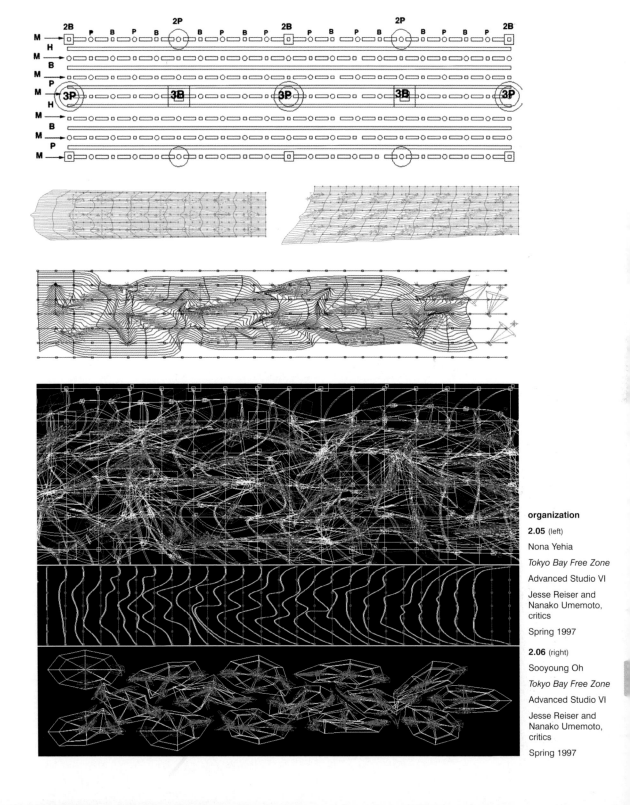

Scenario 1A plan

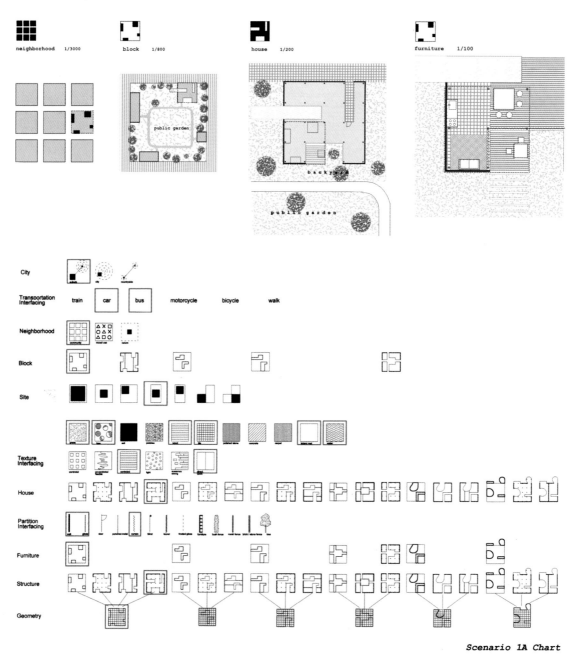

neighborhood 1/3000

block 1/800

public garden

house 1/200

backyard

public garden

furniture 1/100

City

Transportation Interfacing

train   car   bus   motorcycle   bicycle   walk

Neighborhood

Block

Site

Texture Interfacing

House

Partition Interfacing

Furniture

Structure

Geometry

Scenario 1A Chart

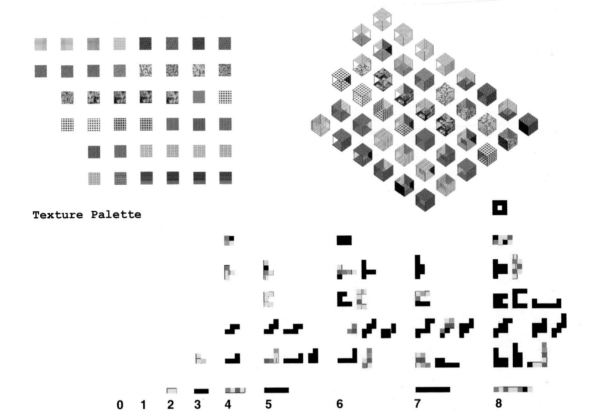

Texture Palette

0 1 2 3 4 5 6 7 8

pedagogy, Columbia

2.07

Kaori Sato

Mail Order House: The Real before the Real

Advanced Studio VI

Stan Allen, critic

Spring 2000

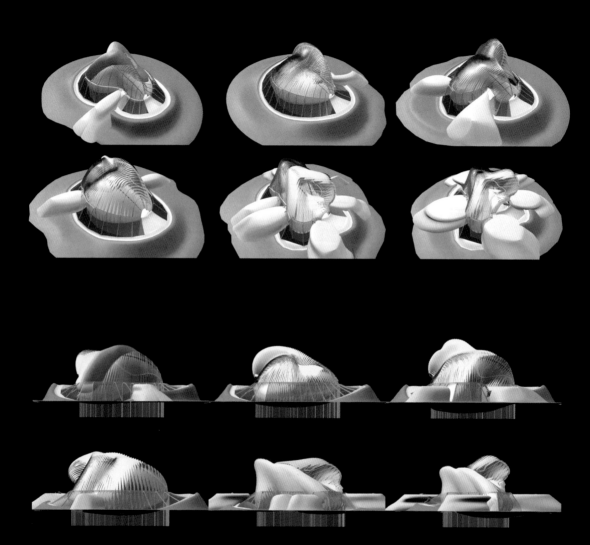

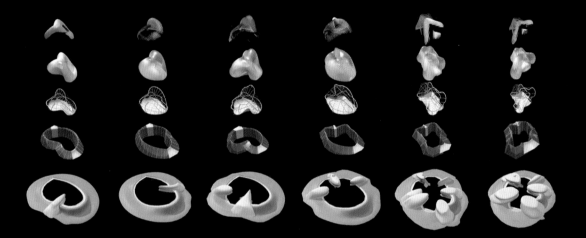

pedagogy, Columbia
2.08
Greg Lynn
Embryonic House
1999

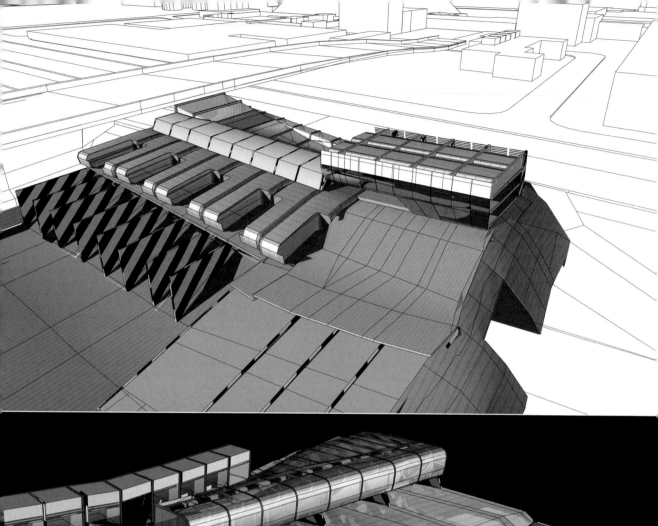

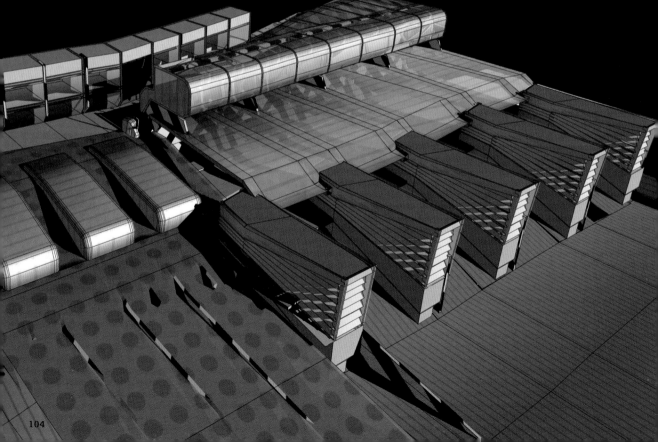

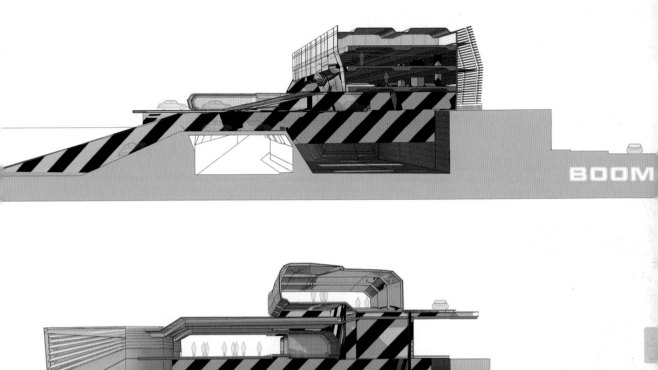

BOOM

BUST

pedagogy, Columbia

2.09

Hugh Hynes

*Back to the Front:
Architecture at Play in
Las Vegas*

Advanced Studio VI

Laurie Hawkinson, critic

Spring 2000

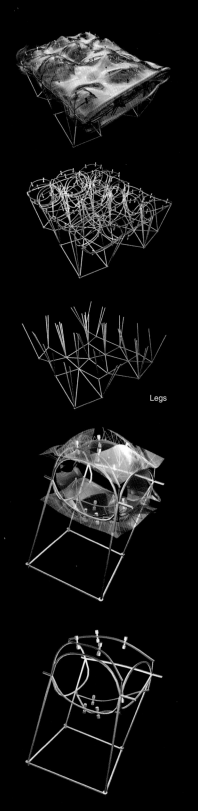

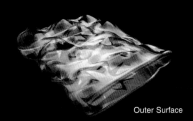

Outer Surface

Inner Cells

Legs

Moving Frames

Basic Frames

Outdoor Surface

Air Valve

Basic Frame

Moving Frames

Elastic Wire

Elastic Cable

Inner Cell

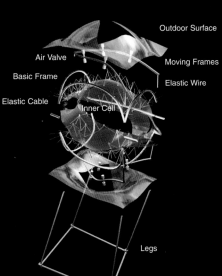

Legs

performance

2.10 (left)

Evan Douglis

Liquid Assets: An Installation

1999

2.11 (right)

Nobu Ota

Liquid Assets: Reassessing Pneumatics as Urban Outfits for the New Millennium

Advanced Studio

Evan Douglis, critic

Summer 1998

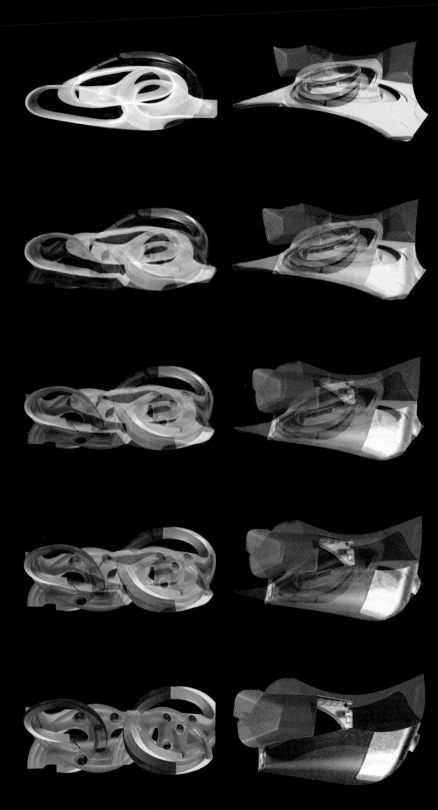

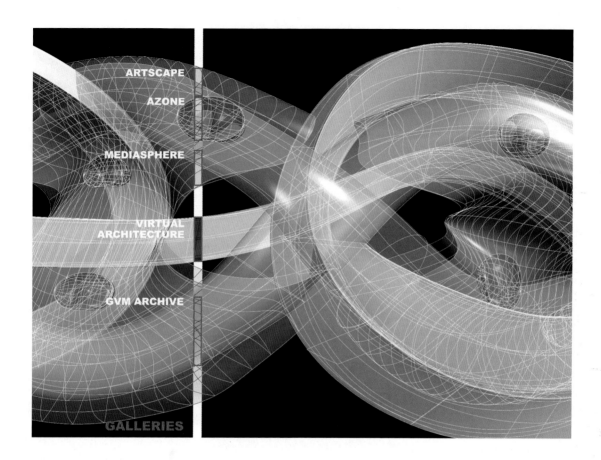

ARTSCAPE

AZONE

MEDIASPHERE

VIRTUAL
ARCHITECTURE

GVM ARCHIVE

GALLERIES

performance
2.12
Asymptote
Virtual Guggenheim
2001

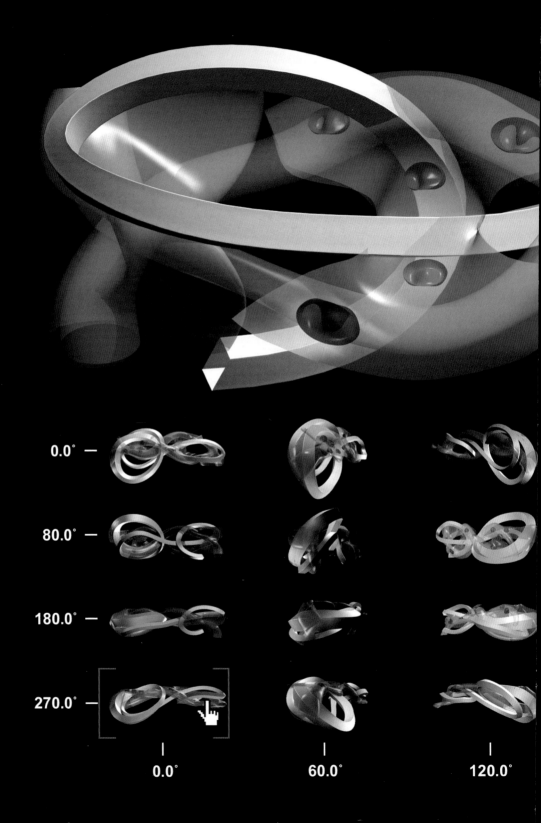

0.0° —

80.0° —

180.0° —

270.0° —

0.0°   60.0°   120.0°

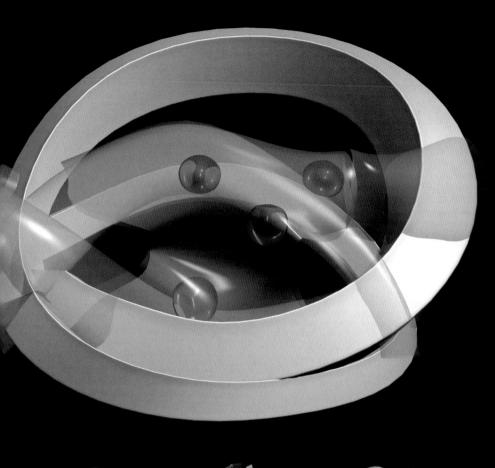

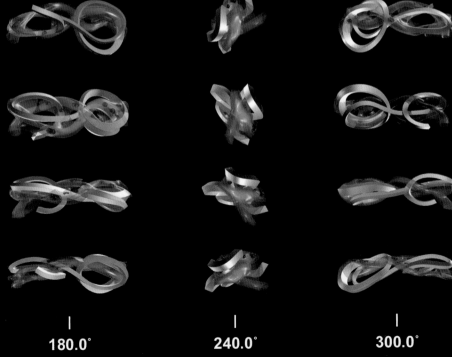

180.0˚   240.0˚   300.0˚

performance
2.13
Asymptote
Virtual Guggenheim
2001

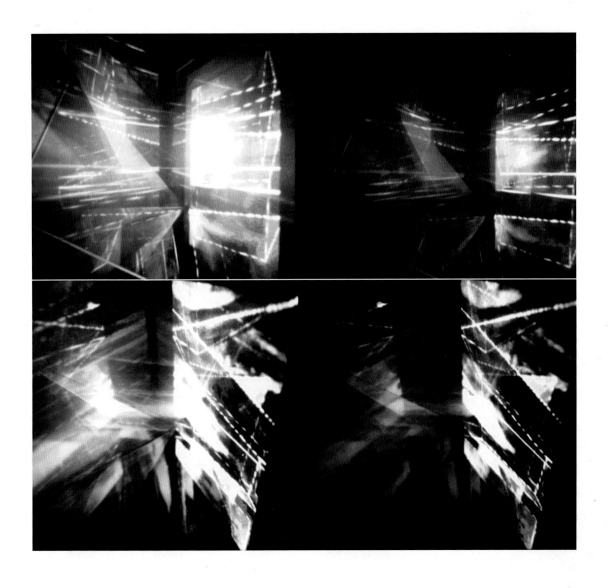

performance

2.14 (left)
Asymptote
Aarhus Univers Theater
Aarhus, Denmark
1997

2.15 (right)
Vasu Virajsilp
E-GORA
Advanced Studio
Hani Rashid, critic
Summer 1997

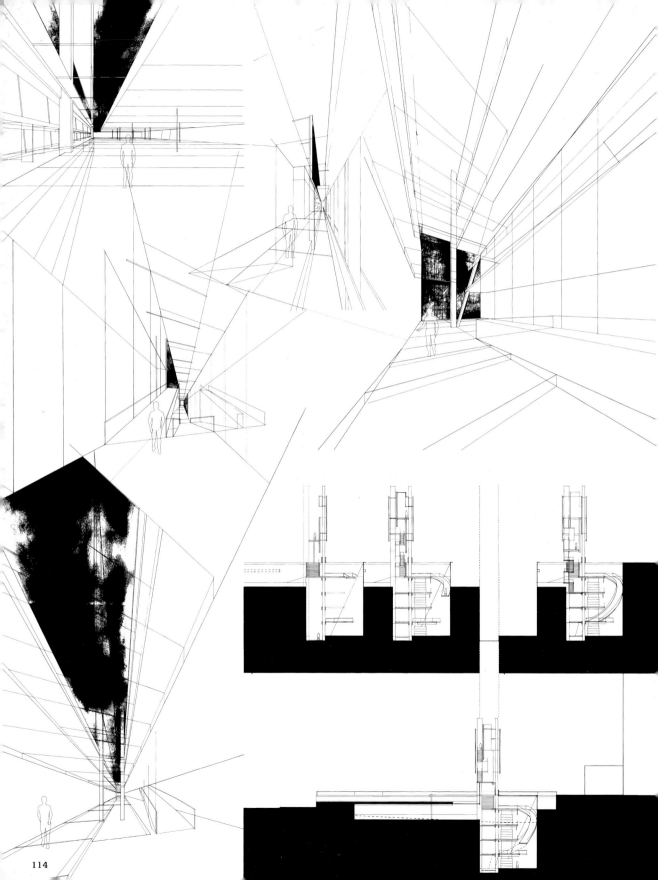

**phenomenon/
phenomenology**

2.16 (left)

Mina Kwon

*Music Library for Lincoln
Center*

Advanced Studio IV

Victoria Meyers, critic

Spring 1994

2.17 (right)

Hanrahan + Meyers

*Chattanooga Nature
Interpretive Center*

Chattanooga,
Tennessee

1998

**phenomenon/
phenomenology**

2.18

Alan Chan

*Music Library:
Los Angeles Performing
Arts Center*

Advanced Studio IV

Victoria Meyers, critic

Spring 2000

K

knowledge

"To design a library today is to contend with an entirely new set of expectations. Above all, it means to recognize an ever-increasing uncertainty about what constitutes knowledge, who has access to it, and how it is distributed."[1]

STAN ALLEN
1. *Logistics of Context: A Library for Columbia University,* Advanced Studio V, Fall 1996.

"[T]he knowledge of the architect must be deployed in a direct and tactical manner, looking pragmatically for opportunities within the constraints of the existing power structure: working 'within the enemy's field of vision.'"[2]

2. "Demarcating Lines: Beirut," *Architectural Design* 65, no. 3–4 (1995): 89.

knowledge
   1. obsolete: cognizance
   2. (a) (1): the fact or condition of knowing something with familiarity gained through experience or association; (2): acquaintance with or understanding of a science, art, or technique; (b) (1): the fact or condition of being aware of something; (2): the range of one's information or understanding; (c) the circumstance or condition of apprehending truth or fact through reasoning; (d) the fact or condition of having information or of being learned
   3. archaic: sexual intercourse
   4. (a) the sum of what is known: the body of truth, information, and principles acquired by mankind; (b) archaic: a branch of learning
  see HISTORY; PEDAGOGY, COLUMBIA; TEACHING

Merriam Webster's Dictionary

kyozone

"Kyozone is a fictional urbanism, an abstraction of contemporary Tokyo formulated as a working prototype of an early 21st-century global urbanism. This architecture emerged as an urban montage construed of events and vivid distortions. The seemingly speculative whims of real estate development; the hallucinatory ethics of consumerism, entertainment, and tourism; and the strange technologies that encapsulate this hypermodern metropolis were all incorporated into the kyozone. These new architectures were not only the outcome of an already entrenched and strange urbanism; they were effectively utterances of a new city space that we have yet to inhabit."[3]

HANI RASHID
3. *Tokyo Extreme,* Advanced Studio VI, Spring 1995.

PLATE 1.24

FIG. 42 Setup sequence, *Tokyo Extreme,* Advanced Studio VI, Hani Rashid, critic, Spring 1995.

L

landmark

REINHOLD MARTIN

We worked on a rooftop addition to a landmarked building that involved intensely theoretical discussions with both the client and the Landmarks Preservation Commission as to the nature of an architectural intervention in the fantasies that institutions like the Landmarks Preservation Commission sustain about what a city is. I cannot tell you whether we were successful in advancing our versions of those fantasies, but I try not to differentiate between the discussions that we have had with Landmarks and the things that we discuss in the academic environment. Even though the languages, the implications, the contexts, and the politics are different, it is as much a research project as our other work. That project involved a lot of historical research on our part in an effort to unravel the apparently firm foundation around which the landmarking of this particular building was structured. It turns out that this building is not a landmark in the conventional sense. It is not a great work of architecture; it was landmarked for cultural reasons. We attempted to integrate those ideas in the way we worked on the project.

landscape

FIG. 43 Dean Wolf Architects, *Spiral House*, Pleasantville, New York, 1994.

PLATE 2.01

Where does your interest in landscape come from?
My ideas about landscape came from several things simultaneously: one was working on interior projects that have no direct grounding in terra firma. Many of my built projects are about ideas of landscape within these interior constructions. I try to understand program spatially by examining representations of the picturesque, sublime, and grotesque within the two-dimensional discipline of painting. I also studied landscape painting traditions and became interested in the American ideology of landscape.

LESLIE GILL

The second was teaching at Harvard where landscape students also take design studios. They come from a very different discipline and think in very different ways. The third was that I had been thinking about landscape in my practice but, without the opportunity to work at a larger scale, the studio became a way of exploring these kinds of extremes.

Why are you specifically interested in the American landscape?

The painting traditions that emerged from the European academy developed very formal and specific ways of representation: there is an iconography, there is a structure, there is a set of parameters. When that tradition came to America it was institutionalized even though it was already beginning to decay in Europe. The American tradition lasted for almost one hundred years and was followed by innovations in 20th-century abstract painting, yet the tools of representation were maintained. In Europe it died away and wasn't as formative. Those images clearly defined and represented an architectural tradition here.

LESLIE GILL

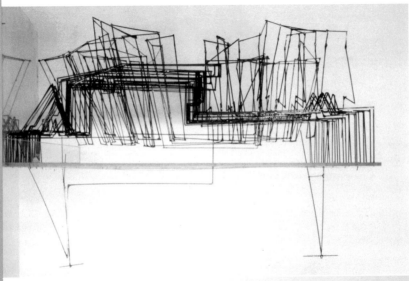

FIG. 44 Anne Chen, *Prototype of a Post-Industrial Resource, Newburgh, NY,* Advanced Studio VI, Leslie Gill, critic, Spring 1996.

FIG. 45 Leslie Gill, *Landscape Paintings*, 1995–2000.

In America, painting was instrumentalized between the two-dimensional and three-dimensional, particularly by Frederick Church, Asher Durand, and Thomas Cole, with Frederick Law Olmsted's Central Park as the most interesting public example. I am interested in that 40-year period where there was a direct relationship between the two-dimensional space of the painting and its three-dimensional application and how it was used in an instrumentalized way rather than as a surface imagery. When you look at the three-dimensional construct and then go back to the painting, you can see the interrelationship. Unfortunately, it turned out to be the imagery of those paintings and their translation into postcards, as well as the domestication of the image over time, that now formulates much of the building today. These painters were sent out on expeditions to paint the first images of the West, of the frontier. When the images went on display on the East Coast, people flocked to them, and because the images defined an idea of place, those places became spaces that the railroads and the highways bypassed. Those very images are still part of this jaded pilgrimage 150 years later. At a certain point, it moved from being an instrumentalized translation into a visually iconic one, and the propagation of the myths that are within the paintings become exclusionary and the countervoices disappear. When you look at its high point, you understand that it's not about surface, it's about the actual production of space. Much later, the highway engineers understood the potential of the relationship between the picturesque and the three-dimensional production of the picturesque. Now it has been obliterated, but it is a tool that can be utilized.

"The landscape is a kind of text, a constructed ground of signification that inevitably speaks of the culture and the natural forces that made it. Specifically we tracked the ways in which landscape is formed through the natural forces of light, wind, and habitation.... Tracking is a means of making a construction within a natural landscape in such a way that it actively engages that landscape."[1]

VICTORIA MEYERS
1. *Reading Landscape: A Library for Crestone*, Advanced Studio IV, Spring 1997.

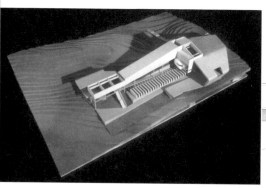 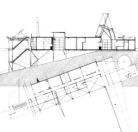

FIG. 46 Randolph R. Ruiz, *Reading Landscape: A Library for Crestone*, Advanced Studio IV, Victoria Meyers, critic, Spring 1997.

FIG. 47 Hanrahan + Meyers, *Chattanooga Nature Interpretive Center*, Chattanooga, Tennessee, 1998.

landscape

    1. (a) a picture representing a view of natural inland scenery; (b) the art of depicting such scenery

Merriam Webster's Dictionary

2. (a) the landforms of a region in the aggregate; (b) a portion of territory that can be viewed at one time from one place; (c) a particular area of activity

see CHIMERA; COLLABORATION; ECOLOGY; LOCAL/GLOBAL; NATURE; STRUCTURE

language

"A dominant pedagogic bias during the years of their architectural formation, the primacy of the linguistic is both a fundamental base for their work and an impediment to be overturned. Perhaps this, along with a reinscribed modernism, explains their interest in optical devices and automatic design procedures: a kind of 'seeing' unmediated by voices spoken or written. The new 'languages' of electronics, biology, mass culture, and urban nomadicism seem to them to escape the relational codes of structuralist linguistics and contribute to their faith that even the most reduced unit of the system can carry elaborate content and valency. Asymptote, then, attempts to penetrate the mutually reinforcing barriers of modernist abstraction and structuralist degree zero."[2]

ASYMPTOTE
2. Introduction to "Analog Space to Digital Field," *Assemblage* 21 (August 1993): 26.

light

"The first premise of this studio was that light is the primary means by which we understand our connection to life. The second premise was that the interaction of space and light convey meaning that is understood viscerally and palpably through the body of the inhabitant. Day space marks an increment of time that we rarely consider, but that develops one of the primary orders of our life and in many ways becomes the way we spend our life. It is a space understood through the passage of one day, in time, light, shadow, and/or reflection."[3]

KATHRYN DEAN
3. *Day Space: Museum for Contemporary Sculpture*, Advanced Studio IV, Spring 1997.

FIG. 48 Jane Kim, *Museum for Contemporary Sculpture*, Advanced Studio IV, Kathryn Dean, critic, Spring 2000.

How do artists who work with light, such as James Turrell and Robert Irwin, begin to create a relationship between art and architecture?
They are more centered in what is possible rather than in a critique of what is already there. They are interested in the visceral response to light, which is absolutely critical to understanding how space is affected by light. It is interesting how little architects think about light. In an environment like this it is one of the only connections you have to the natural cycles of life, which are critical to our states of mind. The visceral approach is something that you know through your emotions, not through your intellect.

see MUSEUM; PERFORMANCE; PHENOMENON/PHENOMENOLOGY; WATERCOLOR

KATHRYN DEAN

PLATE 2.02

L

FIG. 49 Sarah Dunn, *Walking the Edge: A Psychiatric Day Hospital*, Advanced Studio IV, Kathryn Dean, critic, Spring 1993.

line

"A line presents the horizon or the body standing vertically at the edge of the horizon. It forms the most basic formal construct for architecture. The Interpretive Center and Hudson River House allow us to explore all these ideas within an anamorphic envelope. Each of these projects proceeds from an architectural slice that, from certain points of view, projects itself into infinitely deep space. In this sense we are dealing with thickened lines, lines that appear thin but, like a computer chip, contain a density of compacted information."[4]

VICTORIA MEYERS
4. "Geometry and Experience," unpublished article, 1999.

"This studio will be an investigation into how a geometric skin (a line) is challenged in the process of design by the forces of context, site, and program. The experience of inhabiting a line will be questioned."[5]

5. *Line*, Advanced Studio V, Fall 1998.

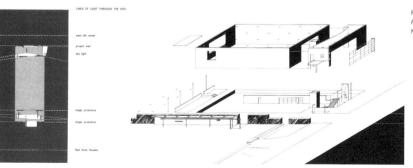

FIG. 50 Hanrahan + Meyers, *Red Hook Center for the Arts*, New York, New York, 2000.

link/linkage

"In the transition from the 'terminal' as train station to the present-day air terminal/port, the notion of the building as 'portal' and 'threshold' to the city is gradually overtaken by the notion of 'building' as 'link' within a global and local system of transportation and communication networks."[6]

WILLIAM MACDONALD
6. *Air/Scape*, Advanced Studio VI, Spring 1994.

"Due to the capacity for linkage, the familiar matrix of global geo-graphics is distorted into new shapes through expansion/contraction/inclusion/ occlusion, etc., on this new map of international cities as they gravitate closer to each other, establishing greater commonalities via linkages that exist between city and regional places of habitation."[7]

WILLIAM MACDONALD
7. *Co-Citational Cities*, Advanced Studio, Summer 1994.

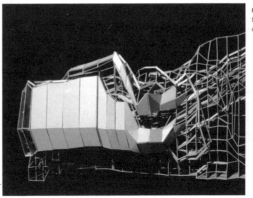

FIG. 51 Mike Pilarski, Core Studio I, William MacDonald, critic, Fall 1998.

link
   1. a connecting structure: as (a) a single ring or division of a chain; (b) an intermediate rod or piece for transmitting force or motion
   2. something analogous to a link of chain: as (a) a connecting element or factor; (b) a unit in a communication system; (c) an identifier attached to an element (as an index term) in a system in order to indicate or permit connection with other similarly identified elements
see CO-CITATION; NETWORK

Merriam Webster's Dictionary

local/global

You often return to the regional landscape and the relationship between that landscape and technology. What is your interest in this relationship?
Technology is allowing for a potential reinvigoration of the frontier. Within the American pathos you have to understand the frontier as a continuum, so as architects, how do we begin to redefine what that is? If you travel out West, it is clear how that is changing and mutating, and it is beginning to reassert itself in different ways. It is an ironic relationship but it needs to be re-engaged on a physical level. The sites that I chose over the last three or four years were valuable a hundred years ago because of their geology and they are currently valuable for those same reasons, but in a very different way. Their economic stability no longer comes from the extraction of natural resources, but from tourists seeking out a more bucolic environment. It is interesting to see how that shift caused the former industrial landscape to become its asset—it is the picturesque rather than the extraction.

LESLIE GILL

How do you define regionalism?
Some time ago I was talking to Nanako Umemoto and Jesse Reiser when they were working on a townhouse, and they said, "There's nothing to do here. We can't do anything because of the bad hierarchical arrangements and geometrical proportions." Fifty to sixty percent of my time is spent working inside existing structures, so I can't escape the regional set of

LESLIE GILL

L

parameters that define how spaces are allocated, how a program is distributed, or how hierarchy and social class are understood. When you work with these parameters, you have to bend the rules, break the rules, or work within them.

FIG. 52 Catherine Jones, *The Evening Redness in the West or the Metallic Frontier, Butte, Montana*, Advanced Studio VI, Leslie Gill, critic, Spring 1995.

You have suggested that a sense of place in the United States no longer exists, or, more precisely, exists at a much deeper level. Fredric Jameson, who also used to speak about global placelessness, is now talking about local practices of space-making.

We go often to Turkey and Germany and it is very interesting to see how global systems take hold locally in different ways. Initially one observes a homogenous global system, but when you begin to look for precise differentiations, you realize that there are very significant variations.

SULAN KOLATAN

One of the interesting things about the studies on Istanbul was my discovery that some of the age-old practices that date from the 1500s correspond and coincide with new global systems and practices. I was interested in ways of appropriating public spaces where the global systems had taken hold because they found correspondences in existing local practices.

How can a work of architecture be globally fluid yet contextually specific?
Wolf Prix once said, regarding contextualism, that it did not matter if the Bilbao Guggenheim was in Bilbao, Bordeaux, or Iceland, but once it gets there it matters where in the city it is located and how it works in that city. There is a difference between position and location. Location is how architecture works in its context; position is more generic. Wolf argued that it didn't matter what shape the Guggenheim was globally, but its relationship to its locale generates the effect that makes people want to go see it. So location is relative and based on adjacency, while position is a more

GREG LYNN

abstract question of the global. I am more interested in location than position, because this is where form makes a difference.

"This studio will seek to harness certain organizational potentials [of Tokyo] as models for the growth of urban form and apply it to systems of organization of multi-dimensional coherence at the middle and large scales. In distinction to the present urban fabric, the global will not simply be an accumulation of the local, that is, global by default, but rather growth will be regulated by structures of continuous variation. The notion of the field gradient is an important paradigm of this approach."[8]

REISER/UMEMOTO
8. *Obayashi Tokyo Experiment: Tokyo Bay Free Zone*, Advanced Studio VI, Spring 1997.

local
1. characterized by or relating to position in space: having a definite spatial form or location
2. (a) of, relating to, or characteristic of a particular place: not general or widespread; (b) of, relating to, or applicable to part of a whole
3. (a) primarily serving the needs of a particular limited district; (b) of a public conveyance: making all the stops on a route
4. involving or affecting only a restricted part of the organism: topical
5. of or relating to telephone communication within a specified area

Merriam Webster's Dictionary

global
1. spherical
2. of, relating to, or involving the entire world: worldwide
3. of, relating to, or applying to a whole (as a mathematical function or a computer program)

see INFRASTRUCTURE; LINK/LINKAGE; NOSTALGIA

love

"Regardless of the medium, be it film, sound, words, movement, paint, or solid mass, the theme of love has been a prevalent preoccupation of the arts since 30,000 B.C. when the Venus of Willendorf was created. Why then is the topic so scarce when it enters the field of architecture? Besides the expression of divine love, memorials for the dead, and occasional houses preoccupied with the theme of Eros or sexuality, little has been investigated. This studio examined the topic of love and its implementation in the spatial medium of architecture. By employing literature, painting, and film as models (Proust, Duras, James, Flaubert, Duchamp, Ingres, Vermeer, and Wenders) we investigated the relationship between the tactile and the intangible, which forms the paradoxical duality of love.... By separating the structure (courtship, mating, childbirth) from its iconography (tokens, signs, and gifts) and surrounding aura (emotion, materiality, color, and light) the spatial properties of love become accessible to the formal properties of architecture.... Using painting and film as catalysts, each student worked through model and collage to develop an architectural vocabulary in an attempt to capture the enigmatic space of the lover. Two parallel researches collided into a fragment or detail of a building, which embodied the unyielding codification of the object together with the aura and materiality of the painted environment."[9]

LESLIE GILL
9. *Love: The Gift, the Dance, and the Enigma*, Advanced Studio VI, Spring 1994.

L

love

Merriam Webster's Dictionary

1. (a) (1): strong affection for another arising out of kinship or personal ties; (2): attraction based on sexual desire: affection and tenderness felt by lovers; (3): affection based on admiration, benevolence, or common interests; (b) an assurance of love
2. warm attachment, enthusiasm, or devotion
3. (a) the object of attachment, devotion, or admiration; (b) a beloved person—often used as a term of endearment
4. (a) unselfish loyal and benevolent concern for the good of another: as (1): the fatherly concern of God for humankind; (2): brotherly concern for others; (b) a person's adoration of God
5. a god or personification of love
6. an amorous episode
7. the sexual embrace
9. capitalized, Christian Science: God

M

"We assimilate knowledge through the dissemination of signs and clues. Though those signs exist with or without our interaction, it is our imaginative interpretation that breathes life into the indexical sign. Traces of architecture exist already within the ruined fragments strewn throughout rural and urban landscapes. They are simply waiting to be decoded. This studio proposes to track the traces of a particular site mimicking the cathartic journey from city to country found within novels and films.... We will investigate man's ability to track information within the disparate environments, focusing on both the physical attributes (movement, duration, sequence, vision, and simultaneity) and the cerebral realm (claustrophobia, agoraphobia, paranoia, segregation, emancipation, repose, and bliss) in an attempt to build a respite for both the pysche and the body."[1]

LESLIE GILL
1. *Without Resting: The Tracking of Home Within the Mystery/Spy Genre*, Advanced Studio, Summer 1993.

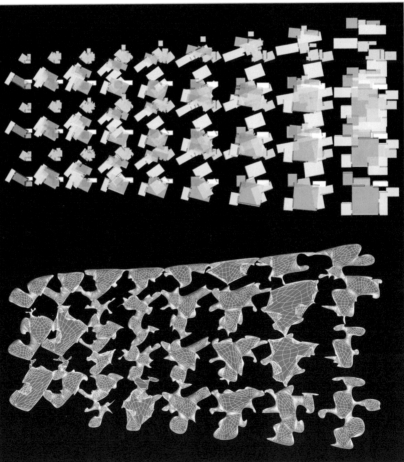

FIG. 53 Sung Kim and Seung-ki Min, *Housing*, Core Studio III, Sulan Kolatan, critic, Fall 1999.

"As individuals, we are in and out of these overlapping dimensions all the time, something which makes an older kind of existential positioning of ourselves in Being—the human body in the natural landscape, the individual in the older village or organic community, even the citizen in the nation-state—exceedingly problematical. . . . The problem [of contemporary 'mapping'] is still one of representation, and also of representability, we know that we are caught within these more complex global networks, since we palpably suffer the prolongations of corporate space everywhere in our daily lives, yet we have no way of thinking about them, of modeling them, however abstractly, in our mind's eye."[2]

2. Fredric Jameson, "Spatial Equivalents: Postmodern Architecture and the World System," in *The States of Theory: History, Art, and Critical Discourse,* ed. David Carroll (New York: Columbia University Press, 1990), 145–146.

map   *Merriam Webster's Dictionary*

    1. (a) a representation usually on a flat surface of the whole or a part of an area; (b) a representation of the celestial sphere or a part of it

    2. something that represents with a clarity suggestive of a map

    3. the arrangement of genes on a chromosome—called also genetic map

see CITY; CO-CITATION; DIAGRAM; PROCESS; STUDIO/PRACTICE

---

margin

see FRONTIER/EDGE/MARGIN

---

mass production

see SERIALITY/MASS PRODUCTION

---

material/materiality

How do you explore materiality?

I often need to build materially to make important leaps and to test new details against the whole. I have always encouraged my students to do the same. At the same time I like to build computer models. I do not really differentiate between the two because both are ways of seeing and investigating in order to get past a particular bias. I'll use any tool to get past what I know.

KAREN BAUSMAN

FIG. 54 Karen Bausman, *Hamlin Chapel,* 2001.

*You talk about a materiality, whether it is a digital materiality or a
physical materiality, that resists a certain typology, and even resists the
tectonic. What exactly do you mean?*

I have been preoccupied in recent years with interrogating hyper-dynamic   EVAN DOUGLIS
materials (i.e. latex hosing, balloons, cast rubber, and spandex) as a source
of speculative "soft-wear." In contrast to generic basswood modeling prod-
ucts, these amorphous membrane materials resist both standard techniques
of assembly and conventional typological precedents, enabling the pursuit
of more radical explorations. The unpredictability inherent within these
materials necessitates a greater deliberation on the means of structural
engagement and the programmatic implications. Through a series of transformational studies that employ a principle of controlled chance, a
reactive topological model emerges.

Because this new tectonic language does not refer to the iconography of
architectural history, the author is challenged to inscribe meaning within
the behavioral logic of the work.

A slightly different set of challenges is encountered when one applies
an operative strategy of material exploration to full-scale construction. For
instance, in conventional modeling techniques the conversion of scale is
reasonably simple, since the object functions primarily on a representational level. In contrast, the physical dynamic model requires a more comprehensive set of adjustments to enable the translation of behavior.

The word "tectonic" in my mind is a language; it is the way in which
meaning embeds itself within the elements of construction. There are
certain tectonics that are more acceptable, popular, and universally prevalent, and there are others that are always emerging and enabling us to
re-address what the body of architecture should be.

PLATES 2.03–2.04

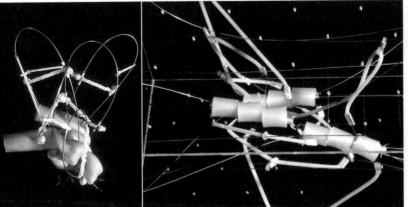

FIG. 55 Keith Kaseman, Core
Studio I, Evan Douglis, critic,
Fall 1998.

FIG. 56 Meiko Sato, Core
Studio I, Evan Douglis, critic,
Fall 1998.

"This politics of materiality is not simply, or even partially, about a clever   LAURIE HAWKINSON
use of materials. It is more cybernetic in the sense that certain material   3. Catherine Ingraham,
(cultural) properties are breached and things drift into the 'wrong' place.   *Smith-Miller + Hawkinson*
Windows become floors and so on. An attenuated posture toward materials   (Barcelona: Gustavo Gili, 1994),
—literally the elongation or distortion of mass, volume, substance—is also   11–12.
a kind of tampering with their proper (genetic) domain."[3]

You taught a studio at Columbia that worked in reverse by starting with a material and ending with architectural space. How does that change the exploration?

The studio is a big experiment. You cannot predict what is going to happen but you learn in the process. The materiality, in this case, became instrumental. When you get to the final review of most studio projects, a common question is, "Well, what is it made of?" and the student's answer is, "Oh, concrete." It is so banal and boring when these computer-generated images with all those wonderful doubly warped shapes don't have any materiality. One of the ways around that is to begin with materials and models.

STEVEN HOLL

FIG. 57 Howard Chu, *From Material to Partial Urbanism*, Advanced Studio V, Steven Holl, critic, Fall 1993.

We do not attach a truthfulness to materials anymore and materials can be understood to represent more than just their physical properties. We discovered molded fiberglass when we were looking for a material to build the O.K. Apartment, and we loved it because it has all of the associations at once and no association whatsoever. Theme parks use it extensively to make forests and animals, so it's a material that simulates other materials very well.

SULAN KOLATAN

"The Holley Loft is a residential project made by carving a new space out of the fabric of an existing city, Manhattan. The only full-height wall in the space is glass.... this thin reflective surface establishes an implication of thinness with an infinite depth of field."[4]

see DRAWING; FIELD; GEOMETRY; MODERN/MODERNISM; PERFORMANCE; PROCESS; REVERSE; SURFACE; TEACHING; WINDOW

VICTORIA MEYERS
4. "Space and the Perception of Time," *Journal of Architectural Education* 53, no. 2 (November 1999): 94.

media

see COMPUTER; IMAGE; PEDAGOGY, COLUMBIA; URBAN

memory

"Shelter as an idea is not only a present necessity but also a vestigial memory. Memory, therefore, contains not only the actual recollections of a human life but also genetic imprints that date back thousands of years. 'Home' is a concept as well as a place, and how successfully it fulfills the needs of its occupants depends at least in part upon its possession of a memory, whether in the real terms of an individual's transient life or in the permanent cultural memory of its many inhabitants."[5]

KAREN BAUSMAN
LESLIE GILL
5. *Memory: Transience and Permanence of Dwelling*, Advanced Studio VI, Spring 1993.

"If architecture is an analogue for human memory, we might well wonder what contemporary minimalist space refers to about human memory today. As a reflection of contemporary life, perhaps it communicates that we are losing access to memory as it was previously understood. We are losing access to memory with any depth of field, but gaining a new intelligence that latches onto several registrations at once, each registration being a superficial and fleeting image."[6]

see NOSTALGIA

VICTORIA MEYERS
6. "Space and the Perception of Time," *Journal of Architectural Education* 53, no. 2 (November 1999): 92.

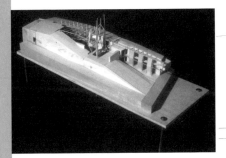
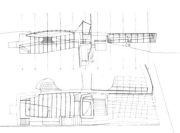

FIG. 58 Woong Yang, *Chapel of the Innocents*, Advanced Studio IV, Victoria Meyers, critic, Spring 1996.

methodology

What happens when conventional methodologies are replaced by technological investigations using the computer?
There are plenty of practitioners who design the same way with the computer as they did before its introduction. It is much more complex than any other tool we have used before and it requires an understanding of its own logic and the logic of the software—it is like working with a third partner rather than working with a pencil. We have found it incredibly productive to work with software that was not developed specifically for architecture. Because of its limitations, it can be thought-provoking with respect to issues that may be taken for granted within architectural processes. Consider the conventional drawing sequence, which moves from plan to section to model. When you work with animation software, it is difficult to get a plan and section, so you have to construct a very different logic for designing. It is not about making the process more complicated, but it has implications in terms of how a building is constructed theoretically and physically, and it allows you to change many of the traditional perceptions regarding architecture.

see ORGANIZATION; RESISTANCE; TEACHING

SULAN KOLATAN

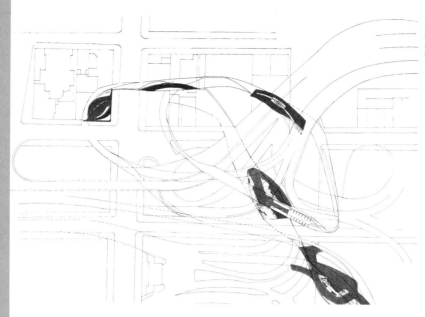

FIG. 59 Julie Salles Shaffer, *Logics and Logistics of Waiting*, Advanced Studio VI, Sulan Kolatan, critic, Spring 1995.

model

Without the advantage of computer technologies in the first year, how is the studio environment different?

In the first year of studio at Columbia, there is an emphasis on physical modeling, which has been greatly influenced by computer-generated wire-frame models in recent years. Building in wire-frame makes you understand the space and structure very differently than if you had constructed it in chipboard and defined the exterior walls. The increased use of wire-frame physical models radically changes the way students think about structure and space from other idioms that were much more popular before the 1990s and the introduction of computer-design programs.

WILLIAM MACDONALD

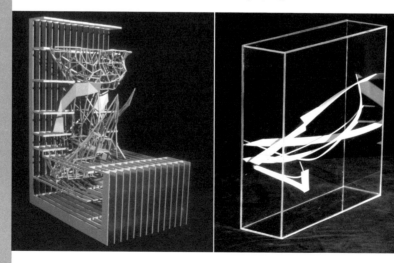

FIG. 60 Robert Holton, Core Studio I, William MacDonald, critic, Fall 1996.

FIG. 61 Christopher Perry, Core Studio I, William MacDonald, critic, Fall 1994.

When we discovered the catenary modeling method, we immediately wanted to see what would happen if we had 13 versions of these models in the

JESSE REISER

studio. We structured the pedagogy such that it would alternate between computer modeling, to develop the geometries relatively quickly, and material modeling, to study the actual catenary curves in the chain models.

We discovered that there are differences between the professional design studio and the academy, especially when you consider the learning curve on the computer and in the modeling. In the best of cases, we found other structural possibilities. One model actually stopped behaving like a catenary and became a funicular, which is related to the catenary but different. Things were developed within the logic of the model that these computers can't predict. Although there's a degree of openness, there's also a need to recognize and define what develops so that we can work through it again.

model

Merriam Webster's Dictionary

1. structural design
2. a usually miniature representation of something; also: a pattern of something to be made
3. an example for imitation or emulation
4. a person or thing that serves as a pattern for an artist; especially: one who poses for an artist
5. one who is employed to display clothes or other merchandise
6. (a) a type or design of clothing; (b) a type or design of product (as a car)
7. a description or analogy used to help visualize something (as an atom) that cannot be directly observed
8. a system of postulates, data, and inferences presented as a mathematical description of an entity or state of affairs

see COMPUTER; DESIGN; GEOMETRY; MATERIAL/MATERIALITY; PARTICLES; PEDAGOGY, COLUMBIA; PERFORMANCE; PROCESS, REVERSE; PROGRAM; STUDIOS, CORE; SURFACE; TEACHING; TECHNOLOGY

modern/modernism

How is your interest in function and performance different from the modern archetype?

At what point did modernism become the bad guy? There are two things at work here that do not get much attention and which I address in a class that I teach during the summer (co-taught in the beginning with Michael Hays). First, Michael and I are both interested in a more complex idea of the modern, an irreducible multiplicity in what we usually call modernism. There are modernities that do not necessarily fit into the simple categories of the totalizing, canonical modernities that often get dismissed today under the umbrella of postmodernism. The early modernist avant-garde project was devoted to coming to terms with the new condition of the city. So much of what animates the speculative and experimental work of the early part of the century was attempting to figure out some kind of artistic response to this monster, which is the modern metropolis. Today, the nature of the city has changed, but the need to come to terms with its demands persists. In this sense, I think we are still operating in terms of some of the modernist dilemmas. This is not to say that we can simply return to the old modernist strategies, but to the extent that we are still dealing with fundamentally modernist issues, many of the modernist strategies are still viable.

STAN ALLEN

M

And that is the second point: Michael Hays argues that the abstraction and instrumentality of modern life have so thoroughly permeated the world around us that we have no choice but to work with techniques that are themselves highly abstract and instrumental. To think that we can refuse that abstraction, or somehow go beyond it through the use of new technologies, is naive. So I do not have a problem identifying myself as a modernist. It is modernism that made it possible to ask these questions in the first place. To think that the game is played out is simply false.

"In Asymptote's reiteration of the modern, two received ideas are jettisoned. First is the contemporary efficacy of modernist practices of negation. The dead end of Malevich's black square, but also of Reinhardt's, are traps to be avoided, as is the newer anti-aesthetic, the critique of form as such.... Negation is understood historically rather than programmatically: negation itself as having already been negated, reified in cultural practices both elite and mass. Asymptote thus maintains a skeptical ambivalence toward the old anarchic object of modernism as well as the logic of that contemporary call to radicality: to construct critically."[7]

ASYMPTOTE
7. Introduction to "Analog Space to Digital Field," *Assemblage* 21 (August 1993): 26.

In your work, there has been an interesting reappraisal of the modern archetype through the use of the diagram. "Function," is reappearing in a novel way that is not a new functionalism, but more of a hybrid of function and design.

My partner, Henry Smith-Miller, and I are interested in pursuing investigations in terms of contemporary culture. It is not the stylistic or the modernist object per se, but an interest and curiosity about the edges, thresholds, and moments of closure of a finite, discrete, *pochéd* space. If the subject of investigation is the house, then what is the house today? How might culture, along with material, production, methodology, and economy have an effect on the house? What would the manifestation of that effect be?

LAURIE HAWKINSON

I am interested in the future, but at the same time I value history. I am especially interested in the history of materials, and how they can carry a particular meaning with them. We designed a canopy for LaGuardia Airport that is made of Kevlar, a material often used in airplane construction and in the space shuttle and the stealth bomber, but which can also be used architecturally. Materials are very important and history can surface through them. We often think of modernism in terms of the International Style, and certain architects of this period were interested in a break with history. We do not have that burden today. I could take a material that we all know and use in a particular way, and completely rethink it by repositioning it in terms of "use." That slippage across disciplines is what is exciting about the "modern" to me.

In your work you speak about seriality and component systems much the same way the Eameses did. Are you returning to a vocabulary of modernism?

I am very interested in how other design fields work, so if we decided that new cars and new athletic shoes were modern, then I would be interested

GREG LYNN

in the language of modern architecture. If you mean the rediscovery of modern architecture, then I am not. Culturally, there seems to be a hiccup in creativity and good taste is taking its place. One reason I am happy to be in L.A. is that I am not immersed in the incipient museum and gallery culture of New York that legislates for austere neutrality and warmed-over modern architecture. What I have heard referred to as "Calvin Klein Modernism" is the avoidance of architectural innovation and it is a capitulation to the worst kind of marketing. I like Los Angeles because there is no disdain for populism so there is no reason to appeal to a culture of mindless good taste. Getting to the epicenter of the culture industry has made me realize how important it is to stay ahead of the culture at a place like Columbia.

see AUTHOR; INDEX; LANGUAGE; ORGANIZATION; STYLE; TIME

montage

"The engineer-monteur is an architect who builds with images. Place is created out of fragments distant in time and space; by constructing 'with intervals,' he recognizes the gap, the lag, which must now be built into the fabric of time and space. The metropolis produces a new subject: the montage eye capable of constructing a new reality out of the barrage of fragmentary, contradictory, and obsolete information which characterizes the modern city."[8]

STAN ALLEN
8. "Projections: Between Drawing and Building," *A + U* 4 (April 1992): 42.

"Times Square is…a vivid paradigm of late-20th-century global urbanism. Here, the city of New York is distilled through an urban montage construed of events and phenomena. Times Square is structured as a cinematic field distorting and conforming to speculative whims of real-estate development coupled with hallucinatory ethics of consumerism, entertainment, and tourism."[9]

ASYMPTOTE
9. "Film as Architecture as Film, Times Square," *Architectural Design* 64, no. 11–12 (November/December 1994): 63.

FIG. 62 Nina Cooke, *Diversionary Tactics: The Architecture of Tourism*, Advanced Studio, Lise Anne Couture, critic, Summer 1997.

"The modernist ideology of film [montage] has given way, in the wake of the universal collapse of ideological structures, to the temporal flow of the

REISER/UMEMOTO
10. *Television Program Mall*, Advanced Studio V, Fall 1994.

M

televisual. The architectural implications of this 'collapse' paradoxically suggests an opening up of possibilities."[10]

see CHIMERA; KYOZONE

movement

"Historically, architects have understood movement as the travel of the moving eye in space. Yet architecture, in both its realization and conception, has been understood as static, fixed, ideal, and inert. Themes of motion and dynamics in architecture are typically addressed through pictorial views of static forms. Not only have buildings been constructed as static forms, but more importantly architecture has been conceived and designed based on models of stasis and equilibrium. Typically, computer-animation software reinforces this normative assumption that architectural design belongs in static Cartesian space waiting to be animated by a mobile view. Instead of using animation software to breathe picturesque movement into Cartesian spaces, this studio investigated motion-based techniques for the generation of architectural projects dynamically. Classical architectural metaphors of stasis and equilibrium were replaced with more vital architectural design processes that are literally and conceptually animated. Building forms and organizations were evolved through the interaction of disparate forces and gradients of influence in time-based environments within which the designer guides their often undecidable growth, transformation, and mutation. This shift from determinism to directed indeterminacy is central to the development of a dynamic design method and will present a new role for design direction and authorship."[11]

see TIME; TRACE; TRANSFORMATION

GREG LYNN
11. *Tate Gallery Competition*, Advanced Studio V, Fall 1995.

multiple

"Corbusier revolutionized the architectural plane by arguing that it supported only one moment of the contiguous space that passed through it. Previously, architecture strove to represent all essential spatial characteristics on a transcendent, reduced plane.... In the Citrohan and Dom-ino types the two-dimensional intersections with the parallel walls are fixed while the spaces between those contours can only be described with probability .... [T]he random section model, as it is known now in biometric science, originated with the development of the Needle Problem by the celebrated naturalist Comte de Buffon in 1777. The Needle Problem is a geometric model used to describe the probability of chance events [i.e. the occurrence of a needle intersecting a parallel series of lines when thrown on a horizontal surface]. As the Citrohan and Dom-ino multiplied the possibilities for programmatic and volumetric events between lateral walls, Buffon's Needle Problem describes a multiplicity of probable occurrences without reducing their chances to any single rule."[12]

GREG LYNN
12. "Probable Geometries: the Architecture of Writing in Bodies," *ANY* 0 (May - June 1993): 47.

museum

"The museum as one of the primary institutions of modern culture has tended to disintegrate into a 'superstore' for consuming artwork. As both critique and provocation of this problematic, the studio seeks to reinvigorate the role of the museum in contemporary culture. It will investigate the ways in which light can create a psychological dimension, resulting in alternative programmatic and spatial propositions for the contemporary museum."[13]

KATHRYN DEAN
13. *Museum for Contemporary Sculpture*, Advanced Studio IV, Spring 2001.

Museums and art institutions occur frequently in your studio programs.
It was a grounding for me that grew out of being at the American Academy
in Rome for a year. When I was there, Bruce Nauman, Martin Furrier, Jackie
Windsor, and Alex Katz were also there. They spoke about work that was
strong because it was of its maker. The only thing you have to offer in the
world is your experience of life, and if your work is not part of your experience of life then it is nothing. I was trying to understand how you could
express the experience of life in sculpture or in painting and translate that
into architecture.

KATHRYN DEAN

The Frank Lloyd Wright Guggenheim Museum took seriously the idea that
art be part of the life of the city. It would not be housed as a sacred icon
in a temple, and yet, Frank Lloyd Wright respected and understood that no
matter how much artists were saying they wanted to be on the street, they
really also wanted to be in museums.

JEFFREY KIPNIS

  He found a miraculous way to synthesize history. He realized a diagram,
but did it in a way that was so specific that it produced the architectural
effect. It's not interesting to talk about the idea. It's only interesting to
see how well he produces the effect.

  Cesar Pelli's idea that the American department store would function as
a diagram that would democratize the reception of art at The Museum of
Modern Art was interesting in that it worked and we didn't like it. It's not
an architecture that failed. It's an architecture that succeeded as an idea.
We just decided that as a culture we didn't like the success of that idea.
We didn't like the idea that when we got off the escalator we saw a painting the same way we would see a dress hanging on a department store
mannequin. It was a successful way of democratizing art that we didn't
want democratized. An architectural study has little to do with how well
the building performs as a building.

see ART/ARTIST; PHENOMENON/PHENOMENOLOGY; REAL

music

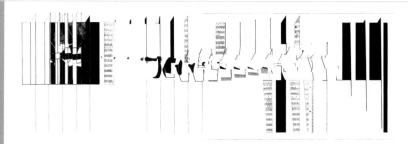

FIG. 63 Rhett Russo, *Music
Library for Lincoln Center*,
Advanced Studio IV, Victoria
Meyers, critic, Spring 1994.

For my studio on the Morton Feldman School of Music, we began by listening to Feldman's work, which is not an easy task. It takes an entire hour
for the nervous system and the brain to adjust to what he's doing, so you
have to listen in silence for an hour. After maybe 60 minutes you begin to
understand something about the space between notes and about the free
structure. Feldman once said, "I chose chance." We wanted to know what
that meant. We listened to Feldman, visited the site, and immersed our-

STEVEN HOLL

M

selves in what could be an inspirational figure in terms of a school of music or a structure of architecture. We also read *Silence: Lectures and Writings by John Cage* and some of the other great Cage texts because Cage respected Feldman. We experimented with the possible inspirations and structural possibilities of music in architecture. Architecture can be inspired by fields outside of architecture, like music or experimental studies of physical phenomena, so I introduce them in each studio.

see GEOMETRY; PROGRAM; SAMPLING

 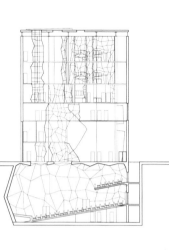

FIG. 64 Amanda Brainerd,
Morton Feldman Music School,
Advanced Studio V, Steven Holl,
critic, Fall 1995.

mutation

"Contingencies compose internal differences that are necessary for unification. Such a network of diagonal alliances is capable of a continual expansion of influence through internal mutation and reconfiguration. '*You will be assimilated; resistance is futile,*' in the words of the Borg. There is an insidious hope that by becoming incorporated within a larger system, there is a possibility to influence that system, not through radical overthrow or revolution but through mutations that might run throughout the system and travel freely; perhaps not even being recognized as radically other."[14]

GREG LYNN
14. *Infesting in New Brunswick through Johnson & Johnson,*
Advanced Studio V, Fall 1993.

mutation
    1. a significant and basic alteration: change
    2. a relatively permanent change in hereditary material involving either a physical change in chromosome relations or a biochemical change in the codons that make up genes

see CITY

Merriam Webster's Dictionary

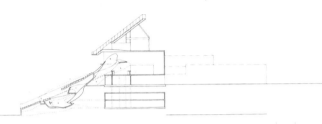

FIG. 65 Grace Cheung and Terry Surjan, *Infesting in New Brunswick through Johnson & Johnson*, Advanced Studio V, Greg Lynn, critic, Fall 1993.

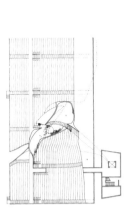

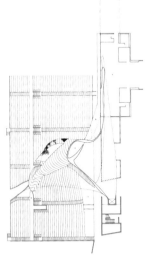

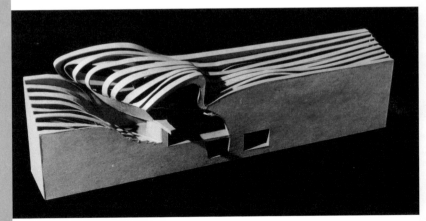

M

N

narcissism

There is an argument that narcissism is no longer a pathology but a contemporary form of positive politics. Koolhaas's Prada store probably fails as a successful boutique if you measure how much it sells, but as an architectural idea it uses the techniques of theater and display to eroticize every object in the store. Jeff Koons makes a similar argument. Narcissism is not a failure in development or a model of regression. We reach adulthood and go to narcissism. If you believe the Freudian model, then that is always regressive and that would be a pathological situation and therefore the store would be a perversion. Rem argues that there is a positive form of social narcissism, which, like it or not, is like shopping, and he's trying to find an affirmative moment for it in the store. It's going to fail as a store, but it's a successful architectural experience.

JEFFREY KIPNIS

nature

"Urban renewal in the later part of the 20th century has sought to restore the character and vision of the earlier ideal [relationship between technology and landscape]. However, restoration is no longer the appropriate means of repair. Instead there is much to be gained by studying America's relationship to the land as a longer-term cultural legacy. Never timid, the pastoral vision bears little resemblance to the contemporary suburban dream of today. The relationship between man and nature debated the issues of the sublime, the grotesque, and the beautiful on a universal scale. Today this landscape has become an isolated view. The wilderness is no longer the natural environment. Instead, it is the abandoned and decaying centers of our urban fabric."[1]

LESLIE GILL
1. *The Evening Redness in the West (or the Metallic Frontier)*, Advanced Studio VI, Spring 1995.

nature
1. (a) the inherent character or basic constitution of a person or thing
2. (a) a creative and controlling force in the universe; (b) an inner force or the sum of such forces in an individual
3. a kind or class usually distinguished by fundamental or essential characteristics
4. the physical constitution or drives of an organism; especially: an excretory organ or function—used in phrases like the call of nature
5. a spontaneous attitude
6. the external world in its entirety
see ARTIFICE; LANDSCAPE; ORGANIC/ORGANICISM

Merriam Webster's Dictionary

network

"How to distinguish between the access functions of the library (compilation and categorizing information) as opposed to the archival functions of the library (protection and storage of rare or historical materials)? What are the spatial implications of the new networks of distribution? How is collective memory constituted under shifting definitions of culture and knowledge?"[2]

STAN ALLEN
2. *Library, Archive, Atlas*, Advanced Studio V, Fall 1995.

"Asymptote explicitly refuses to configure architecture in a representational fashion and strictly avoids making a building into a metaphor for collision, fragmentation, discontinuity. And, correspondingly, there is a displacement of creative effort toward planning and programming, a suggestion that architecture itself can become a facilitating network for a complex series of events, encounters, and programs that normally take place *within* or even *in spite of* built form."[3]

ASYMPTOTE
3. Introduction to "Analog Space to Digital Field," *Assemblage* 21 (August 1993): 26.

"The terminal is a place, a provisional terminus to the trip. It is also a link, a single stop amidst a network of many. It is a singular building, yet together with highways and buses it constitutes an expansive infrastructure. It is in and of the city, yet it indicates the suburban."[4]

SULAN KOLATAN
4. *Logics and Logistics of Waiting*, Advanced Studio IV, Spring 1995.

"One of the emerging spatial paradigms is that of the network as a system of interrelations between dissipative processes and aggregative structures that shape new spatial patterns and protocols. How does this network logic affect space and its making? Our work focuses in particular on the network model's capacity to facilitate cross-categorical and cross-scalar couplings whereby the initial systems/morphologies are not merely interconnected, but form new hybrid identities."[5]

KOLATAN/MACDONALD
5. "William MacDonald and Sulan Kolatan: Recent Work", *Columbia Documents of Architecture and Theory*, vol. 6 (1997): 121.

"We began with the proposition that architecture be understood as a set of 'relationships,' rather than as an autonomous object. To that end, the studio explored ways of producing architectural interventions based on an understanding of the city as a field of dynamic, cross-referenced organizational networks."[6]

WILLIAM MACDONALD
6. *Channel Surfing: Urban Networks*, Core Studio I, Fall 1997.

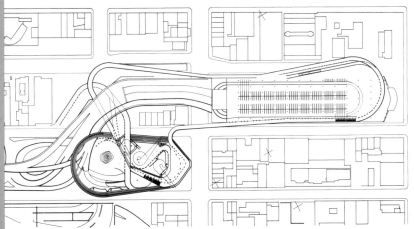

FIG. 66 Michael Su, *Logics and Logistics of Waiting*, Advanced Studio IV, Sulan Kolatan, critic, Spring 1995.

"As the computer is rediscovered on saliva-drenched glossy pages featuring the excited commentary of breathless critics, networks are portrayed as playgrounds of the future. Young designers are persuaded that they are pioneer explorers, shockingly oblivious of how well traveled are their paths and how many architects went so much farther. In the face of destabilizing

MARK WIGLEY
7. "Network Fever," *Grey Room* 4 (Summer 2001): 114.

forces, the romantic figure of the architect as stabilizer is reasserted. Now digital architects have moved into housing, with competitions on the virtual house, house forms inspired by information flows, mass-production techniques for infinite variations of housing forms within generic parameters, and so on. Electronic space is being settled. The architect is once again a figure of order, of pattern within chaos, of comfort. The architectural species have survived by ignoring a century of intense discourse about networks. In a kind of Warholian dream, every echo has become an original artwork."[7]

"The networks of these moving intersecting writings compose a manifold story that has neither author nor spectator, shaped out of fragments of trajectories and alterations of spaces: in relation to representations, it remains daily and indefinitely other. Escaping the imaginary totalizations produced by the eye, the everyday has a certain strangeness that does not surface, or whose surface is only its upper limit, outlining itself against the visible. Within this ensemble, I shall try to locate the practices that are foreign to the 'geometrical' or 'geographical' space of visual, panoptic, or theoretical constructions. These practices of space refer to a specific form of *operations* ('ways of operating'), to 'another spatiality' (an anthropological, poetic and mythic experience of space), and to an *opaque and blind* mobility characteristic of the bustling city. A migrational, or metaphorical, city thus slips into the clear text of the planned and readable city."[8]

8. Michel de Certeau, *The Practice of Everyday Life*, trans. Steven Randall (Berkeley, Calif.: University of California Press, 1984), 93.

"By means of such surveillance, disciplinary power became an 'integrated' system, linked from the inside to the economy and to the aims of the mechanism in which it was practiced. It was also organized as a multiple, automatic, and anonymous power; for although surveillance rests on individuals, its functioning is that of a network of relations from top to bottom, but also to a certain extent from bottom to top and laterally; this network 'holds' the whole together and traverses it in its entirety with effects of power that derive from one another: supervisors, perpetually supervised."[9]

9. Michel Foucault, *Discipline and Punish: The Birth of the Prison* (New York: Vintage Books, 1977), 176–177.

network

Merriam Webster's Dictionary

    1. a fabric or structure of cords or wires that cross at regular intervals and are knotted or secured at the crossings

    2. (a) an interconnected or interrelated chain, group, or system; (b) a system of computers, terminals, and databases connected by communications lines

    3. (a) a group of radio or television stations linked by wire or radio relay; (b) a radio or television company that produces programs for broadcast over such a network

see CITY; CO-CITATION; FIELD; TECHNOLOGY

New York

see ARCHITECTURE CULTURE; BUILDING/CONSTRUCTION; FRAME; MODERN/MODERNISM; MONTAGE; NOSTALGIA; PEDAGOGY, COLUMBIA; REAL; SPACE; STUDIO/PRACTICE; STUDIOS, CORE; TREND; URBAN

nonlinear

"Underlying all of the contemporary animation software is a mathematics of the infinitely small interval which simulates actual motion and time through keyframing. These transformations can be linearly morphed or they can involve nonlinear interactions through dynamics. These sequential transformations are possible because the formal entities themselves are described using flexible topological surfaces made of vector splines rather than points."[10]

GREG LYNN
10. *Animate Form* (New York: Princeton Architectural Press, 1999), 23.

"We are all familiar with linear systems that have been the mainstay of science for more than three hundred years: because one plus one equals two, we can predict that the volume of water flowing down a drain is doubled when a tap drips for twice as long. Nonlinear systems do not obey the simple rules of addition. Compare the simple flow of water down a drain with the complex nonlinear phenomena that regulate the quantity of water in the human body, or the movement of water vapor in the clouds overhead. Nonlinearity causes small changes on one level of organization to produce large effects at the same or different levels. This is familiar to most of us through the example of positive feedback, which turns amplified music into a deafening howl, but the same effect is present in the propensity of plutonium atoms to fall apart during an explosive nuclear chain reaction. In general, nonlinearity produces complex and frequently unexpected results."[11]

11. Peter Coveney and Roger Highfield, *Frontiers of Complexity: The Search for Order in a Chaotic World* (New York: Fawcett Columbine, 1995), 9.

"If one allows an intense flow of energy in and out of a system (that is, if one pushes it *far from equilibrium*), the number and type of possible historical outcomes greatly increases. Instead of a unique and simple form of stability, we now have multiple coexisting forms of varying complexity (static, periodic, and chaotic *attractors*). Moreover, when a system switches from one stable state to another (at a critical point called a *bifurcation*), minor fluctuations may play a crucial role in deciding the outcome.... Attractors and bifurcations are features of any system in which the dynamics are not only far from equilibrium but also *nonlinear*, that is, in which there are strong mutual interactions (or feedback) between components."[12]

12. Manuel De Landa, *A Thousand Years of Nonlinear History* (Cambridge, Mass.: MIT Press, 1997), 14.

"We can develop an intuitive idea of nonlinearity by characterizing the behavior of a system in terms of stimulus and response: If we give the system a 'kick' and observe a certain response to that kick, then we can ask what happens if we kick the system twice as hard. If the response is twice as large, then the system's behavior is said to be linear (at least for the range of kick sizes we have used). If the response is not twice as large (it might be large or smaller), then we say the system's behavior is nonlinear. In an acoustic system such as record, tape, or compact disc player, nonlinearity manifests itself as a distortion in the sound being reproduced....
The study of nonlinear behavior is called *nonlinear dynamics*."[13]
see INTERFACE; SYMMETRY

13. Robert C. Hilborn, *Chaos and Nonlinear Dynamics*, (New York: Oxford University Press, 1994), 3.

N

normative

"As excess of repetition oscillating between complicity and resistance in the rehearsal of life, the new architecture will serve as a reminder of contradictions invading the constituency of the norm. Deployed as moving targets across the entire subway system, a new theater will emerge as testimony to the 'spectacles of accidents' missing in time."[14]

EVAN DOUGLIS
14. *Screamscape of the Invisible City: A Museum of Accidents*, Advanced Studio, Summer 1997.

For the Housings project (1999), you created a series of experimental designs for pre-fabricated homes. How did you approach the idea of the "normative" versus the "experimental" housing type?
We began with normativity. The possibility, both conceptual and literal, of working with ideas of houses that are globally normative but locally experimental, or globally experimental and locally normative, is interesting. It is also a way of experimenting with mass customization—one could customize by normalizing certain aspects of the house, but have much more liberty with others.

SULAN KOLATAN

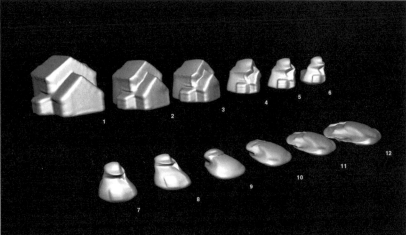

FIG. 67 Kolatan/MacDonald Studio, *Housings*, 1999.

In Housings, we took a normative building structure from a normative design-your-own home computer program and targeted conditions of desire that we could find from real-estate pages in different areas of the country. We then developed ranges according to the particular attributes and characteristics that we found in these real-estate ads. While retaining the original information from the normative house we applied degrees of influence on this kernel of information. At that point it began to yield new identities and relationships that we developed into architectural responses. In our case we're striving for mass customization, meaning multiple and unique, but not multiple as a kind of standardization.
see ORGANIC/ORGANICISM

WILLIAM MACDONALD

nostalgia

How does your nostalgia for popular Americana figure into your work?
In my studios we use nostalgia as a way to understand our past and build our future. To move away from nostalgia is shortsighted because it can be

LESLIE GILL

used as a critical tool. Few people of my generation have built in America or in New York because it is very hard to work within this cultural program. I am trying to take on these issues and build a critical practice while still accepting that these are the parameters. I use them as a way to define my architecture.

With respect to this idea of nostalgia, you talk about the reworking of the memory that is produced from a narrative event. How do you do this?

We live in a culture that is simultaneously transient and culturally nostalgic. How do you reconcile these two things because they are obviously intrinsically linked? How do you reconcile those within a program and a practice? If you want to build here, it is a question that you are going to have to answer.

LESLIE GILL

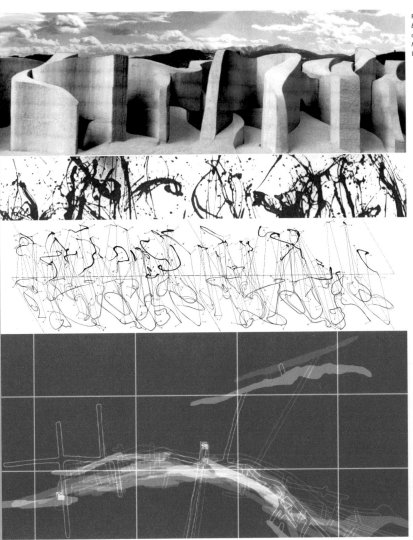

FIG. 68 David Pysh, *The Evening Redness in the West or the Metallic Frontier, Butte, Montana*, Advanced Studio VI, Leslie Gill, critic, Spring 1995.

How does that nostalgia reconcile itself with the influences that come from outside the local condition?

One of the issues I have been trying to explore is how to pair a regional identity with the abstraction of the larger infrastructure, whether it is the physical roadway or highway system, or an abstract sense of a global identity.

see TIME

LESLIE GILL

organic/organicism

How does your concept of the "organic" differ from that of others who use the term to imply something that is simply amorphous or non-Cartesian? I want to connect discordant points for a transformation of architectural language that builds a new reality. This is not about the amorphous.

KAREN BAUSMAN

I am interested in the generative potential of detail that comes as the result of analyzing composite systems. For example, flowers are exuberantly designed: saturated with color, dynamic in form, and have complex surfaces incorporating structure. Flowers are functionally efficient; they

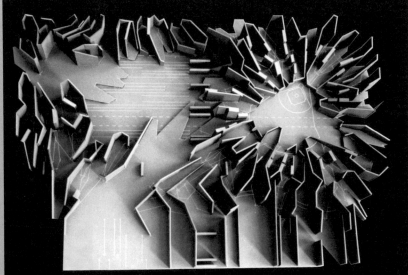

FIG. 69 Flor Crespo, *Yankee Stadium*, Advanced Studio V, Karen Bausman, critic, Fall 1998.

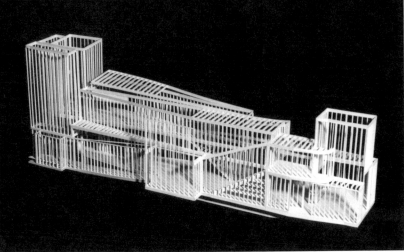

FIG. 70 Simon Eisinger, *Omphalos: The Thickened Present: A Montage of Dwelling*, Advanced Studio V, Karen Bausman, critic, Fall 1993.

exhibit no excess. It is interesting to note that nature is not uncomfortable with color. One could say a beautiful iris is a proven design. I am now trying to find ways to recast that as a given so that it no longer falls under the trope of the "organic."

"The speculative nature of these projections [for the incorporation of entertainment into eating and shopping programs] reopens established definitions of building categories such as type and program for debate. Thus begging the question: if normative identities are being conflated with and contaminated by elements and influences outside their defined boundaries, what other criteria can be used for identification and differentiation? What kind of new design methods might be suggested?

These issues [are addressed] through the notion of the *organic* hybrid, with organic implying here not a reference to formal qualities but a structural and operational unity absent in the mechanical hybrid. The concepts and methods used in the production will be developed through close examination of chimerization (biology) and, to some degree, of co-citation mapping (information system theory)."[1]

SULAN KOLATAN
1. *Movie Theater + ...*
Advanced Studio IV, Spring 1998.

"[W]e should beware of any architecture described as wholesome or organic, for the logic of the organism is the logic of self-enclosure, self-regulation and self-determination. Organic types that are whole to the fullest extent are full to the point of exclusion. Buildings are not organisms but merely provisional structures that are already multiplicitous. Where the organic is internally consistent, the inorganic is internally discontinuous and capable of a multiplicity of unforeseen connections. To disentangle the pact between organic bodies and exact geometric language that underlies architecture's static spatial types is a monumental task. Any attempt to loosen this alliance must simultaneously deterritorialize the autonomy of whole organisms and replace the exactitude of rigid geometry with more pliant systems of description. . . . In architecture, the present static alliance between rigid geometry and whole organisms cannot be entirely overcome but may be made more flexible and fluid through the use of more suppler, deformable geometries."[2]

GREG LYNN
2. "Multiplicitous and Inorganic Bodies," in *Folds, Bodies, and Blobs* (Brussels: La Lettre Volée, 1998), 41.

The subject of biology is recurring at a time when we are still saddled with the term "organicism," which has come up around computing. Organicism is a classic example of a disciplinary panic converted into an aesthetic discourse. It may not even be restricted to a disciplinary panic, because this digital organicism, to give a general umbrella, is something that can be found in American culture during the 1990s and that one can still find now.

Digital technologies give us ways to model complex behavior in accessible visual form. It is another version of the behaviorism of the 1960s projected onto an economic rather than a social referent. Its function is to naturalize what we call globalization now. And when something is naturalized it's as if there is no alternative. It's like nature. You can't argue with nature. It's just there. It's just truth.

REINHOLD MARTIN

organic

1. (a) (1): of, relating to, or derived from living organisms; (2): of, relating

Merriam Webster's Dictionary

to, yielding, or involving the use of food produced with the use of feed
or fertilizer of plant or animal origin without employment of chemically
formulated fertilizers, growth stimulants, antibiotics, or pesticides;
(b) of, relating to, or containing carbon compounds
2. (a) forming an integral element of a whole; (b) having systematic coor-
dination of parts; (c) having the characteristics of an organism: developing in the manner of a living plant or animal
see ENTROPY; ORGANIZATION; PERCEPTION; ROMANTICISM

organization

"The notion of the field gradient is important because it eludes definition
either as the sum of discrete particles amounting to a whole or as an organism simply constituted out of many parts.... This involves the interaction
of differentiated systems that are coherent but not simple."[3]

REISER/UMEMOTO
3. *Tokyo Bay Free Zone*,
Advanced Studio VI, Spring
1997.

PLATES 2.05–2.06

*Christopher Alexander once said that every component has a dual nature
—one, as a unit that fits into a larger hierarchy, and the other, as a pattern
that itself is made of smaller components. How do you relate to this idea?*
Alexander would still be talking about a modern hierarchy—components
that become patterns or components within patterns of order, above and
below. Although we're looking at a hierarchy similar to the one Alexander
is describing, they wouldn't simply be slotted into their position as pattern
or as element. There is a larger pattern, but there is a very different notion
of how exchanges occur; whether it's by direct impress to those components
above and below it, or whether it occurs through notions of feedback that
jump scales in the hierarchy. There is a commonality in recognizing those
systems as important.

JESSE REISER

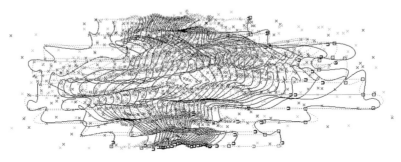

FIG. 71 Ciro Najle, *Tokyo Bay
Free Zone*, Advanced Studio VI,
Jesse Reiser and Nanako
Umemoto, critics, Spring 1997.

organize

Merriam Webster's Dictionary

1. to cause to develop an organic structure
2. to form into a coherent unity or functioning whole: integrate
3. (a) to set up an administrative structure for; (b) to persuade to
associate in an organization; especially unionize
4. to arrange by systematic planning and united effort

see CO-CITATION; COMPLEXITY; DIAGRAM; ENTROPY; IMAGE; LOCAL/GLOBAL; NONLINEAR;
ORNAMENT; PARTICLES; TECHNOLOGY

ornament

"Prominent among the dualisms that have regulated Western architectural
thought has been the opposition between ornament and structure. The aim
of the studio was to seek new architectural potentials arising out of a

REISER/UMEMOTO
4. *Ornament and Conformity*,
Advanced Studio, Summer
1995.

o

fundamental reappraisal of the status of ornament and its implications for architectural organization. Axiomatic to this approach is the critique, and ultimately the dismantling, of the dualistic structures that have heretofore regulated these conceptions. First and foremost, we assume, contrary to the classical formulation, that ornament is not subservient to structure, but in fact ornament is preeminently structure in itself. And furthermore, we posit that what classically would be understood as structure [is] an inherent subset of the general ornamental organization. This collapsing of the duality has potentially far-reaching architectural consequences—though not, as one might immediately suppose, as a vehicle for producing yet another ornamentalized architecture. Rather, it employs the ornamental as a graphic instrument capable of engendering complex organizations and spatialities, i.e., those that would foster unforeseen interruptions of institutional forms and programs."[4]

ornament

Merriam Webster's Dictionary

1. archaic: a useful accessory
2. (a) something that lends grace or beauty; (b) a manner or quality that adorns
3. one whose virtues or graces add luster to a place or society
4. the act of adorning or being adorned
5. an embellishing note not belonging to the essential harmony or melody

other

"One of the primary preoccupations of contemporary architectural theory is the concept of 'other' or 'otherness.' Members of the so-called neo-avant garde—architects and critics frequently affiliated with publications such as *ANY* or *Assemblage* and with architecture schools such as Princeton, Sci Arc, and the Architectural Association—advocate the creation of a *new* architecture that is somehow totally 'other.' While these individuals repeatedly decry utopianism and the morality of form, they promote novelty and marginality as instruments of political subversion and cultural transgression. The spoken and unspoken assumption is that 'different' is good, that 'otherness' is automatically an improvement over the status quo.... Foucault's conception of 'other' stands apart from Lacanian and Derridean models in that it suggests actual places, in actual moments in time. It acknowledges that power is not simply an issue of language. And this insistence on seeing institutions and practices in political and social terms has been welcomed by many feminist theorists. Yet one of the most striking aspects of Foucault's notion of heterotopia is how the idea of 'other,' in its emphasis on rupture, seems to exclude the traditional arenas of women and children—two of the groups that most rightly deserve (if by now one can abide the term's universalizing effect) the label 'other.' Women are admitted in his discussion primarily as sex objects—in the brothel, in the motel rented by the hour. (And what might be even harder for most working mothers to accept with a straight face is his exclusion of the house as a heterotopia on the grounds that it is a 'place of rest.') Foucault seems to have an unconscious disdain for sites of everyday life such as the home, the public park, and the department store that have been provinces where women have found not only oppression but also some degree of comfort, security, autonomy, and even freedom."[5]

MARY MCLEOD
5. "'Other' Spaces and 'Others,'" in *The Sex of Architecture*, ed. Diana Agrest, Patricia Conway, and Leslie Weisman (New York: Harry N. Abrams, 1996), 15, 20.

P

painting	see ART/ARTIST; LANDSCAPE; WATERCOLOR

particles

"Themes of particle and topological modeling were thematic in the studio. The ability for semiautonomous particles or agents to interact, through limited feedback with one another to develop second-order coupling or emergent organizations was investigated using particle-based modeling software. In particle-based environments space and form are defined not by points, lines, planes, and volumes but rather by the varying densities and relations between particles with differing attributes—more precisely, elements within gradient fields. Space is defined in a more meteorological fashion as clouds of particles with densities and shapes that can only be defined through the relationships between a multiplicity of differing particles. These particle-based organizations, in some situations, develop large-scale, singular characteristic forms and organizations. Blob, slug, clay, and shrink-wrap software were used for their ability to fuse these aggregate, particulate systems into provisional unities. Common to these processes is the development of larger-scale collective patterns that cannot be attributed to a single part or module but are instead a relational or collective effect. These second-level organizations or phenomena also typically occur in phases of development and are prone to evolutionary change over time."[1]

GREG LYNN
1. *The Topological Organization of Free Particles: Parking Garage Studio*, Advanced Studio V, Fall 1994.

particle
1. (a) a minute quantity or fragment; (b) a relatively small or the smallest discrete portion or amount of something
2. archaic: a clause or article of a composition or document
3. any of the basic units of matter and energy
4. a unit of speech expressing some general aspect of meaning or some connective or limiting relation and including the articles, most prepositions and conjunctions, and some interjections and adverbs
5. a small eucharistic wafer distributed to a Roman Catholic layman at Communion

Merriam Webster's Dictionary

pattern	see CYBERNETICS; FIELD; ORGANIZATION; TYPE

**pedagogy,
Columbia**

How would you characterize the approach at Columbia?
When I first arrived at the School in the late 1980s, the atmosphere was more polarized, while I think now there is a shared idea about what the important issues in architecture are. We are not necessarily in agreement about exactly how to address those issues, but we have a loose understanding that there are certain crucial questions that need to be addressed today.

  In 1989, we were still working through debates regarding the critical practices of the 1980s, even to the extent of asking whether—if you are

STAN ALLEN

after a critical, radical practice—it was appropriate for an architect to be building at all. There was a focus instead on theoretical work, gallery installations, and virtual architecture. The shift that occurred in the early 1990s was the emergence of a shared sense of purpose in dealing with urban issues, questions of technology (both building technology and computer technology), and addressing real problems of building construction and performance. In other words, while there is still a commitment to speculation and experimentation, that experimentation is directed toward real problems and within what are conventionally understood as the limits of architecture as a discipline.

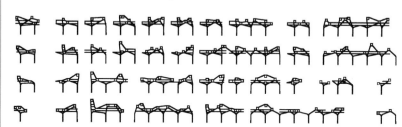

FIG. 72 Richard Garber, Sebastian Khourian, and Rajeev Thakker, *Event/Infra/Structure*, Advanced Studio VI, Stan Allen, critic, Spring 1998.

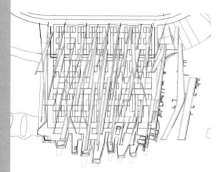

Some people would say that the discourse has turned inward; I think there is now a clearer sense of the necessity to bring that experimental attitude back to bear on real architectural issues. In my own work, for instance, I've been concerned with issues relating to field conditions, contextual tactics, and infrastructural urbanism. These are all ideas that were brought up in practice, and elaborated in studios during discussions with students, colleagues at Columbia, and visitors who passed through. It was not simply a reiteration of the same academic concerns; rather, they were modified and transformed in the arena of competitions and large-scale speculative urban work, which lies somewhere between the more experimental academic discourse and the really hard-nosed constraints of actual building projects.

PLATE 2.07

I have been given a great deal of latitude to explore and experiment, although there were several times along the way when my methods were criticized because they were seen as precarious. Despite that, I have stubbornly stuck to the notion that the School remain as experimental

HANI RASHID

and polemical as possible in order to inform new definitions and forma-
tions of both practice and design. I am committed to detaching my studio
from the day-to-day drudgery of clients and budgets, instead cultivating
an experimental laboratory for architecture on many levels.

The AAD students often come with somewhat superficial expectations,   LISE ANNE COUTURE
developed from reading the School's publications, such as *Newsline* and
Abstract. The new students tend to adopt a formal language or process-
oriented methodology that is not always grounded in wider culturally based
issues. Many come from backgrounds where an "ism" conditioning is
accepted and encouraged. They've been trained to accept that architecture
is all about categorization. In some ways, they are looking for another
form of legitimization, having been nurtured on a system that is structured
that way in the first place. The problem starts at the undergraduate level
and exists within the profession itself. I encourage my students to question
their backgrounds similar to the way Hani has students in the upper
years question their trajectory through the School. I also encourage them
to assume responsibility for the ways that they condition themselves
architecturally.

The majority of the people that Bernard has invited to Columbia, both the   HANI RASHID
people who have been there a long time and the visitors, come from diverse
backgrounds and interests, and have propagated a culture that opposes
categorizations and "isms." And yet the irony persists; Columbia is often
perceived as a place spawning yet another style. Columbia has often found
itself in the dubious position of propagating certain stylistic genres,
which has created an interesting dynamic at the school—the ever-changing
landscape of what is "hot." I have always perceived myself as being more
of a curious spectator and reluctant participant in that phenomenon.

Columbia's strange relationship to style and fashion is caught between
the romantic idea of Alvin Boyarsky's AA model and the very market-driven
situation that defines the New York cultural scene. The School is an interesting hybrid of idealism and pragmatism—a strong desire to teach coupled with the very real need to survive in a tough city.

When I started at Columbia, there was more Manfredo Tafuri than Gilles
Deleuze; there was more of an emphasis on the history of theory and a
great deal of interest in the works of the heroic moderns. As strange as this
may sound, the School became more theoretical and realistic at the same
time, and that has tempered it as a critical place for the reality of architecture, a reality well beyond good design and academic refuge.

*Does Columbia have the same strong underpinnings and personalities that
you had at the Cooper Union?*
It is more pluralistic. At eighteen, I was a beneficiary of a group that studied   KAREN BAUSMAN
at Cooper Union and the Institute for Architecture and Urban Studies, whose
ranks included Evan Douglis, Stan Allen, and Jesse Reiser. Columbia is
the next round, and the dialogue there is so open that it can only flourish.

The high priority that Bernard has placed on media has contributed to the international reputation of the School. More important, the increased rate of publications has enabled the various critical practices within the institution to reach a far larger architectural audience within a short period of time.

EVAN DOUGLIS

If you look at the whole bandwidth of teachers, I think that Columbia has stronger teachers than other places, and there is a place for each of these unique ambitions to exist, as well as a mutual respect for each other's ideas within their individual studios. That started to shift when the computer was introduced into the studio and people jumped on the bandwagon because they just didn't know what to do. Using the computer became a method rather than an exploration. Fortunately the School is starting to find a balance. I appreciate the independent visions and the discussions that allow for interconnections to take place.

LESLIE GILL

Do the students tend to produce a certain type of imagery?

It shifts quite dramatically. The students who are really independent thinkers become the leaders of the next generation. Really good students at Columbia are far superior to ones at other schools where I have taught because they are really able to think on their own terms and they are able to produce a body of work that represents those ideas. When you get to Columbia the rug gets pulled out on day one so the people who manage, after six semesters, to come out with a body of knowledge and a body of ideas are prepared to define their own vision and their own kind of pedagogy about architecture.

LESLIE GILL

What are the differences and similarities between Columbia and Harvard, where you also teach?

Each school has its strengths. Columbia is educating the leaders of the next generation. The School makes the students look at a much more diverse set of theoretical and seminal propositions about what constitutes architecture. Harvard has a far narrower set of limitations that are much more defined, which leads to a much more rigorous exploration. Conversely, at

LESLIE GILL

FIG. 73 Stephen Wang, *Without Resting: The Tracking of Home within the Mystery/Spy Genre*, Advanced Studio, Leslie Gill, critic, Summer 1993.

154

Columbia I think there are many people who fall through the cracks and there is a lot of pastiche. That does not happen at Harvard because the boundaries have been defined and, ultimately, institutionalized.

Does Columbia train architects for the profession?
Critics have to find ways to link professional issues to the studio problems in ways that seem relevant, which is always a balancing act in any school. A good way to engage students in these issues often begins with a consideration of architectonic ideas about structure and the construction of enclosure, which are theoretical in their own right. We always stress a relationship between concept and its architectonic expression. In our office we begin with a strong concept that relates to the culture of the moment, but without structure and without some sense of enclosure, volume, and materiality, it is difficult to imagine architecture taking place. These issues are communicated in a complex, nonlinear way during the first year. At Columbia we saw a variety of students, both in terms of experience and thought. Students did not have to be taught how to draw and they learned quickly from each other, which allowed critics to focus more on ideas than on technicalities. Even with the more advanced paperless studios, there was a tangibility to the models, drawings, and computer renderings; there was a desire to present something that could be discussed.

THOMAS HANRAHAN

FIG. 74 Darryl Ohlenbush, *Montessori School, Staten Island, New York,* Core Studio II, Thomas Hanrahan, critic, Spring 1991.

What are your criticisms of Columbia's program?

We still need to learn how to sketch because there is a very strong connec- LAURIE HAWKINSON tion between the hand and the mind, but now I am just as affected by computer software as I am by a 9H pencil. As Catherine Ingraham has said, the computer is both very smart and very dumb. We are teaching students to construct a visual argument for a project, so it should be rigorous. We need to be more expansive with our software instead of being invested in just a few programs because product and process are the result of limita- tions of a particular software. Form Z, for example, can do certain things very well while other operations are not possible. The software should facilitate your idea, so you need choices. Visual studies is an important complement to the studio because it is an opportunity to work specifically on representation. Many first-year students have no knowledge of modern buildings when they arrive at Columbia. As a student at Cooper, I could not wait to find out about those buildings, but you had to wade through the early periods before you actually got to something that was really relevant to what you were doing as a designer. I don't understand why history needs to be taught chronologically. PLATE 2.09

When the computer initially appeared, faculty and students wanted to see how far they could push it. Now that we have a better idea of what to expect, you suggest that many of the faculty are frustrated. Why is this so?

The trap of having a successful school is continued change and evolution GREG LYNN in the face of imitation and duplication. There were particular canonical elements that attracted people to the School—I remember the horror of having a student tell me he wanted to end up with a project similar to one on some page of *Abstract*. For example, after teaching three studios using a specific digital technique of mapping particles I decided to aban- don the experiment. I told the next incoming batch of students the limits of that approach, yet they asked me to teach another particle-mapping studio because that was what they had seen and that was what they wanted to learn.

I hope there are some issues that are agreed upon so that we can move forward. For instance, the consensus on how and why deformable surfaces should be used for architectural design has opened up recent investigations of variable or nonstandard design approaches. The ability to teach milling classes was a direct result of the agreement on the usefulness of paperless studios and moreover, the need to take the next step and investigate robo- tic fabrication of architectural models and full-scale components.

There is no curse greater than the nostalgia of having to relive the birth of a school every term in perpetuity. Bernard has been able to keep Colum- bia evolving. The School does not appeal to simple diversity as a method of change either; the stakes are much higher as the School trades diversity for evolution. The whole academic project could be scratched and rebuilt every two years in an attempt to figure out what constitutes a successful school, because that is how quick things are changing these days. Bernard's commitment to ongoing research has been amazing and I am glad to be part of it. PLATE 2.08

**phenomenon/
phenomenology**

3.01

Steven Holl

*Kiasma, Helsinki
Museum of
Contemporary Art*

Helsinki, Finland

1998

**phenomenon/
phenomenology**

3.02 (left)
Antonella Mari
A Collection
Advanced Studio VI
Steven Holl, critic
Spring 1997

3.03 (right)
Steven Holl
Museum of the City
1996

CIRCULATION SYSTEM ON AND THROUGH
HABITABLE SPACEFRAME

HABITABLE SPACEFRAME ROOF

ELEVATED PUBLIC GARDENS
ATTACHED TO EXTENSION OF WEST
SIDE PARK

CULTURAL PROGRAMS + MEZZANINE WITH
HOTELS AND LEASABLE OFFICE
TOWERS CONNECTED BY WAY OF
MALL ARMS

MAJOR AND MINOR EVENT SPACES
WITH SEVEN FLOORS OF LEASABLE
OFFICE SPACE ATTACHED

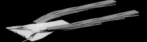

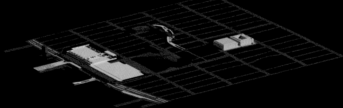

CITY GRID WITH JACOB JAVITS
CONVENTION CENTER EXTENSION +
LINCOLN TUNNEL ENTRANCE EXTENSION

SHOPPING MALL ATTACHED DIRECTLY
TO NEW PENNSYLVANIA STATION

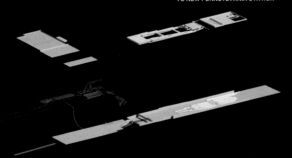

SUBSURFACE RAILCUT AND TRACKS WITH LINCOLN TUNNEL

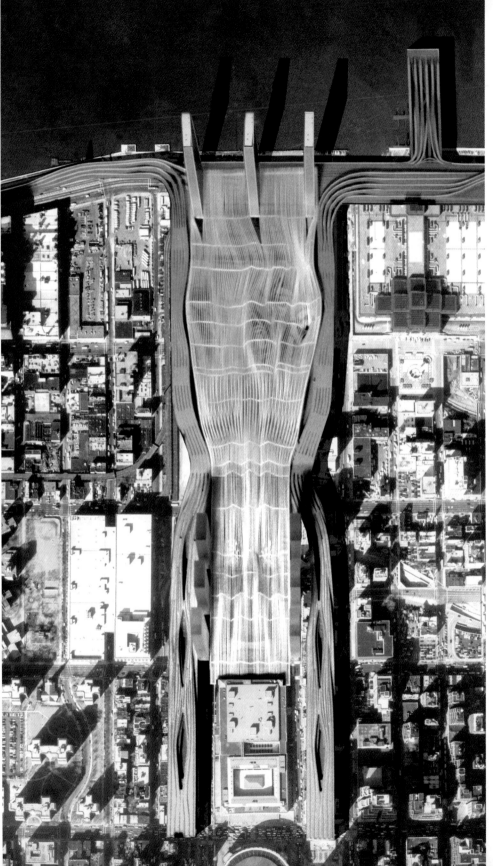

potential
3.04
Reiser + Umemoto
West Side Convergence
2000

practice/clients
3.05
Hanrahan + Meyers
*Red Hook Center
for the Arts*
New York, New York
2000

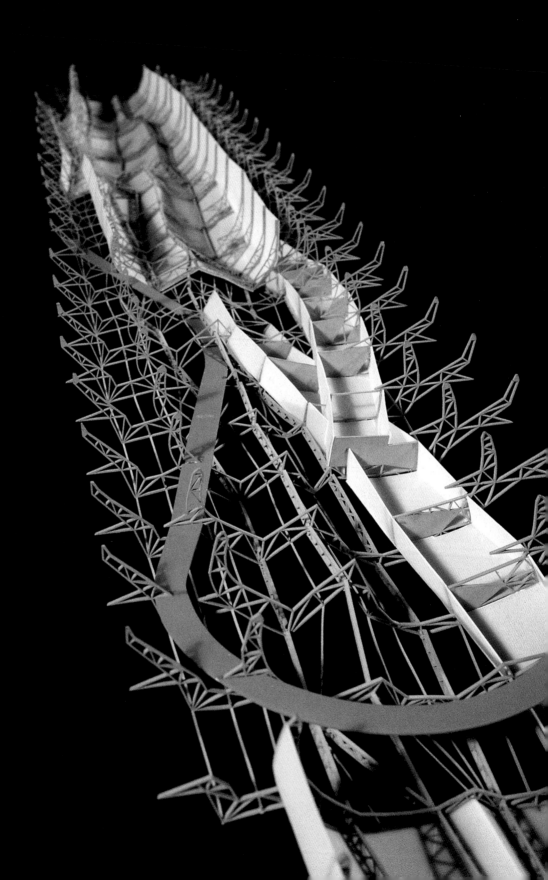

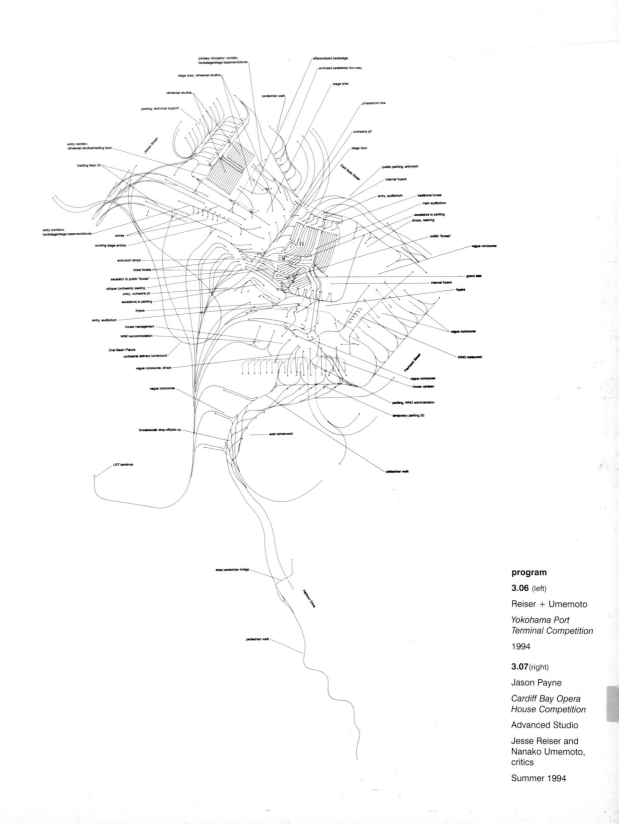

primary circulation, corridor,
backstage/stage basement/stores

differentiated backstage

enclosed pedestrian thru-way

stage area, rehearsal studios

stage area

rehearsal studios

pedestrian walk

proscenium line

parking, technical support

orchestra pit

James Street

stage door

entry corridor,
rehearsal studios/loading bays

public parking, entry/exit

East Bute Street

internal foyers

loading bays (4)

entry, auditorium   traditional boxes

main auditorium

escalators to parking
shops, catering

entry corridors,
backstage/stage basement/stores

public "boxes"

vague concourse

stores

working stage entries

entry/exit ramps

grand stair

ticket kiosks

escalator to public "boxes"

internal foyers

oblique (orchestra) seating

foyers

entry, orchestra pit

escalators to parking

foyers

vague concourse

entry, auditorium

house management

WNO accommodation

WNO restaurant

Oval Basin Piazza

Pierhead Street

orchestral delivery turnaround

vague concourse

vague concourse, shops

house canteen

parking, WNO administration

vague concourse

temporary parking (6)

limosine/cab drop-off/pick-up

auto turnaround

LRT terminus

pedestrian walk

steel pedestrian bridge

Harbour Drive

pedestrian walk

program

3.06 (left)

Reiser + Umemoto

*Yokohama Port
Terminal Competition*

1994

3.07 (right)

Jason Payne

*Cardiff Bay Opera
House Competition*

Advanced Studio

Jesse Reiser and
Nanako Umemoto,
critics

Summer 1994

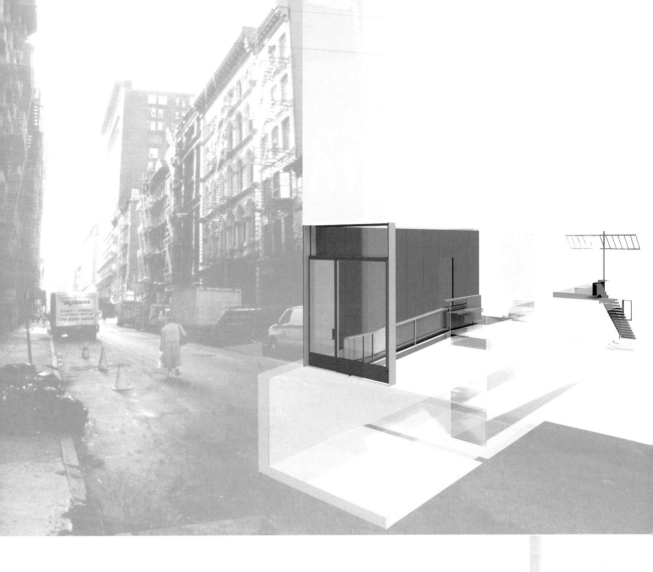

public/private
3.08 (left)
Dean Wolf Architects
Ethan Cohen Fine Arts
New York, New York
2000

3.09 (right)
Dean Wolf Architects
Urban Interface Loft
New York, New York
1997

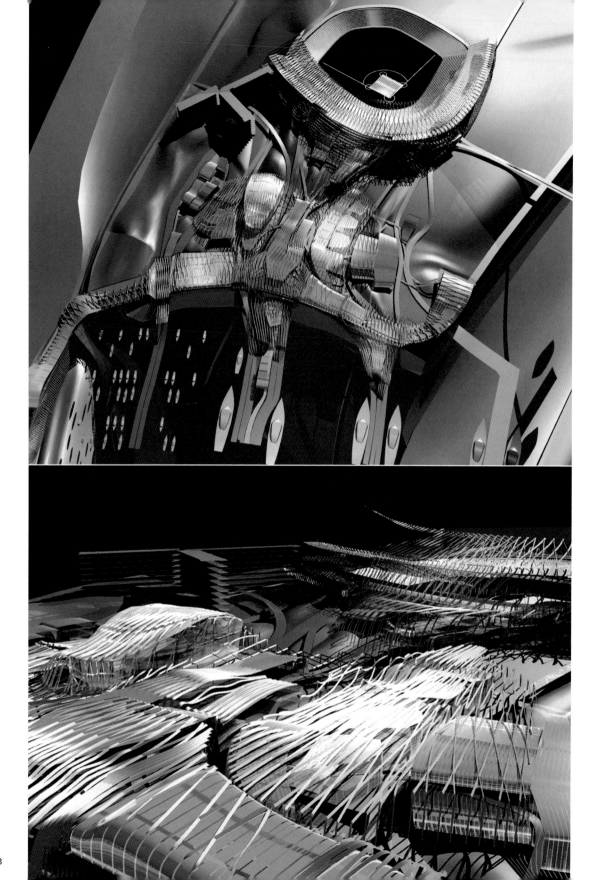

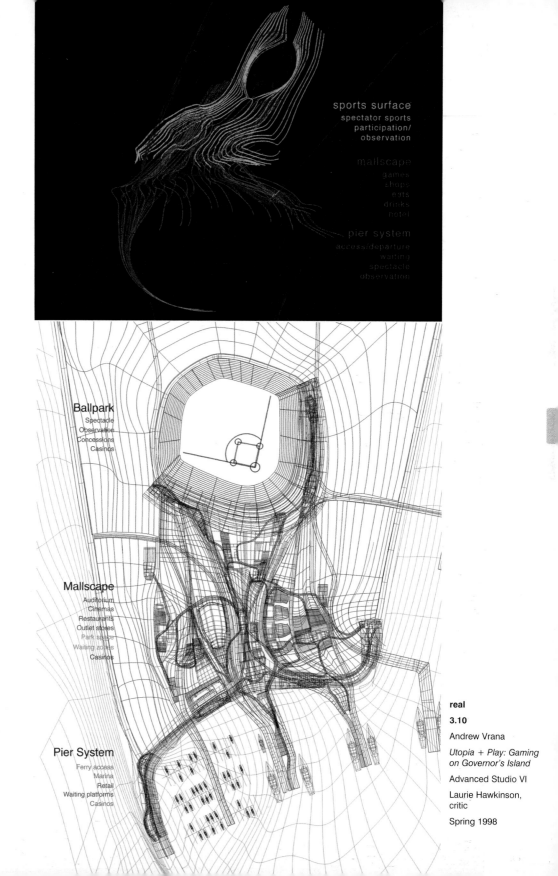

sports surface
spectator sports
participation/
observation

mallscape
games
shops
eats
drinks
hotel

pier system
access/departure
waiting
spectacle
observation

Ballpark
Spectacle
Observation
Concessions
Casinos

Mallscape
Auditorium
Cinemas
Restaurants
Outlet stores
Park space
Waiting zones
Casinos

Pier System
Ferry access
Marina
Retail
Waiting platforms
Casinos

real

3.10

Andrew Vrana

*Utopia + Play: Gaming
on Governor's Island*

Advanced Studio VI

Laurie Hawkinson,
critic

Spring 1998

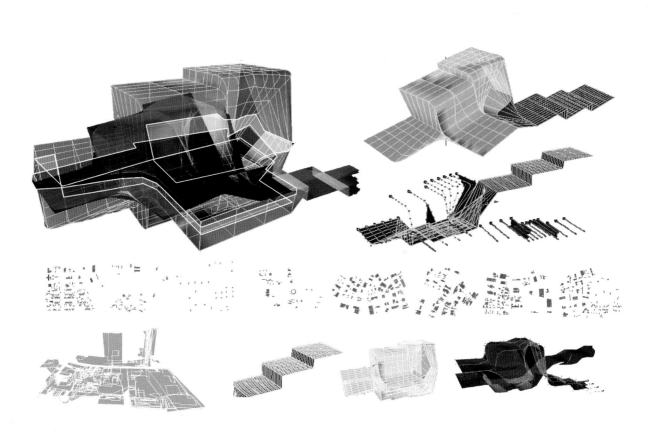

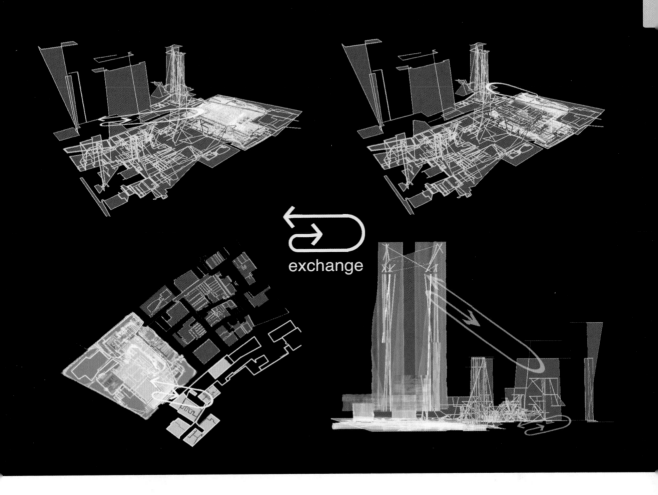

exchange

real

3.11

Thunyalux Hiransaroj

City as Artificial Ecology
Case Study: Port
Authority of New York

Advanced Studio V

Stan Allen, critic

Fall 1999

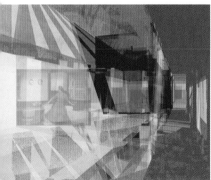

real

3.12 (left)
Martin/Baxi Architects
Entropia: Embassy
2001

(right top)
Martin/Baxi Architects
Entropia: Homeoffice
2001

(right bottom)
Martin/Baxi Architects
Entropia: Open House
2001

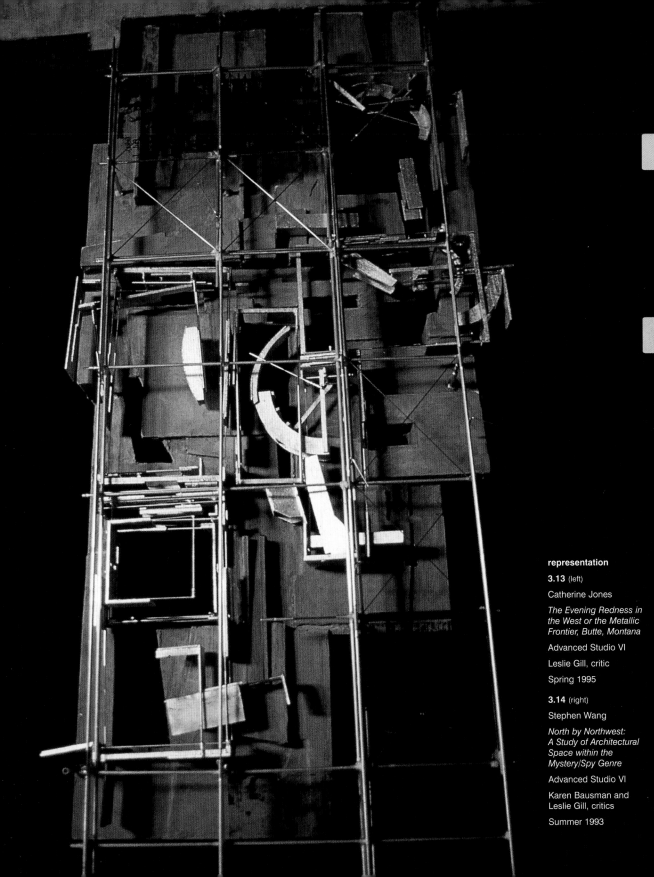

scale

3.15

Leslie Gill

*Watrous Weatherman
Residence*

New York, New York

1998

seriality/ mass
production

3.16 (left)

Francesco de Fuentes

*Rutgers University
Vision Plan*

Advanced Studio V

Greg Lynn, critic

Fall 1998

3.17 (right)

Greg Lynn, Michael
McInturf, and Douglas
Garofalo

*Korean Presbyterian
Church*

New York, New York

1998

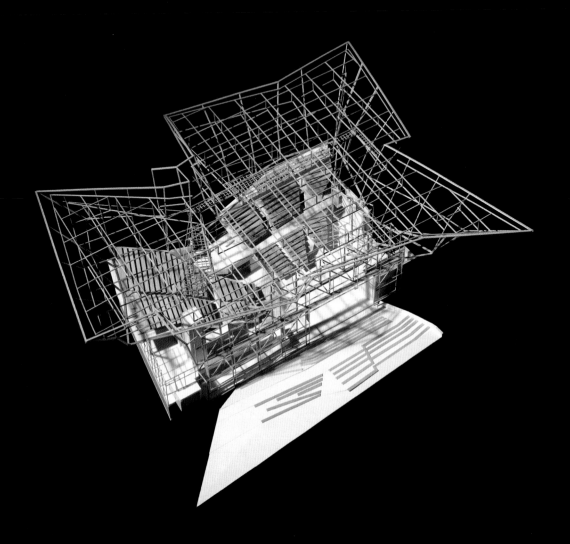

structure

3.18 (left)

Karen Bausman

Performance Theater

1998

3.19 (right)

Shirley Tsou

A Thickened Present and the Architecture of Meditation

Advanced Studio V

Karen Bausman, critic

Fall 1999

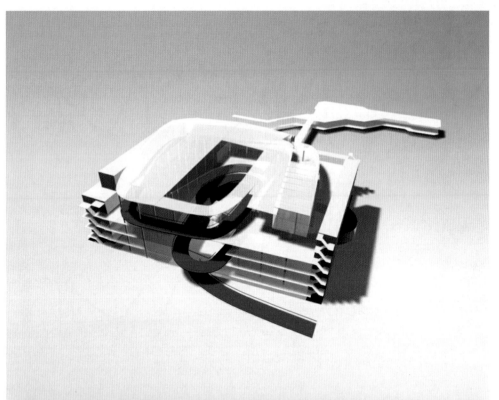

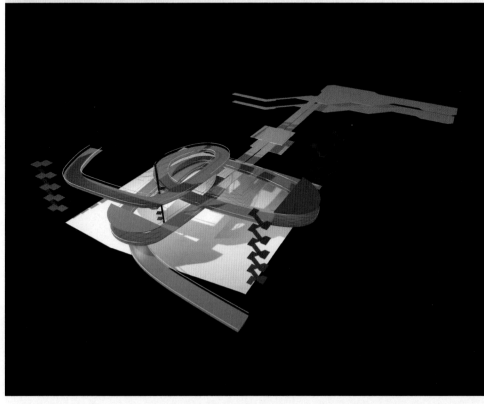

studio/practice

3.20 (left)
Carmen Carrasco
Advanced Studio VI
Bernard Tschumi, critic
Spring 1995

3.21 (right)
Bernard Tschumi
K Polis
1995

studio/practice
3.22
Bernard Tschumi
Lerner Hall
New York, New York
1999

For too long, architectural education has been about teaching recipes.
I have always felt that this was a restrictive and unintelligent way to go
about learning architecture. I would rather acknowledge that we are
attempting to reinvent the world every day.

BERNARD TSCHUMI

Do the students and faculty coalesce around certain trends?
At Columbia, my observation is that ideas are moving much faster than
in the outside world. It is a liquid process that you cannot let freeze or
solidify. The intent is to keep adding new ingredients to the mix or to
make sure that the flow never stops.

BERNARD TSCHUMI

At no moment do we want to canonize a given style or a given ideology.
Architecture is about dynamics and is constantly in motion. The students
are quite aware of this evolution and little by little the ideas of previous
years evolve into something altogether different. The studio research is
never exhausted and is constantly moving forward, which is true of the
faculty work as well.

Literary criticism, philosophy, art, film, physics, chemistry, and other
fields have been explored by architects throughout history and these other
fields have consistently borrowed architectural concepts and metaphors
to establish their own foundations. A school of architecture is an ideal
place for exploring these modes of interchange, allowing import and export
between different areas of knowledge.

The nature of questioning implies a very broad and liberal approach, but
there also has to be a rigor and discipline. How is that balance found?

One way is through the mix of the faculty. I have always been very careful
to try to balance out the physically minded, architectonic faculty members
with the virtual, conceptual, abstract types. The individual faculty members
are highly conscious of what everybody else is doing and tend to position
themselves in relation to the others, and try to assert their differences.

BERNARD TSCHUMI

Ultimately, the only thing that they have in common is that they are a part
of a school of architecture. At times in the history of architectural education, there were schools that were governed by one person or one dogma.
Architecture, however, is not a knowledge of form; it is a form of knowledge.
There needs to be a rich mix of competitive faculty and a competitive
dialogue with other disciplines to do this.

If architecture is a form of knowledge, what exactly do you want students
to learn?

I often have that argument with some of my colleagues who want to teach
architecture through canonic buildings. I have no problem with teaching
key historical concepts that have developed in architecture, but call them
concepts, not canons. Freedom of thought and questioning is our priority.

BERNARD TSCHUMI

I was pleased when certain faculty members started to talk about notions
of continuity and fluidity in ways that were very different from earlier
notions of discontinuity. These debates are more interesting and more important within the history of architectural thinking than the teaching of
canonic buildings.

A school of architecture does not represent a single ideology or religion.
It is about polemics, creative arguments, and conflicts of opinion. A school

should welcome people with diverse views, provided they are willing to engage in debate.

When you arrived at Columbia, you undertook what Vincent Scully called "an exploration of extreme silliness." He was referring to the transition between what might appear to be an aesthetic historicism into something that could be considered no longer grounded in anything historical. At first these explorations bordered on the ephemeral, yet in the past ten years, there is a conceptual underpinning that seems to be both strong and real. How did this transition occur?

People like Scully simply did not know what we were doing. When I arrived, the school was very formulaic. In the third semester, you did the housing type, in the fifth semester, the long span type, and in the sixth semester, you did the monastery type. These typologies were not quite canons, but they were a secondary set of frozen rules that were being used as a way to teach.

  With this old system the faculty member was setting an answer or model as a goal and the students would work twelve to fourteen weeks to arrive at that predetermined goal. It was a difficult situation because I was adamantly opposed to this method of teaching. I felt that faculty members ought to ask a question and explore that question through a project with their students.

BERNARD TSCHUMI

My approach to teaching is first and foremost to encourage and enable students to develop a level of criticality. All of the rather tepid hype about the post-critical approaches to the new economy—surfing the wave and going with the flow—seem to me not only hopelessly irresponsible, but naive. At every level I would like to be able to operate both inside and outside of this institution, informed by the need to continue to develop critical consciousness with respect to what contemporary architecture is and could be.

  The funny thing about the image that the School has acquired is that it reduces the actual diversity within the School. When I arrived, I was happy

REINHOLD MARTIN

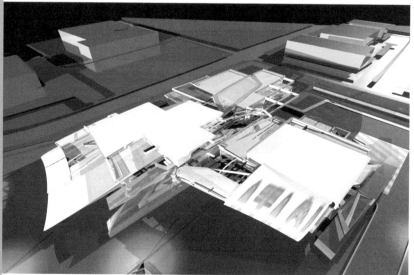

FIG. 75 Anthony Burke, *Entropy Lab*, Advanced Studio V, Reinhold Martin, critic, Fall 1999.

to see that the School was not this monolithic thing devoted to some rather clichéd image of what to do with computers. That has enabled a range to emerge and proliferate in different directions, rather than to continue to reinforce the party line.

see BUILDING/CONSTRUCTION; STUDIO/PRACTICE

perception

"The interrelationships between the organic and the inorganic, the micro-cosmos and the cosmos, and matter and energy must be expressed, which raises questions concerning limits of knowledge and the way the physical world is shaped by our perception."[2]

STEVEN HOLL
2. *Experimental Studies for a Museum of Science*, Advanced Studio VI, Spring 1993.

"Experience of phenomena—sensations in space and time as distinguished from the perception of objects—provides a 'pre-theoretical' ground for architecture. Such perception is pre-logical, i.e., it requires a suspension of a priori thought. Phenomenology, questions of perception, encourage us to experience architecture by walking through it, touching it, listening to it."[3]

see VIRTUAL/ACTUAL

3. "Phenomena and Idea," <www.stevenholl.com/writings/phenomena.html> (8 July 2002).

performance

"The Aarhus Theatre…emerged from a number of investigations into the making of fluid and transitional space. The building emerged not so much as a direct result of computer-generated images and studies, but rather as a space aspiring to contain the dynamics and possibilities inherent in computer modeling and simulation.

This process of speculating on the possible uses of digital technologies enables us to investigate the merging of architecture, city, and event through the use of modeling, [and] animation software."[4]

ASYMPTOTE
4. Georgi Stanishev, "Designing the Unpredictable" (interview), *World Architecture* 54 (March 1997): 74.

PLATES 2.14–2.15

There is a performative aspect to the studio and professional work that you do, yet at the same time architecture, at least in a Vitruvian sense, is static. What is the performance?

It goes back to a couple of things, one of which is Aldo Rossi's *A Scientific Autobiography*. In it he refers to buildings as carcasses, and he develops the notion that architecture is nothing more than a harness in which things unfold. The idea of architecture as a scaffolding for everything from dialogues to events has developed to the point where we have fused the performative aspect of space with the actual. In the last couple of years, with the advent of digital technologies, we have been producing virtual environments that are really the seamless fusion of a number of our interests. Our architecture has changed as we have been able to reject the Vitruvian model of architecture as static and immutable and we are able to now conceive of and construct liquid and mutable space, a kind of performing architecture.

These interests actually preceded our use of computers; we produced projects like the Los Angeles West Coast Gateway around the same time that I started teaching at Columbia. The project was thought of as an agglomeration of parts within an open scaffolding situated above the Hollywood Freeway, which included hanging hinged theaters and oscillating aquariums, parks as samples of various American landscapes, and

HANI RASHID

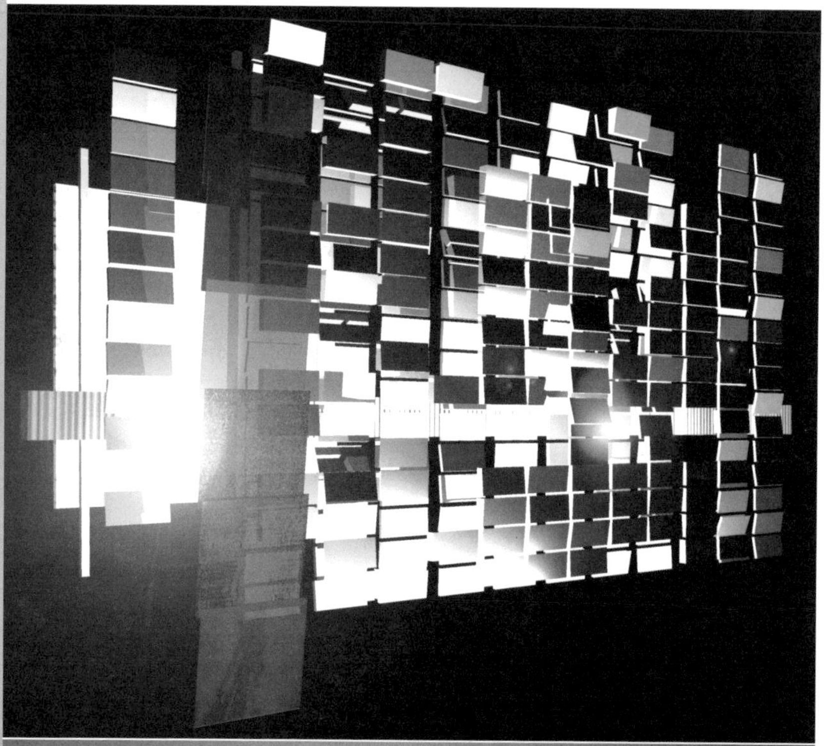

FIG. 76 Peter Dorsey, *Columbia@AlphaWorld*, Advanced Studio V, Hani Rashid, critic, Fall 1996.

FIG. 77 Asymptote, *Steel Cloud*, 1989.

so on. This project was already a departure from a grounded, stationary building and in some ways made explicit our search for a performative aspect to building. We talked about the building at that time as being absent of facades and instead enveloped in streaming text. When it was proposed in 1989, we scrambled to justify and locate those types of very new and unknown technologies, but we knew that the information and digital ages would allow us to start thinking of architecture in a more mutable way. It was one of the first large-scale proposals for an architecture that is more plausible today, well over a decade later.

Our work on the Virtual Guggenheim Museum has allowed us to get rid of not only the diagram but also the notion of architecture as a frame or place for program. The moment where the body of architecture is able to be eliminated and subsumed into experience is very important to us, which goes back to the way we confront the city as a place that invokes performance, spectacle, and fluidity.

PLATES 2.12–2.13

I remember studying Palladio one day in Vicenza when we were students. We were walking down the street listening to a dry lecture about the different orders, the columns, the proportional systems, the various hierarchies, and when we went into the Teatrò Olympico, we saw another example of the work of that period that had very little to do with the mathematical certainty we were being shown. It was not a static, dead, well-proportioned building after all, but a space of event that was capable of constant transformation. The city as event was inverted and contained in this place in a fantastic way.

When did your interest in the performance of buildings first appear?
The first time we talked about this was for a building we designed in Tours, France, about four or five years ago for an invited competition, the Contemporary Cultural Center (1993). The competitors were from a slightly older generation, which included Daniel Libeskind and Wolf Prix, a generation that we got tagged onto for years. We recently jumped ship and are now becoming appropriately associated with our own generation of architects. They were all making formal proposals, and we started looking toward other nuances through the implementation of new technologies. For example, for the music pavilion at the Cultural Center we proposed a glass case around the theater that would be constructed of malleable joints at each of the vertices. The music inside would generate a computer program that would make the joints produce an oscillation in the structure; the building itself would move during performances. On the other side of the site, for the art building, we were more interested in the history of vision and seeing in the 20th century. We designed the building in such a way that artists and curators could filter light into the galleries in different ways by changing the roof structure, effectively breaking down the idea that art galleries should contain a kind of sacred light devised by the architect—what we call the Kimbell effect.

Our music theater proposal for Graz, Austria (1998), also attempted to be usable outside of its program with an entirely operable facade that literally changed the acoustics of the music hall within and allowed composers to "tune" the building prior to performances.

That building was based on physical movement, but in the building we are doing in Kyoto, the glass changes density and coloration. We are all familiar with the pragmatic modernist interest in light, opacity, and translucency, but we thought of using the technology to communicate the rate of occupancy and fluctuating interiority. As the building's occupants leave at night, a gradient of colored light fills the facades from the first floor up. The building appears as if it is being filled with a liquid and, in the morning, as people arrive to go to work, the building's "light" empties out and the windows become transparent. We are interested in implicating technology into building in unorthodox ways.

I often tell my students that our role is that of a spatial engineer. There are spatialists in the world of sculptural art and interiors, but the engineer-

HANI RASHID

FIG. 78 Asymptote, *Graz Music Theater*, 1998.

P

ing of space falls into our discipline. If you are going to use new technologies, how do they allow us to engineer space, not simply engineer better buildings?

What do you mean by performance?

Each botanical specimen is designed to function in a highly specific way, which allows for all manner of things, including each specimen's unique form. Nevertheless, by reorganizing information a new language evolves that allows for the performance of functions wholly unrelated to the original program and form. In short it is a transformation of function through the development of an architectural language leading to new form.

KAREN BAUSMAN

With your installations, the object has a very powerful presence, but how and when does it begin to cross the line from sculpture to building?

I have always been a proponent of the "presence of the absence": the capacity of architecture to project its influence without actually having to occupy a particular territory of space. Space, whether it is delineated as material or immaterial, ultimately must become performative in order to arrive at a transcendental state. There are countless examples of how the ideological intentions embedded within a work of architecture have asserted significant influence over the political ethos of civilizations.

EVAN DOUGLIS

In both the Pesce and *Liquid Assets* (1999) installations, the material practices imply a self-regulating system that accommodates to a variety of contexts. In other words, the organizational logic intrinsic to methods of production refer to a more complex set of relations beyond the object.

In the Pesce exhibition that I organized, the relentless inscription of homasote profiles layered over one another enabled the incremental unit of time attributed to the duration of construction to be placed in juxtaposition to an opposing desire for a continuous performative surface. By strategically adjusting the variables within the rules of the game a momentary agreement was obtained, conflating the distinction between aesthetics and labor. In contrast, *Liquid Assets* explored the properties of suspension and levitation utilizing pneumatic technology. Utilizing a system of controlled chance, the opposing forces of growth and immobility were summoned together to create a range of topological variations.

PLATES 2.10–2.11

FIG. 79 Evan Douglis, *Liquid Assets*, 1999.

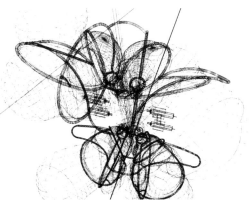

How does the idea of performance surface in your Arts International project?

Arts International (2000) is interesting because it is a gallery, a conference room, a performance space, and a workshop. We try to focus on the notion of performance, specifically music and cinema. Victoria is very interested in these dynamic art forms in particular, and I have learned a lot from her. People participate in the dynamic quality of those art forms as both spectator and actor very differently from other, more contemplative art forms. Music and dance in particular resist a simple, one-liner interpretation. There are role reversals, different and multiple points of view, different stories told.

THOMAS HANRAHAN

performance

    1. (a) the execution of an action; (b) something accomplished

    2. the fulfillment of a claim, promise, or request

    3. (a) the action of representing a character in a play; (b) a public presentation or exhibition

    4. (a) the ability to perform; (b) the manner in which a mechanism performs

    5. the manner of reacting to stimuli

see PHENOMENON/PHENOMENOLOGY; PROCESS; REAL; SERIALITY/MASS PRODUCTION; SURFACE; TYPE

Merriam Webster's Dictionary

periphery

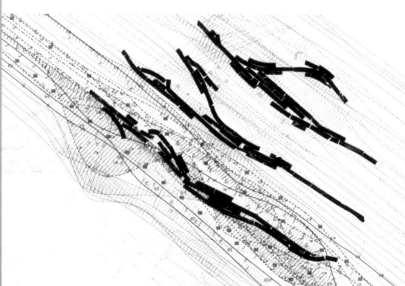

FIG. 80 Andreas Quednau, *A Museum in the Suburbs*, Advanced Studio VI, Stan Allen, critic, Spring 1997.

**phenomenon/
phenomenology**

"[Holl's] architecture [is] a phenomenological elaboration about the passage of a subject within the flux of a continuous temporal wave, in which architectural 'anchoring' is an oscillation between passivity and activity. His accomplishment lies in maintaining a palpable tension between the experiential articulation of certain conditions and the definition of their geometrical necessity."[5]

STEVEN HOLL
5. Sandro Marpillero, "Steven Holl's Anexact Geometries," *Lotus International* 94 (1997): 106.

P

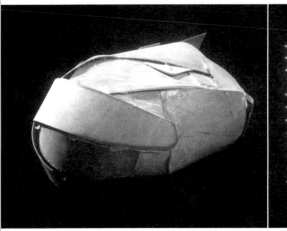

FIG. 81 Morgan Fleming and Erik Languden, *Urban Insertions: Experimental Teaching Center,* Advanced Studio V, Steven Holl, critic, Fall 1996.

"I want to work on…the phenomenological dimensions: how we experience things like light and material. I think that this is a powerful means to open up a whole new sense of time and space. This is something that is real and visceral. You can't simulate it, you can't draw it and you can't model it on a computer."[6]

STEVEN HOLL
6. Aaron Betsky, "Steven Holl" (interview), *Metropolitan Home* 30, no. 6 (November/December 1998): 66.

PLATES 3.01–3.03

"The studio stressed the phenomenal experience of art objects, using the concept of 'ambient installation.' This idea guided the studio projects, which investigated the uses of light, sound, and other ambient qualities for a definition of museum spaces."[7]

GREG LYNN
7. *The Third Millennium Art Museum,* Advanced Studio V, Fall 1992.

FIG. 82 Emil Grieco, *The Third Millennium Art Museum,* Advanced Studio VI, Greg Lynn and Shoei Yoh, critics, Fall 1992.

FIG. 83 George Murillo, *The Third Millennium Art Museum,* Advanced Studio VI, Greg Lynn and Shoei Yoh, critics, Fall 1992.

Your work points to a difference between understanding light and sound as phenomenon and documenting light and sound as an event.
I am interested in the translation between very precise analytical concepts, like lines and waves, and built form, because they are not necessarily build-able things—it is a cerebral construct. I think that there are highly effec-tive ways of doing it and highly affected ways. I am only interested in space if you do it in ways that are affecting, because to me that is architecture. I have probably referenced Michelangelo more than any other architect

VICTORIA MEYERS

because I think that his work is the most phenomenological and visceral. If you go into one of his spaces, you can feel his body there, you can feel him grieving. That is why you can look at the *Pietà* and cry. I try to teach my studio how to bridge the gap between these abstract cerebral things and what happens in a space that someone enters.

As much as you can have an incredibly visceral architecture, you can have an experience as a performer in which you throw energy out and the audience pushes it back. To me when a performer gets that going, it's like going into the space of Michelangelo. You stand there and you're being pressed and pulled by what you see. Really great performers can almost reach out and grab you by the shirt and pull you in and push you back. They hold you in their hand and manipulate you the whole time. That's a very interesting experience and that's what great art does—it grips you and holds you and pushes you, and I think that's what architecture is supposed to do if it's performing correctly.

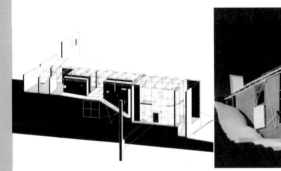

FIG. 84 Hanrahan + Meyers, *Hudson River House*, 1990.

What interests you about the phenomenon of water?

It stems from Marcel Duchamp. Water is important as a natural element and as it relates to life and sexuality. We proposed a small addition to an existing house (Fleischmann Residence, 1999, unbuilt) that has a swimming pool that extends into the house. I was going to blacken the floors and polish them and put a bathroom, which was the width of the room, in the back. The floor of the bathroom would be of the same plaster that would be used for the pool, to continue the idea of walking on water.

VICTORIA MEYERS

I am very interested in expanding people's sense of spaciousness. The house was actually very small—too small—and cramped. The gift of the architect is the ability to make, through careful design, a tiny space feel enormous. I attribute that less to Mies and more to Japanese architecture, which is very successful at doing that. We did an apartment that I call "Swift and Slow Space" that investigated quickness, slowness, and entropy. Like Duchamp, I think about digital things, light waves, entropy, and physics when I am designing.

PLATES 2.16–2.18

see INTERDISCIPLINARY; PERCEPTION; REAL

picturesque   see LANDSCAPE; LOCAL/GLOBAL

place   see LOCAL/GLOBAL

postmodernism	"When I started working, postmodernism was just beginning. Everybody was interested in 'complexity and contradiction,' a phrase from Robert Venturi. But I was after clarity and simplicity....I tried to transform vernacular knowledge into something modern."[8] see HISTORY; MODERN/MODERNISM	STEVEN HOLL 8. Aaron Betsky, "Steven Holl" (interview), *Metropolitan Home* 30, no. 6 (November/December 1998): 66.

potential	"The structures and components that comprise buildings are capable of lateral communication *through one another,* provoking developments that, while inherent within the definition of the structure itself, remain only unfulfilled potentials without the provocation of some outside force (of an adjacent structure). The demand here is to invigorate the entire range of possibilities contained within a given material logic. Further, these material logics and potentials are rooted in the very real structures and matter comprising building elements."[9]	REISER/UMEMOTO 9. *Convergent Structures,* Advanced Studio V, Fall 1998. **PLATE 3.04**

FIG. 85 Reiser + Umemoto, *West Side Convergence Competition,* 2000.

potential
    1. existing in possibility: capable of development into actuality
    2. expressing possibility; specifically: of, relating to, or constituting a
    verb phrase expressing possibility, liberty, or power by the use of an
    auxiliary with the infinitive of the verb

Merriam Webster's Dictionary

practice	see STUDIO/PRACTICE

practice/clients	In addition to a more traditional client base, we now have clients engaging us to produce digital environments. This intrigues us because we were trained during the reign of postmodern discourses and were taught that the only viable way to unravel the institution and its stranglehold on architectural production was through a narrow band of investigation. Now, our clients recognize and acknowledge the impact of media and digital cultures on the human condition and they push us to reevaluate the situation and	HANI RASHID

formulate a response. In the studio, I try to devise ways to facilitate this
type of dialogue between my students and future clients and colleagues.

THOMAS HANRAHAN

We are not different from other people who try to practice architecture on
their own terms. That is a big difference from fifty years ago when the
architect was supposed to come in, wave a wand, and provide a solution. At
this point in our careers we are trying to achieve a level of excellence at
larger scales, which is presenting another set of challenges. When I was
younger and teaching core studio, I was involved in more theoretical work
because I was not building as much. As I become more experienced as a
practitioner, I began to look for something a bit more substantial.

FIG. 86 Hanrahan + Meyers,
Red Hook Center for the Arts,
New York, New York, 2000.

Do you think that communication is an inherent problem?
You communicate to the degree that you can. I have had clients say, "I don't
want to do this. It's too expensive," but if it does get built as designed,
clients often love it and say that they wish they had understood what I was
talking about. The models we build are very specific, very carefully crafted,

VICTORIA MEYERS

and require hours and hours of time. Space is a very abstract art form and it is very difficult to communicate to a client ahead of time what they are buying into. We will build very specific physical models and computer models, we'll do renderings, we'll provide material samples, and I know exactly what the space consists of before it goes into construction. Still it's always a shock for the client.

PLATE 3.05

I started teaching at the School shortly after the MoMA exhibition *Deconstructivist Architecture* in 1988 and witnessed the dramatic effects of that show on the School. Three or four years after the show, several large corporate offices began to pluck our graduates out of school and drop them into their offices to run competitions and work in model shops, overseeing massing and schematic design. It used to happen at Princeton when I was a student there and postmodernism was hot. They wanted to start winning competitions again and Columbia was the school to recruit from. I miss those days of predatory recruitment and seeing student projects shaping the world of practice so instantaneously.

GREG LYNN

Columbia does not teach you how to work in a conventional practice, yet all of the studio critics practice and they all define themselves first, and foremost, as practicing architects. What does practice mean in this case?
The issue is not whether to practice but how to practice critically. I would assume that by the time a student gets to Columbia, he or she has the opportunities, intelligence, and resources to hang up a shingle, get some work, and start a practice. The difficult thing is to have a critical and experimental practice that contributes to the intellectual culture of architecture. One of the School's agendas has been to redefine architectural practice, which assumes that when practices form they will emerge from a research agenda and intellectual position that exceeds conventional practice and makes significant contributions to the field. Of course, this is an incredibly ambitious agenda.

GREG LYNN

see ARCHITECTURE CULTURE; EPIPHANY; PROCESS; REAL; STUDIO/PRACTICE; STUDIOS, ADVANCED; VIRTUAL/ACTUAL

---

prefabrication

see SERIALITY/MASS PRODUCTION

---

pressure

Do the students grasp the ideas that you are investigating in the studio?
They do, although the toughest thing to simulate is the pressure of constraints. Most architects do not value their time, so if you tell them they have twenty minutes to present, they talk for forty minutes because a minute is only worth a dime anyway so they are happy to give you double for free. I have recently found that to have successful studios I need to simulate pressure. Once you pressurize a studio, you begin to see invention and creativity. By introducing the constraints and pressures from practice I put the students into a situation where creativity is the only way to solve intractable problems.

GREG LYNN

---

pressure

Merriam Webster's Dictionary

   1. (a) the burden of physical or mental distress; (b) the constraint of circumstance: the weight of social or economic imposition

2. the application of force to something by something else in direct contact with it

3. (a) the action of a force against an opposing force; (b) the force or thrust exerted over a surface divided by its area

private

see PUBLIC/PRIVATE

process

STAN ALLEN

I believe that the design process has very little to do with architecture per se. You experience a building in the world, and it makes very little difference what the steps were that brought it into being. That information simply doesn't persist in the building. If the architect needed it to get to the final configuration, fine, but unless you have the script, there is no way for the visitor to know that. What is interesting about architecture is not how well or how accurately the designer's script is followed; it is all the other unexpected things that people who use the building or the space bring to it. It's about the *performance* of the space, not about the process that led to its configuration. Moreover, the process-based designers tend to rely on a representational model. They basically say that the primary information you're going to receive from a building is the formal trace of the designer's operations in making that building. That is to me the least interesting information that a building can transmit. What's more interesting is the new field of possible events that are opened up by a building.

There is a pedagogical issue here. Process has very little to do with architecture, yet we need to talk about process in school because that's what we do here. This is a paradox of education; we have to foreground process in school, but in so doing we run the risk of forgetting that the design

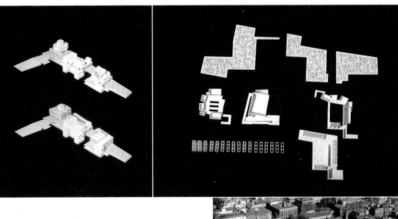

FIG. 87 Stan Allen, *Extension of the Museo del Prado Competition*, Madrid, 1995, reworked 1997.

P

process means very little once architecture is built, once it gets out of that limited academic context. A process-based architecture is trivial unless it produces new effects in the world; all it can do is point back to the author. Frank Gehry, for example, manages to do both. You could say that the Guggenheim Museum in Bilbao points back to Gehry as an author. If that were the only thing it did, it would not be a terribly interesting building, but it also produces other effects that range from the economic benefit for the city and region of Bilbao to the individual encounters between works of art and the space, and its urbanistic effects.

You have said, "Architects have a stopping problem, not architecture." What did you mean?

The stopping problem is a discussion that is fairly specific to Columbia. It pertains to the ambition of the designer to use the dynamic capacities of the computer to generate formal configurations, and the problem with that model is you have got to freeze it at some point. As soon as you freeze it, the building becomes a representation of those forces; it becomes a representation of that frozen moment. What I am pushing for is a shift from representation to performance: hence in my mind, it is architects who have a stopping problem, not architecture. The dynamism of the events that play out in architecture, in the city, can never be frozen. It is the physical form of the building that gets frozen in the design methodology. For me the mistake is to think of the architecture itself as that which is in motion and dynamic rather than about the dynamic of events and experiences that play out within architecture's spaces.

STAN ALLEN

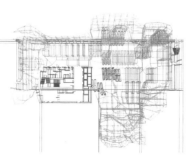 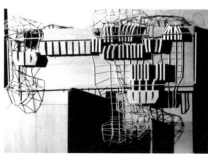

FIG. 88 Nona Yehia, *Logistics of Context*, Advanced Studio V, Stan Allen, critic, Fall 1996.

"The formal strategies...are not autonomous from other aspects of the architectural projects. Rather the process of generating form cannot be seen as separate from the process of generating programs or responses to other, contextual issues..."[10]

ASYMPTOTE
10. Georgi Stanishev, "Designing the Unpredictable" (interview), *World Architecture* 54 (March 1997): 74.

"Notes on the design process:
– transform abstractions into space.
– transform program into ideas that begin to enclose the transformations.
– rediscover space within the conceptual framework, its qualities of light, its boundaries, its force.
– transform 'program' into a poetic narrative."[11]

THOMAS HANRAHAN
11. Core Studio II, Spring 1992.

*What did the introduction of computer technology do to the status
of process?*

It made process the method for discerning architectural quality. I remember GREG LYNN
my first review at Columbia while working for Peter Eisenman, and the
similarities between the ways the students worked and the way that Peter
worked. It was the apex of textuality and semiotics in architecture and the
base drawing reigned supreme. At that time in Peter's office, we would
begin projects by producing drawings out of context and other forms of
textuality that would then be interpreted and transformed materially and
formally through architectural techniques. In Peter's office that strategy
required incredible talent and training—people like Thomas Leeser and
Hiroshi Marayama were experts in this transformational design strategy.
When I first came to Columbia every interrogation by a juror was always
responded to with a trip back to the base drawing and its genesis and
interpretation. This model produced exemplary work, but it waned for two
reasons: first, the primacy of theory over design began to turn around to
an extent where, for the last several years, design has been provoking architectural theory; second, there was no way to teach the intermediate stages
of design that occur between base drawing production, through mapping,
and the interpretation of these maps architecturally. Although most faculty
were using the same generative mapping techniques, there was much diversity in the architecture that emerged, from neo-modernism to collage to
expressionism. These base drawings were neither devolvable nor evolvable
in any rigorous way. The first experiments in the paperless studios adopted
this sensibility and most discussions were about step-by-step procedures.
It is very difficult to have the students depart from procedural processes
and talk about architectural design as being distinct from computer simulation. I take much responsibility for this problem but, nonetheless, it does
frustrate various faculty and myself as it continues to be the dominant
mode at the School.

Why do you think they are more interested in a procedural operation?

If you take a conservative student from a technical university who believes GREG LYNN
they already know what architecture is, but who comes to Columbia to
learn the latest thing, which happens to be computer-aided design, they will
tell you things like, "I am just doing this diagram on the computer and it
does not matter what shape it is. I will interpret it as architecture later."
Some people are really invested in a non-material architecture, but I think
the majority of the students are interested in supplementing their existing
education. They learn an incredible amount very quickly without having to
rethink what they bring with them to the School. Students with this background usually spend several years resolving their very compressed experiences at the School with their previous design tendencies. This only explains a percentage of the student body but it is an important constituency.

*Do you think it is a default response or excuse that allows them to step
away from their responsibilities?*

No, it is more that once a happy accident appears during an automatic or GREG LYNN
procedural design process one learns pretty quickly how to replicate it. The
conventional description of this would be intuition about process. The

longer these experiments run at the School, the more facility and expertise the faculty and students develop and the less important process becomes, and the more important technique becomes.

There has been a notion at the School that suggests that form can emerge as a by-product of a formula that is not controlled by the individual. You began experimenting with these ideas with your project for the Korean Presbyterian Church. How do you feel about that project and about your discoveries now?

Processes act as both a displacing agent and as a generator but there is a caution about investing in experimental forms. Jeff Kipnis uses the example of somebody deciding to cook a meal with every ingredient in the recipe starting with the letter "A." Cooking exclusively with letter "A" ingredients could produce an interesting result, but the only thing that would make it edible, let alone culinary, is the skill within the discipline of cooking that would come in contact with that kind of displacing strategy. Instead of looking at the algorithmic processes as a displacing agent, something changed and it became generative, and everybody has been very cautious about staying invested in some form of experimental, radical practice, and avoiding recipes.

In the Korean Presbyterian Church project (1998) I found the emergence of a new organization of the practice and a new relationship to our clients. Because there was little precedent for a church addition on top of a factory, the formal techniques and research worked to give a new kind of identity to a new kind of project. I would have thought patronage was the only venue for experimental architecture and this first project changed my view of contemporary culture and the role of architectural research. We worked with clients who had no interest in patronizing architecture but who needed a new identity and, therefore, we were able to practice in a way that I would not have thought possible on a low-budget project with clients that neither supported nor understood design philanthropy.

GREG LYNN

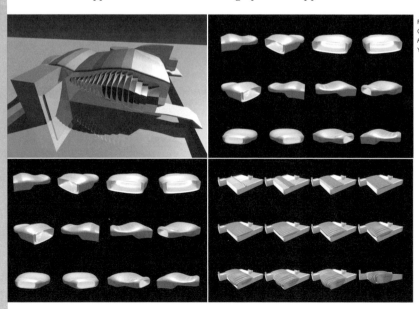

FIG. 89 Greg Lynn, Douglas Garofalo, and Michael McInturf, *Korean Presbyterian Church*, New York, New York, 1998.

The scene of architectural production is enormously complex and varies with the diverse characters and influences involved. No one ever knows how a project comes about, yet somehow, unclear procedures result in strikingly clear objects.

MARK WIGLEY

process

1. (a) progress, advance; (b) something going on

2. (a) (1): a natural phenomenon marked by gradual changes that lead toward a particular result; (2): a natural continuing activity or function; (b) a series of actions or operations conducing to an end; especially: a continuous operation or treatment especially in manufacture

3. (a) the whole course of proceedings in a legal action; (b) the summons, mandate, or writ used by a court to compel the appearance of the defendant in a legal action or compliance with its orders

4. a prominent or projecting part of an organism or organic structure

see ARCHITECTURE CULTURE; AUTHOR; CHIMERA; CITY; COLLAGE; COMPUTER; ECOLOGY; EVOLUTION; IMAGE; METHODOLOGY; PEDAGOGY, COLUMBIA; PROCESS, REVERSE; PROGRAM; RESISTANCE; STUDIO/PRACTICE; TEACHING; TRACE

Merriam Webster's Dictionary

process, reverse

"The focus of this studio, that of developing spatial, material, and structural thought at the small scale which can be extended to the large scale, was made possible through a process of working 'backward' from the particular to the general."[12]

KATHRYN DEAN
12. Advanced Studio IV, Spring 1995.

 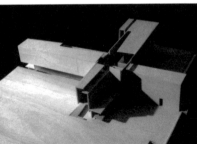

FIG. 90 Karel Klein, Advanced Studio IV, Kathryn Dean, critic, Spring 1995.

FIG. 91 Shirley Leong, Advanced Studio IV, Kathryn Dean, critic, Spring 1995.

"Traditionally, design instructors define a building program and a site and ask the student to produce a form and indicate materials and construction. This studio attempted a reverse process. First we chose a material and then an action, and finally joined the two with a concept. Later a site was selected and then a building program was defined. Material to be selected: concrete, brick masonry, wood, canvas, wax (resin), glass, asphalt, felt, steel, aluminum, stone. Action to be selected: burning, twisting (torque), blowing, inversion, bulging, concave-convex flutter, hinging, sinking/floating, rotation, connecting, centrifugal push-pull."[13]

STEVEN HOLL
13. *From Material to Partial Urbanism: Far West Village, NYC* Advanced Studio V, Fall 1993.

"Instead of making plans and finding perspectives in building models of those concepts, we did the reverse, we *first* drew perspectives and *then* cast them into planned fragments. We were then able to weave these fragments together in a series of overlapping perspectives. We devised what we call

14. "Pre-Theoretical Ground," *Columbia Documents of Architecture and Theory*, vol. 4 (1995): 30.

'semiautomatic programming,' in which we put these cast perspectives together with suggestive images, thus indicating possible programming."[14]

"This new focus was initiated through a disciplined process that began with the particular and projected toward the general. In this sense we reversed the normal process of beginning with a general sketch and moving toward the particular detail as final product. It was intended that this method would force a studio focus on material and detail."[15]

VICTORIA MEYERS
15. *Visibility/Invisibility*, Advanced Studio V, Fall 1994.

program

"This studio was engaged in three principal investigations in an effort to recast space, power, and authority. Beginning with the site of the Cathedral of St. John the Divine, with its incomplete Neo-Gothic edifice, we examined the social and historical relationships of evolving networks, both real and virtual, global and local."[16]

KAREN BAUSMAN
16. *Gotham Gothic: Unpacking the Cathedral*, Advanced Studio V, Fall 1996.

Both conceptual and spiritual underpinnings together with project require-ments are all but a part of the process in the authoring and development of program. Perhaps unlike a building, program is essential to the design and construction of a work of architecture. One part of the program is the type—stadium, for example—and the other part is surface and structure and the development of a relationship. We might propose a zoo, but first we have to create the creature. The creature is based on an investigation of structure and surface and its emergent behavior. That kicks off an explo-ration of a place or site. The emergent behavior is brought about through structure and surface and then it's located in a particular condition that starts to bring about a chain of reactions and thoughts.

KAREN BAUSMAN

I am interested in the process of unpacking and reassembling. In the case of the Eastern State Penitentiary, which I used as a studio program in Fall 1994, my goal was to gain insight into how one responds to being confronted with a building and a site that were already overly determined and fixed.

Eastern State Penitentiary was America's first private penal institu-tion and had been shuttered since 1974. While the prison today is in an extremely advanced state of deterioration, it is still possible to read the figural landscape and contemplate the reality of such an unyielding domain by experiencing the panoptic view, walking the hallways, visiting the central observation station and occupying inmate cells. Interestingly, the inmate cells each included an outdoor space. Many of the spaces were used as private gardens, which was a prescriptive programmatic element and unique to the Eastern State facility.

The Penitentiary was conceived of and operated by the Quakers who were pacifists trying to preserve the "soul" of the inmate. Each inmate was viewed as a special case requiring a specific rehabilitation that could only be attained through personal industry. Interestingly, these 19th-century Quakers did not recognize that the pathology of their inmates was driven more often by nature rather than by nurture and environmental circum-stances. The prisoner was often in poor mental health.

FIG. 92 Danielle Etzler, *Eastern State Penitentiary: Discipline and the Architectural Space of Production*, Advanced Studio V, Karen Bausman, critic, Fall 1994.

My students were greatly affected by the imprint of solitary confinement. Gathering prison artifacts was very much a part of their deeply personal inquiry. Working from the infinitesimal to that which encompassed the human figure engaged in work allowed the students to recast specific artifacts through drawing. This reading of artifacts allowed for the establishment of an architectural language overall and a subsequent strategy to override the original plan and strong typology of the penitentiary.

"Prompted by a 'program' of a single word or theme, a body of rigorous ideas and analyses are projected into the work. However, as the project progresses, manifesting itself in scale and measure, a set of images, drawings, and models are extracted from each successive development. A reciprocal tension is established between the hypothesis and experiment, one challenging the other, a continuous research into the sources of the architectural idea."[17]

THOMAS HANRAHAN
17. Core Studio I, Fall 1992.

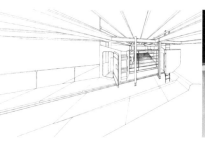 

FIG. 93 Rhett Russo, Core Studio I, Thomas Hanrahan, critic, Fall 1992.

"The basis of this studio asks students to consider architecture as an aspect of time and experience, where the starting point may be reduced as a single

18. Core Studio I, Fall 1995.

'momentary program.' Architectonic constructions and large-scale models are analytical and visceral at the same time. These investigations have a purity and freedom that often demand the engagement of intuitive and imaginative thought processes, leading from one unexpected invention to the next."[18]

"Program is understood as multiple possible scenarios that have an oblique, indirect relation to space and form. It is part of the speculative dimension of the project. Program thus is not equal to function."[19]

SULAN KOLATAN
19. *Logics and Logistics of Waiting*, Advanced Studio IV, Spring 1998.

"'Program is to architecture what lyrics are to music.'. . . The ancient and perhaps questionable analogy between forms of architecture and forms of music finds its most recent formulation in the loose fit between program and form. Loose fit of course involves a spectrum of congruencies ranging from the tight fit of the rhyming lyric to the loose fit of the dissonant one. In both cases, however, contingency is a fundamental condition as the rhyming or lack of rhyming is not in any meaningful way attached to form."[20]

REISER/UMEMOTO
20. "Jesse Reiser and Nanako Umemoto: Recent Work," *Columbia Documents of Architecture and Theory*, vol. 6 (1997): 158.

What are the differences or similarities between actual programs like the Cardiff Bay Opera House and pedagogical programs like Space Frames or One-to-One?
The two types are similar at the level of the brief or the studio. Neither is compromised by practice or somehow modified by the so-called "real world" versus the world of the academy. The competition situations are different because the constraints are spelled out, but both investigate the impact of certain contingencies on speculative models. The models in the studios reflect a dominant idea or theme and in a competition situation or in a real project, larger themes can be subordinated by other themes that are mixed in.

JESSE REISER

PLATES 3.06–3.07

Columbia's faculty sometimes uses the design studio as a laboratory environment for their own investigations. How do you feel about that?
Some students come to the School because they are interested in joining a new architecture culture and have a desire to work with a certain person and explore a certain area. Some of the faculty members try to stimulate the students to come up with their own ideas, while others will set the parameters of their research in a very strict manner that enables the students' research to be an extension of their own. Both are absolutely correct.

BERNARD TSCHUMI

However, I am not terribly comfortable with faculty members who give a competition as a student project. The reason is that the competition has been framed elsewhere by others with an enormous number of preexisting constraints. It is too restrictive. I would rather have the faculty set the parameters around a theme or around their past research rather than around other people's restrictions.

program
1. (a) a brief usually printed outline of the order to be followed, of the features to be presented, and the persons participating; (b) the performance of a program; especially: a performance broadcast on radio or television

Merriam Webster's Dictionary

2. a plan or system under which action may be taken toward a goal

3. (a) a plan for the programming of a mechanism; (b) a sequence of coded instructions that can be inserted into a mechanism (as a computer); (c) a sequence of coded instructions (as genes or behavioral responses) that is part of an organism

see IDEA/CONCEPT; PERFORMANCE; SITE; STUDIOS, CORE; TEACHING

propaganda   see COMMUNICATION

public/private

"The specific program of dormitory is understood as having two very different starting points. The first is the dormitory as interconnected social structure—the space of many—and the second is the dormitory as intimate personal space—the space of one. The space of many starts with the most fundamental understanding of the nature of public space with its inherent continuities, overlaps, and linkages. It springs from the desire to connect us to what is outside ourselves. Its counterpart is the space of one with its interiority, enclosure, and a desire for intimacy, quietness, and introspection."[21]

KATHRYN DEAN
21. *Campus Housing*, Core Studio III, Fall 1996.

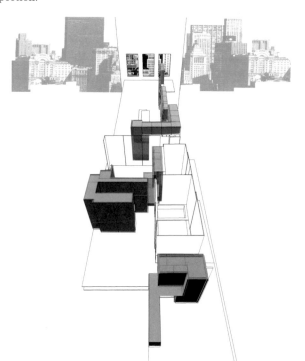

FIG. 94 Dean Wolf Architects, *Skyline Loft*, New York, New York, 2001.

The work that came out of my studio was still very much grounded in my own practice, which is about private experience and the ability of a single individual to create larger understanding. Our own work has always been about understanding the people that inhabit spaces and their state of mind. The latent conditions in the private realm were expanded to the way people exist in the public realm, and to how structures affect the lives of a larger body of people.

KATHRYN DEAN

PLATES 3.08–3.09

FIG. 95 Robert Holton and Sumana Sermchief, *Housing for Hell's Kitchen*, Core Studio III, Kathryn Dean, critic, Fall 1997.

FIG. 96 Dean Wolf Architects, *Urban Interface Loft*, New York, New York, 1997.

"The building of form out of the ground plane relates to the necessity of placing the architecture of the Holley Loft within a 'prepared' ground. To achieve this placement, two actions were necessary. First, the space of the loft was 'cut' conceptually and removed from the field of the city. Then a new ground was constructed within which a new terrain and language of architectural operations could take place. At the Holley Loft, as at Duplicate House, the programmatic necessity to delineate public and private interrupts the purely conceptual diagrams populated by selected architectural samplings.

Wood cabinetry, glass planes, and even mobile wall elements demonstrate a play between thick and thin, while respecting the domains of public space and boudoir. The glass wall within the loft and the reflections it contains were designed as an anamorphic device. Anamorphism allows the loft to contain an extreme depth of field within the confines of a relatively small space. The glass plane sets up an opposition between profile and elevation similar to the juxtaposition of thick and thin at Duplicate House. It is this play between the two-dimensional flatness of the profile view and the depth of field of the elevation view that links this wall to an anamorphic idea."[22]

VICTORIA MEYERS
22. "Space and the Perception of Time," *Journal of Architectural Education* 53, no. 2 (November 1999): 94–95.

R

In your studio programs, you keep coming back to the word "real" and the word "function." How would you define these words?

STAN ALLEN

Both of those concerns have always been present, even in the most specula-tive work that I have done at Columbia. Part of what has motivated my teaching is that reality is often a lot more interesting and surprising than anything we could invent. For example, one studio I taught dealt with a courthouse based on an actual federal government courthouse program located on an irregular, highly restricted lot in lower Manhattan. Something very interesting resulted from the intersection of three variables: the actual demands of the judicial system today, the restricted real estate available in New York City, and the desire for a conventional image of a classical courthouse. The resulting 40-story building with courthouses stacked on top of one another was a radical proposition and it had very interesting, complex consequences. The prisoners, the public, and the judges, for exam-ple, have to move through this building, this vertical structure, without meeting one another. Complex functional problems are played out in rela-tionship to demands that do not come from a critical or speculative aca-demic point of view, but from out-of-control forces like real-estate econom-ics, crime, and new construction technologies. Of course, as built by Kohn Pederson Fox Associates, all this is masked by a conventional facade, but if you look at the internal organization of that building, it is very interest-ing and fairly radical. If you pay attention to the real, it is continually going to surprise you; it is much more radical than anything we could think up in our world of the studio.

Another related concern of mine (one that perhaps does not play out in the studios so obviously) is to redefine function, not in terms of a return to *functionalism*, which was all about minimum standards and efficiency, but in terms of *performance*, that is to say the capacity of architecture to engender multiple functional and programmatic possibilities. Michael Speaks describes this as a shift from issues of representation to questions of performance—how things work as opposed to what things means. That is a key shift.

PLATE 3.11

FIG. 97 Luis Rueda, *Courthouse: Complete and Austere Institutions*, Advanced Studio VI, Stan Allen, critic, Spring 1993.

FIG. 98 Curtis Wagner, *Courthouse: Complete and Austere Institutions*, Advanced Studio VI, Stan Allen, critic, Spring 1993.

You both address reality much more than the imagery that comes out of your studios might suggest, and your work is described as being critical of the margin yet still existing within it. Where does the real find itself within the margin?

Both of us understand architecture as being more than mere material fabrication. Through architecture we build the world that we live in, as a sociopolitical construct as much as a built artifact. We are complicit with the manufacturing of institutions as political bodies as much as physical buildings. Building architecture is always a critique of the history of architecture and it is also a critique of the housing and legitimizing of these institutions. The construction of architecture cannot be separated from the act of rethinking and redefining the global and local parameters. Issues of program and site need to be scrutinized as well as the social, cultural, and political dimensions. When I did the museum studio, we investigated notions of authority, issues of marginality, and how the housing of objects of display can support particular ideas. We are interested in working with clients who are open to our methods. With them we work toward redefining their needs, and they have all encouraged us to attack the architectural problem from the ground up, conceptually and theoretically.

LISE ANNE COUTURE

In 1992, I taught a studio entitled "Distraction City," which was based on the idea that any study of new spatialities today should look at phenomena and situation instead of history and precedent. I asked my students to seek out what I ambiguously called "vectors of distraction," from which they were to distill an architecture. We are already in "real" space. We can work from the source instead of delving into a philosophical text as an a priori activity. It is inverse to what I saw as a fashionable methodology at the School and is more reminiscent of teaching methods used by painters, philosophers, and others. We have tended to overemphasize a body of theory, predominantly located within certain texts, and that dislocated experience in many ways has proved to be irrelevant to much of contemporary experience.

HANI RASHID

FIG. 99 Group project, *Distraction City*, Advanced Studio V, Hani Rashid, critic, Fall 1992.

In almost all of your studio programs you talk about real proposals. What is your interest in the "real"?

There is nothing more fantastic than the real. When I was in Tucson I went to the mirror-casting lab at the University of Arizona, which makes very

LAURIE HAWKINSON

large 22-foot mirrors like the one exhibited in our Corning Museum of Glass project. The mirror-casting lab is under the football stadium, which, because it is a very large column-free space, has been retrofitted into a scientific instrument laboratory. I find this incredibly interesting and un-believable. One of our clients, Samsung, came to us with a program for a restaurant/gym with a car showroom on the ground floor. There are certain-ly no precedents for this kind of building, but this is the world we live in and these are the kinds of programs that should be part of the studio.

 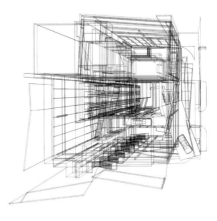

FIG. 100 Smith-Miller + Hawkinson, *Samsung Corporation, Shilla Daechi Building, Car Showroom and Four Restaurants*, Seoul, Korea, 1996.

How do you carry that multiplicity over into the studio?
When I used Governor's Island as the site for a studio, the New York Yankees (and Mayor Giuliani) were also thinking of moving their stadium into Manhattan. Andrew Vrana decided to investigate the implications of incorporating a baseball stadium into a program that could also accommo-date gambling. (He needed a studio "variance" for this.) His proposition presented very interesting formal and logistical problems. Part of the logis-tics involved determining how to get all of the people to the island for a game. He studied the ferry schedules, and demonstrated through diagrams and drawings that it could be done.

LAURIE HAWKINSON

In Spring 1999, the topic for the studio investigation was again Las Vegas —with a particular focus on two downtown sites on Fremont Street. Peter Sokoloff and Vivian Fu worked together and combined the two sites both thematically and programatically, by proposing a water reclamation plant that was also a recreational park. They researched water reclamation issues and the technique of recycling water into various states for irrigation, for making snow or ice, and for drinking. They claimed that their project could provide 100 percent of Las Vegas's water, which they substantiated with their design and their data. The project required 40 acres to accomplish this goal and Peter and Vivian demonstrated that this could be done with the combined acreage of the two sites. The project explored the potential for different spaces in which a visitor could engage the water reclamation process through programs of passive and active recreation—from park to ski slope to aquarium to beverage.

PLATE 3.10

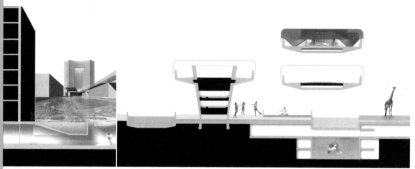

FIG. 101 Vivian Fu and Peter Sokoloff, *NEONOPLIS*, *re:SURFACE*, Advanced Studio VI, Laurie Hawkinson, critic, Spring 1999.

How has the computer changed the perception of real space?

I see the computer as a tool, a dumb tool, that is controlled by your brain, hand, and heart. Although this technology is exciting, it is a poison gas that must be carefully controlled and resisted because it can lead to a pollution of real experience. In other words, the real, tactile experience of space— the experience of acoustic reverberation as you walk through a room, the wonderful phenomenological dimensions of real architectural experience— is gradually being erased by the idea that the total horizon of architecture exists inside the screen. It is fantastic that I can e-mail my consultants, but beware, the real problem in the twenty-first century will be an erasure of the great actual experiences of architecture. Eventually, everybody could be sitting in windowless, lightless, sheetrocked boxes, looking at fabulous images in cyberspace. Where is the skin; where is the flesh; where is the smell; where is the sound; where is the life of architecture?

STEVEN HOLL

How does the work in your office mediate between the virtual and the real?

Our installation in the Angelika Film Center (1995) was one of the projects that introduced our thinking about the relationship between real and virtual. We were trying to set up an extended movie theater condition that also involved the Web. It was very important for us to establish a hybridization between different protocols—protocols that happen in a real, physical context and protocols that happen in the virtuality of the film and on the Web. It has always been interesting to think about the incredible expansion into the virtual realm in relation to its impact on the physical world. The ATM machine has always fascinated me because it involves an abstract operation that takes place in a digital domain, but then you get real money, which is dirty, used, and handled by people, so there is a contradiction. It is never about exclusivity. Ideas that try to deal with notions exclusively are always somewhat boring. We are living in a transitional period and it's much more interesting to see these new hybrid conditions in terms of operations and methodologies.

SULAN KOLATAN

You have said that you operate within reality. How is something like your Entropia project (2001) understood as being part of a reality?

The three projects in the *Entropia* series begin with existing buildings, which are real things built by real architects. We just borrowed, reinvented,

REINHOLD MARTIN

and virtualized them. Digital technology has enabled the freedom to recycle and sample existing material. Many other fields besides architecture have understood this. Architecture, however, seems more preoccupied with inventing because we are hanging onto this early-20th-century version of the avant-garde that has to do with inventing the new. There is nothing older than the idea of the new. We prefer to begin with reality, as it were.

The embassy project that is in *Entropia* begins with the U. S. Embassy in Saigon, and finishes after the bombings of the U. S. embassies in Africa. The conversion of that embassy into a digital bunker reflects and represents a hopefully critical reflection on the nature of institutional representation and globalization. These efforts are in a relatively abstract medium as compared to so-called built architecture. We want to experiment with that.

The *Entropia* work is one example of projects that we invented for very specific reasons. They have both a historical/analytical dimension and a projective one. Those two are deliberately wound around one another in such a way that it is difficult to see which way the arrow is pointing, forward or backward. For us, that is a way of thinking about what architecture is, including architectural practice and speculation in today's environment.

PLATE 3.12

FIG. 102 Martin/Baxi Architects, *Entropia: Embassy*, 2001.

There were two studios that I did in which we looked at situations in Silicon Valley. One was a biotechnology lab, the other was a more general laboratory. In each case, we attempted to start with something resembling reality, if only to understand how theoretical reality is. This studio directly addressed the so-called digital revolution in architecture. Rather than saying how metaphorically we can rehearse our old desires for architecture in new media, we actually understand the realities of new media in their depth as they intersect with architecture and urbanism. It's interesting to me that the most literal sense in which architecture and urbanism come into contact with digital technologies is in places like Silicon Valley.

real

Merriam Webster's Dictionary

    1. of or relating to fixed, permanent, or immovable things

    2. (a) not artificial, fraudulent, illusory, or apparent: genuine; also: being precisely what the name implies; (b) (1): occurring in fact; (2): of or relating to practical or everyday concerns or activities; (3): existing as a physical entity and having properties that deviate from an ideal, law, or standard; (c) having objective independent existence; (d) fundamental, essential; (e) (1): belonging to or having elements or components that belong to the set of real numbers; (2): concerned with or containing real numbers; (f) measured by purchasing power; (g) complete, utter

see DRAWING; PEDAGOGY, COLUMBIA; PHENOMENON/PHENOMENOLOGY; PROGRAM; STUDIO/PRACTICE; VIRTUAL/ACTUAL

regionalism

see LOCAL/GLOBAL

representation

"The principle of continuous representation, the inclination to review, as in film or cinematic space, all the particular phases of an event, the readiness to overlay what Edwin Panofsky called the 'pregnant moment' with an expansive wealth of detail comes to the forward in this cyclical type of composition."[1]

KAREN BAUSMAN
1. *Gotham Gothic: Unpacking the Cathedral, Desire and Technique*, Advanced Studio V, Fall 1996.

Whether modeling in two or three dimensions, it is important to understand that the parameters of representation are maintained by a class and social structure. It is important to question those parameters, and understand the myths associated with them. I work hard to get people to understand this relationship of translations and I try to bring to the academic environment an understanding that the medium of the academy—drawing and building models—is not the end product but a middle condition. Many people of my generation have not taken that path toward being architects and it leads to a very different way of thinking about space and architecture.

    I try to get students to understand the plasticity of a medium through an emphasis on optical projection and surface, or understand material as a tool, so that they eventually realize that how they choose to represent their work is as formative as the concepts they employ. It is seen pedagogically as anti-computer, but the computer simply becomes another tool within the entire array of choices. I am against using a single tool to work on a project.

LESLIE GILL

PLATES 3.13–3.14

representation

Merriam Webster's Dictionary

    one that represents: as (a) an artistic likeness or image; (b) (1): a statement or account made to influence opinion or action; (2): an incidental or collateral statement of fact on the faith of which a contract is entered into; (c) a dramatic production or performance; (d) a usually formal statement made against something or to effect a change

see DRAWING; PROCESS; REAL; STUDIOS, ADVANCED; STUDIOS, CORE; TEACHING

research	see LANDMARK; PEDAGOGY, COLUMBIA; STUDIO/PRACTICE; THEORY

resistance

Do you meet a lot of resistance at Columbia?

There are many forms of resistance in architectural education, some of which are actually quite important in the sense that they can be constructively mined for their potential. Explicitly installing methodological delays within the learning process, for example, enables the student to be more rigorous within the development of the work.

EVAN DOUGLIS

Another form of resistance concerns an unwillingness to commit oneself to the studio pedagogy. I can't say I remember someone outwardly declaring that they refused to participate, but as teachers, we have all experienced individuals over the years that had difficulty adjusting. One generally finds this with the student who is unfamiliar with this way of working and, to a certain extent, is intimidated. It's a natural reaction and the real question is how to work together to get beyond this stage.

Ultimately it's my responsibility as a teacher to find a way to reach every one of these students. This is the discipline within which I am committed, and I have a responsibility as an educator to somehow inform others; it's part psychology, part diplomacy, and part seduction.

I have had students tell me that I have talked to them about things that they had not heard from other critics. That always shocks me because I think that the things that I speak about are so obvious.

VICTORIA MEYERS

romanticism

There is a reemergence of romanticism in a weird way, to which the computer has contributed. In the highly differentiated work being produced today there is an elevated regard for nature, or more specifically for organic structures, along with an emphasis on individual expression of imagination and a freedom from the rules of form. Emerging in parallel are ever advancing breakthroughs in hardware and software development. The result of this furious pace of development is that the criteria of aesthetic values is shifting. Is innovation itself, with its inherent condition of obsolescence built in, driving the design process and becoming its own subject in the process?

KAREN BAUSMAN

R

S

sampling

"The electronic eye is a sampled eye which annihilates difference in the digitalization and simulation of information. It is the vision produced out of the unreal spaces of the postmodern city. Frontiers shift and reform, new spatialities emerge, sometimes unrecognized."[1]

STAN ALLEN
1. "Projections: Between Drawing and Building," *A + U* 4 (April 1992): 42.

"Digital technology in particular has led to the prominence of 'sampling' within music as well as formal quotation within architecture. As an exploration of the strategies of this phenomenon, the focus of this studio was on sampling. We attempted an understanding of the spatial strategy of sampling and its structural effect on the development of a contemporary language of architecture...sampling changes the numerical spatial analysis from one of proportion to one of fluid dynamics."[2]

see ENTROPY; INTERDISCIPLINARY; REAL

VICTORIA MEYERS
2. *Sampling: Architecture and Music*, Advanced Studio V, Fall 1997.

scale

There is a continuity of concept and of formal resolution from small scale to very large scale. Over time that has changed from looking at an institutional scale to, more recently, looking at the balance between architecture and landscape. That kind of integration—from the scale of a piece of furniture to a landscape or an urban system—is something that I stress both in my own practice and in my teaching.

LESLIE GILL

PLATE 3.15

FIG. 103 Leslie Gill, *Watrous Weatherman Residence*, New York, New York, 1998.

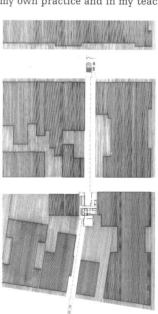
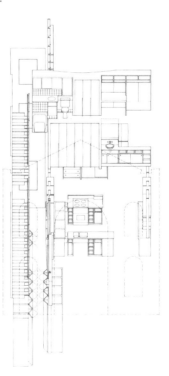

FIG. 104 Leslie Gill, *Watrous Weatherman Residence*, New York, New York, 1998.

GREG LYNN

There was a moment at Columbia where Jesse Reiser, Stan Allen, Bill MacDonald, Sulan Kolatan, Evan Douglis, and I were all giving the same projects, usually megascale problems solved with some kind of intricate giant object. They were big envelopes of architectural and urban potential. There were discussions about whether these large-scale projects should be considered architecture, information for an architect to use, or programmatic zoning envelopes. We all started to shift away from intricate gigantism to projects that were more conventionally within an architectural scale. Recently, I decided to return to urban planning, but from the scale of building components. This mapped a significant change, from the statistical data envelope to more instrumental architectural components. This was also tied to the milling equipment that the School received and the milling course I was teaching.

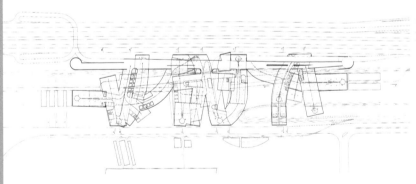

FIG. 105 Robert Vertes, *Smooth Urbanism*, Advanced Studio VI, Greg Lynn, critic, Spring 1993.

Why do you think there was a move away from the macroscopic urban scale while at the same time people are still employing all of the macroscopin urban influences?

Bernard Tschumi and Rem Koolhaas were probably responsible for the shift in similar ways. When Rem coined the term "bigness," a parallel was drawn with work at the School and that discussion could be agreed upon and closed in a way. A less obvious yet significant impact was the discovery that both he and Bernard are incredibly good architects. Many of their large-scale projects were resolved with extremely elegant architectural moves.

GREG LYNN

Moreover, it was clear that they had a proclivity, as ironically critical as it is, for modernism. When that happened everyone realized that large-scale urban projects are about the opportunities to utilize architectural design. Most of the faculty began to invest more heavily in architecture and divest themselves of programming and zoning.

see CHIMERA; COLOSSAL; DIFFERENTIATION; E-GORA; LANDSCAPE; MATERIAL/MATERIALITY; ORGANIZATION; STUDIO/PRACTICE; STUDIOS, CORE; TEACHING

science	see COMPLEXITY; TEACHING

seriality/ mass production	The difference between existing notions of customization or prefabrication and our notion is the idea of exchangeable parts; the more customization you offer, the more parts you have to produce. Contemporary software programs permit structural changes and transformations that allow each piece its own mold through CAD/CAM interfacing. The idea of producing a typical or prototypical mold, which is reproduced en masse, as well as the idea of customization through the creation of extra parts, is in question. The potentials of the new technology haven't been conceptualized. It's similar to Henry Ford's initial horseless carriages that contained all of the leftover pieces of carriages—the car hadn't really been conceptualized. Prefabrication is in a similar phase right now.	SULAN KOLATAN

You're suggesting that the conventional notions of standardization and prefabrication are no longer applicable, but unless the designer customizes every single piece, isn't something going to be mass-produced or standardized?

We are not saying that everything is going to be completely customized, but advances in prefabrication have led to significant changes in construction practices with standardized parts. One would have to conduct a lengthy investigation of different variables in order to pin down which parts want to remain fixed and which parts want to remain customizable.

SULAN KOLATAN

The car industry works entirely within the paradigm of exchangeable parts. I discovered that a car actually has more parts than a typical house, which I thought would be the most complex product. Toyota does something called cross-platforming between its prefabrication plants and its car plants. It would be interesting to see what kind of architectural potentialities lie in that, and whether the way various parts are conceived, designed, and produced could have greater influence across the board.

"The intent of the studio was to research iterative organizational techniques that involve repetition with differentiation. This objective draws upon the new logic of the series, which assumes that there can be continuity between specific elements when they are seen in duration while maintaining differentiation when seen individually. In order to elaborate this concept, the studio task was twofold: first to develop a design problem which is programmed and assembled without a specific site. These manifold decisions were designed in what was termed a 'performance envelope.' This term connoted a rigorously delimited, but not yet exact, network of variables defining an envelope of potential. Instead of designing a fixed prototype, each student was asked to design a more open network or

GREG LYNN
3. *Fast Food*, Advanced Studio VI, Spring 1997.

multitype. This design of a virtual range of possibilities was then unfolded within the specificity of at least three sites. The functions, areas, and construction techniques of the series had to be equivalent. The design of both the multitype and the three particular instances were dependent on a serial design strategy that exploits local variations and fluctuations between elements. The relationships between these components can be understood as elastic."[3]

"The variation in requirements between a classroom for seven-year-olds and a classroom for eighteen-year-olds is radical both in program and ergonomics. This studio emphasized these variations in the design of classroom components including: structural, mechanical, electrical, audiovisual, lighting, fixtures, and finishes. Each project posed a logic of serial variation in dimension and proportion."[4]

GREG LYNN
4. *Rutgers University Vision Plan*, Advanced Studio V, Fall 1998.

PLATES 3.16–3.17

FIG. 106 Francesco De Fuentes, *Rutgers University Vision Plan 2000*, Advanced Studio V, Greg Lynn, critic, Fall 1998.

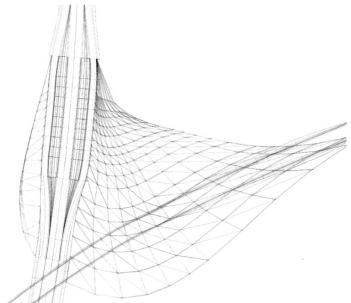

"Time can be marked through sequence or serial repetition. Sequences and serial repetitions can be stretched, shortened or overlaid to read as rapid or slow time passages."[5]

VICTORIA MEYERS
5. *Time: Passage Way*, Advanced Studio V, Fall 1995.

shelter   see MEMORY

site   "This project [for the Croton Aqueduct] proposes as its primary strategy programmatic grafts: readings of the site and context developed through a mapping procedure, which seeks to uncover shifting site histories, patterns of land use, and changing articulation of public and private uses as encoded in place names and street designations.... Architectural models are not seen as scalar reductions for individual projects, but as nomadic 'props' to

STAN ALLEN
REISER/UMEMOTO
6. "RAAUm: Croton Aqueduct," *Architectural Design* 63, no. 3–4 (March/April 1993): 87.

be used in multiple contexts and interchangeable combinations. Working in a very direct manner with the particularities of the site, a field of complex and unexpected exchanges develops as a result of these grafts, suggesting in turn a further reprogramming of the architecture, and a redefinition of the site itself."[6]

FIG. 107 RAAUm, *Croton Aqueduct*, 1992.

"Site is a continuum that grounds the investigation. Perceived from the train tracks (a spine that scores its midst), the site unfolds space through our understanding of time. The journey or itinerary is seen through the varying speeds of contemporary motion, alternately extending or compressing our notion of events. Slow travel (at stations and intermittent stops) is understood in direct relationship to the movement of man—a time that unfolds in rhythm to our heartbeat."[7]

LESLIE GILL
7. *Without Resting: The Tracking of Home Within the Mystery/Spy Genre*, Advanced Studio, Summer 1993.

"Physical dislocation from the earth forces the 'interpretation' of the site to occur within the spatial and technological constructions of the building. In doing so, the building proposes a contemporary, more complex understanding of the natural world, while at the same time acknowledging that such constructions represent an 'artificial' division from an 'original' relationship to nature."[8]

HANRAHAN/MEYERS
8. An *Interpretive Center* (New York: Columbia Graduate School of Architecture, Planning and Preservation, 1989).

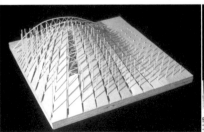
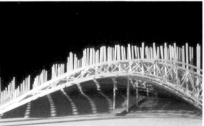

FIG. 108 Clarissa Matthews, *Gate/Garden/Basin*, Core Studio I, Thomas Hanrahan, critic, Fall 1990.

site

1. (a) the spatial location of an actual or planned structure or set of structures; (b) a space of ground occupied or to be occupied by a building 2. (a) the place, scene, or point of something; (b) one or more Internet addresses at which an individual or organization provides information to others often including links to other locations where related information may be found

see CITY; FRONTIER/EDGE/MARGIN; HISTORY; STUDIOS, CORE; TEACHING; TECHNOLOGY

Merriam Webster's Dictionary

FIG. 109 Christopher Perry, *The Container: Coliseum Convention Center @ Columbus Circle*, Advanced Studio IV, Sulan Kolatan, critic, Spring 1996.

"Is it possible to think of the convention center as not a neutral container, which through its neutrality accommodates complexity, but rather as a kind of cumulative index of this complexity? The notion of the container inevitably provokes questions regarding the envelope, commonly understood as skin wrapped around space and skin stretched over structure. In place of the distinct and separate categories of skin, space, and structure, the studio tested a concept of 'deep skin,' which looks at the differences between these constituent elements as effects of (small) degrees of transformation."[9]

SULAN KOLATAN
9. *The Container: Coliseum Convention Center @ Columbus Circle*, Advanced Studio IV, Spring 1996.

skin
1. (a) (1): the integument of an animal separated from the body usually with its hair or feathers; (2): a usually unmounted specimen of a vertebrate; (b) the hide or pelt of a game or domestic animal; (c) (1): the pelt of an animal prepared for use as a trimming or in a garment; (2): a sheet of parchment or vellum made from a hide
2. (a) the external limiting tissue layer of an animal body especially when forming a tough but flexible cover relatively impermeable from without while intact; (b) any of various outer or surface layers
3. the life or physical well-being of a person
4. a sheathing or casing forming the outside surface of a structure

Merriam Webster's Dictionary

slice

"Modern mathematicians have developed equations that, projected into form, yield figures exceeding three dimensions. Assuming the fourth dimension represents time, students will be encouraged to investigate these forms. These include the hypercube, the hypersphere, and complex torus configurations. Because we understand three-dimensional space, these can be studied through 'slices and shadows.' Slices and shadows allow four-dimensional form to be projected into three dimensions."[10]

VICTORIA MEYERS
10. *Time: Passage Way*, Advanced Studio V, Fall 1995.

slice
1. (a) a thin flat piece cut from something; (b) a wedge-shaped piece
2. a spatula for spreading paint or ink
3. a serving knife with wedge-shaped blade
4. a flight of a ball that deviates from a straight course in the direction of the dominant hand of the player propelling it; also: a ball following such a course

Merriam Webster's Dictionary

space

"As the Internet and other public-domain applications reaped from advanced information technologies become exceedingly pervasive and accessible, promises of fluid interactive environments filled with endless streams of information are imminent. The space of interactivity coupled with the prospects of multimedia are inevitably opening the way for architects to operate within folds of information space, developing and devising as of yet unforeseen territories for human interaction and dwelling."[11]

HANI RASHID
11. *http://www.interactive.architecture.com*, Advanced Studio VI, Spring 1996.

"[T]he design of the Yokohama Port Terminal was influenced by...what we perceived as the ineffable space located within media domains such as the televisory or cinematic. This revealed to us an architectural apparatus closer to an atmosphere than to the traditional Euclidean sense of space. The inherent instability of the resultant space opened it to the possibility of intrinsic multiple readings, which influenced actual projects."[12]

ASYMPTOTE
12. Georgi Stanishev, "Designing the Unpredictable" (interview), *World Architecture* 54 (March 1997): 73–4.

"The Big Door Big Wall takes very seriously the idea that architectural space, as a conceptual or experiential entity, can never be located once and for all.... the Big Door Big Wall acts as an urbanistic figure [that speaks to] the post-historic New York: compression of space, potency of spatial difference, material weight hinged to complex infrastructures, the politics of space, a provisionality about most things, resourcefulness, protection. And finally, the Big Door Big Wall pressures the scale and pitch of typologically correct space by attenuating both door and wall, making them stretch beyond themselves. The wall is made slender and sent behind the lines of its traditional domain."[13]

LAURIE HAWKINSON
13. Catherine Ingraham, *Smith-Miller + Hawkinson* (Barcelona: Gustavo Gili, 1994), 9–10.

"The shift from determinism to directed indeterminacy is central to the development of a dynamic design method.... Rather than being designed as stationary inert forms, space is highly plastic, flexible, and mutable in its dynamic evolution through motion and transformation."[14]

GREG LYNN
14. *Tate Gallery Competition*, Advanced Studio V, Fall 1995.

"The nature of the project and the site required an interpretation of the built environment as an interface between three ideas: industrial packaging and capitalist consumption of a vital element; 'nature,' or the contemporary reading of a natural element within a managed ecosystem; and liquid space, or the spatial interpretation of water as a flowing/wet element."[15]

VICTORIA MEYERS
15. *Water Bottling Plant*, Advanced Studio V, Fall 1993.

space

1. a period of time; also: its duration

2. (a) a limited extent in one, two, or three dimensions; (b) an extent set apart or available

3. one of the degrees between or above or below the lines of a musical staff

4. (a) a boundless three-dimensional extent in which objects and events occur and have relative position and direction; (b) physical space independent of what occupies it—called also absolute space

see ARCHITECTONIC; ART/ARTIST; CITY; COLLAGE; E-GORA; ELECTRO-SPHERE; GEOMETRY; LANDSCAPE; PERFORMANCE; PHENOMENON/PHENOMENOLOGY; PRACTICE/CLIENTS; REAL; TIME; TREND; VIRTUAL/ACTUAL

Merriam Webster's Dictionary

space frame

"This studio is about the development of the space frame as an extended structural field punctuated by differentials rather than as a structural technique of simple modularity. More than a proposal for extending an uninflected matrix throughout the world, the space frame is a comprehension of the fullness of the world as a field of ubiquitous difference.... The space frame would become an all-purpose but differentiated spatial sponge for

REISER/UMEMOTO
16. *Space Frame*, Advanced Studio VI, Spring 1998.

programs to be associated with the millennium.... The systems then were more about responsiveness and flexibility in relation to vicissitudes of program, rather than simple, program-derived mono-functionalism."[16]

FIG. 110 Alex Loebell, *Housing on the River Plate, Argentina*, Advanced Studio VI, Jesse Reiser and Nanako Umemoto, critics, Spring 1999.

frame

Merriam Webster's Dictionary

1. (a) something composed of parts fitted together and united; (b) the physical makeup of an animal and especially a human body;
2. (a) the constructional system that gives shape or strength; also: a frame dwelling; (b) such a skeleton not filled in or covered
3. obsolete: the act or manner of framing
4. (a) a machine built upon or within a framework; (b) an open case or structure made for admitting, enclosing, or supporting something; (c) (1): a part of a pair of glasses that holds one of the lenses; (2) plural: that part of a pair of glasses other than the lenses; (d) a structural unit in an automobile chassis supported on the axles and supporting the rest of the chassis and the body

spectacle

see E-GORA; PERFORMANCE

standardization

see SERIALITY/MASS PRODUCTION

stopping problem

see PROCESS; TIME

structure

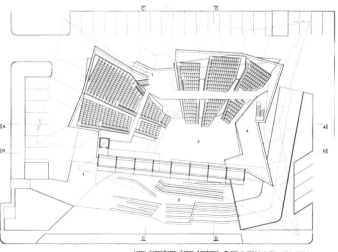

FIG. 111 Karen Bausman, *Performance Theater*, 1999.

1 entry 2 amphitheater 3 stage 4 backstage *SEATING*LEVEL

For both the U. S. Currency and Performance Theater commissions, I attempted to resolve the relationship between the art (desire) and engineering (technique) of architecture and of nature, and the inner systems of order that are intrinsic to the structure of botanical specimens.

KAREN BAUSMAN

For the currency design I chose a Los Angeles freeway on-ramp structure and its highly organic organization to symbolize a commitment to a dynamic network of distribution both physically, as with roadways and freeways, and ephemerally, as with new information technologies. Juxtaposed with that image are detailed engravings of American cash crops—tobacco, cotton, and soybeans—to symbolize the nation's continued and opportunistic wealth, of which currency serves as the means of transaction.

PLATES 3.18–3.19

Both projects are aligned in their relationship to a specific inquiry of a particularly American landscape, and as such attempt to cultivate a singular capacity to support structure. The image of the colossal L.A. freeway

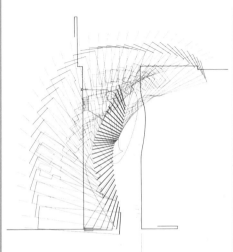
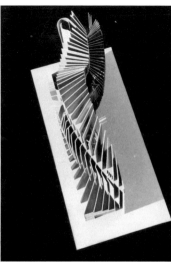

FIG. 112 Simon Eisinger, *Omphalos: The Thickened Present: a Montage of Dwelling*, Advanced Studio V, Karen Bausman, critic, Fall 1993.

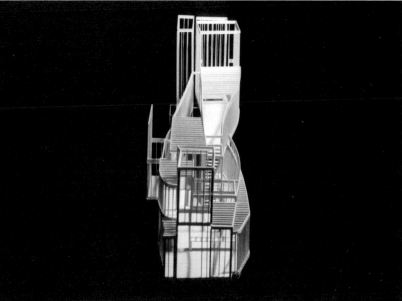

FIG. 113 Guy Maxwell, *Omphalos: The Thickened Present: a Montage of Dwelling*, Advanced Studio V, Karen Bausman, critic, Fall 1993.

S

on-ramp structure that I incorporated into the currency design also represents man's heedless impulse to constantly erect a manufactured landscape against archetypal, as well as material, obstacles. I am interested in reintroducing value to tossed-off plots and barren asphalt surfaces.

"Geodetics…acts as a structural tissue, or flesh—an intermediate structure capable of assembling heterogeneous agglomerations of space, program, and path. Geodetics is protean—in the sense that the structure can change and adapt to the space it develops by:

    a. Changing the fineness or coarseness of its reticulations.

    b. Growing or multiplying the number of struts or crossovers.

    c. Mimicking the surfaces of, for example, conventional structures into or onto which it is projected.

    d. Changing by degrees the type of infill or skinning that it carries."[17]

REISER/UMEMOTO
17. "Jesse Reiser and Nanako Umemoto: Recent Work," *Columbia Documents of Architecture and Theory*, vol. 6 (1997): 165.

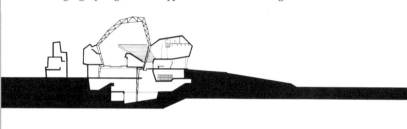

FIG. 114 Michael Su, *From Type to Schema*, Advanced Studio V, Jesse Reiser and Nanako Umemoto, critics, Fall 1995.

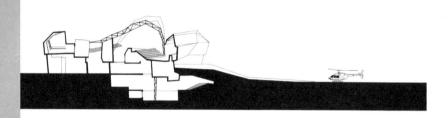

CHASE TICKETS

PROG

studio/practice

4.01

Smith-Miller +
Hawkinson

*Ticketing Counter at
Continental Airlines*

New York, New York

1990

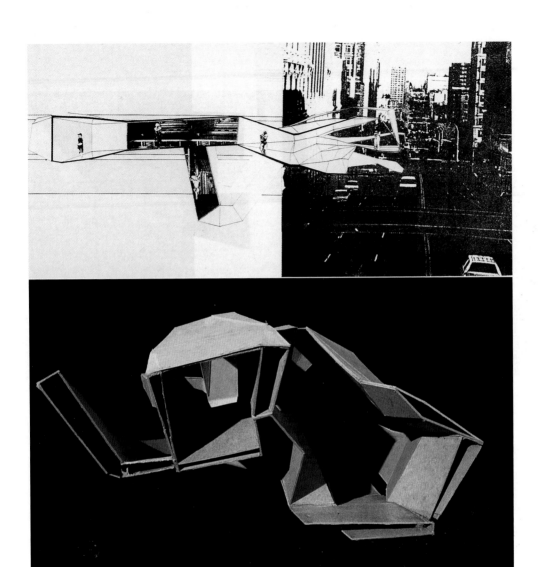

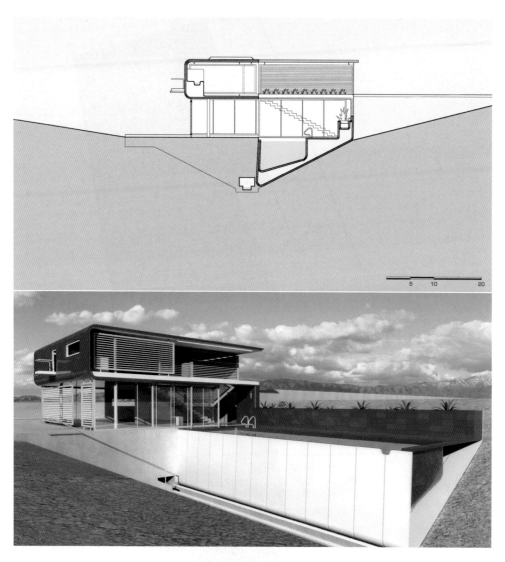

studio/practice

4.04 (left)

Leslie Gill

edLab: Edison School

2000

4.05 (right)

Joseph Kosinski

*Looking Forward,
Looking Back:
Nostalgia/Shafter
Ghost Town*

Advanced Studio VI

Leslie Gill, critic

Spring 1999

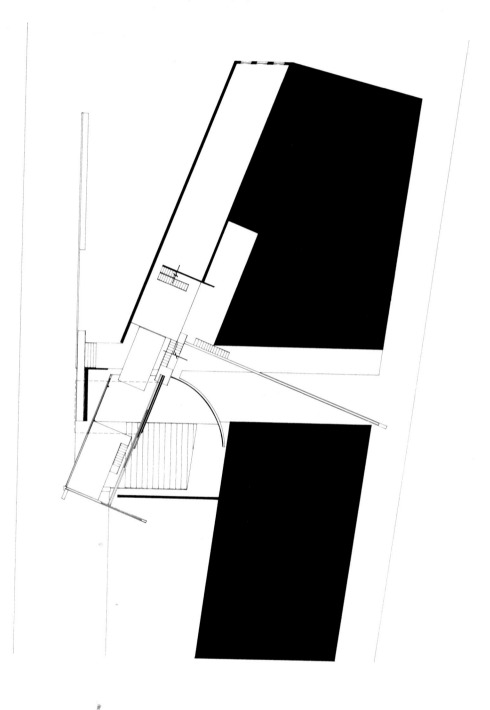

studios, core
4.06
Todd Cossman
Core Studio II
Thomas Hanrahan, critic
Spring 1995

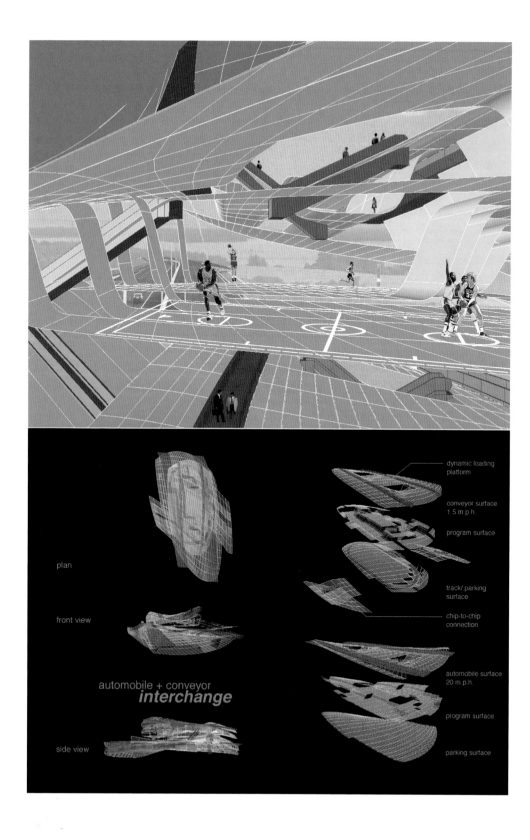

plan

front view

automobile + conveyor
interchange

side view

dynamic loading
platform

conveyor surface
1.5 m.p.h.

program surface

track/ parking
surface

chip-to-chip
connection

automobile surface
20 m.p.h.

program surface

parking surface

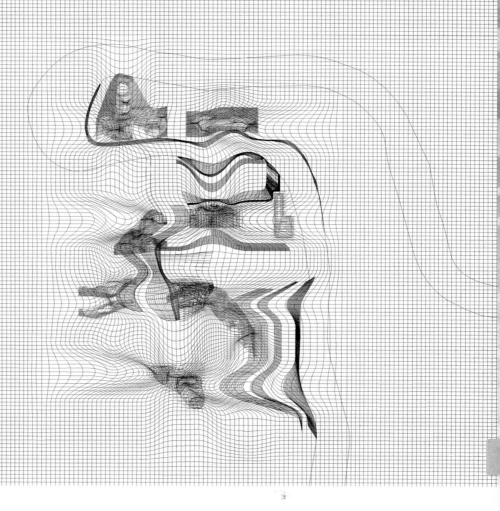

system

4.07 (left)

Emmanuelle Bourlier
and Robert Holton

*Rutgers University
Vision Plan 2000*

Advanced Studio V

Greg Lynn, critic

Fall 1998

4.08 (right)

Emmanuelle Bourlier,
Robert Edmonds, Dan
Gonzalez, Vincent Pang,
and Maia Small

Advanced Studio VI

Greg Lynn and Jeffrey
Kipnis, critics

Spring 1999

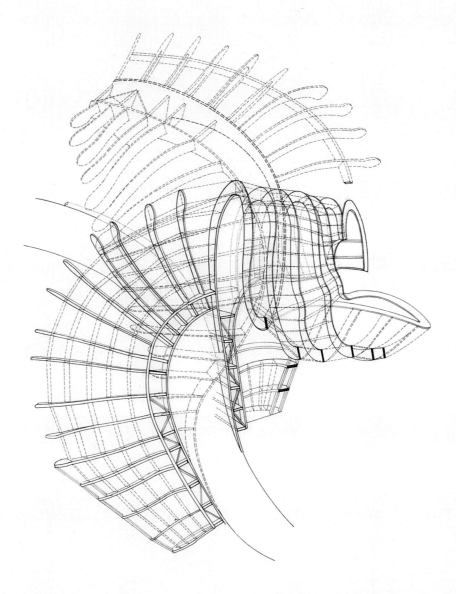

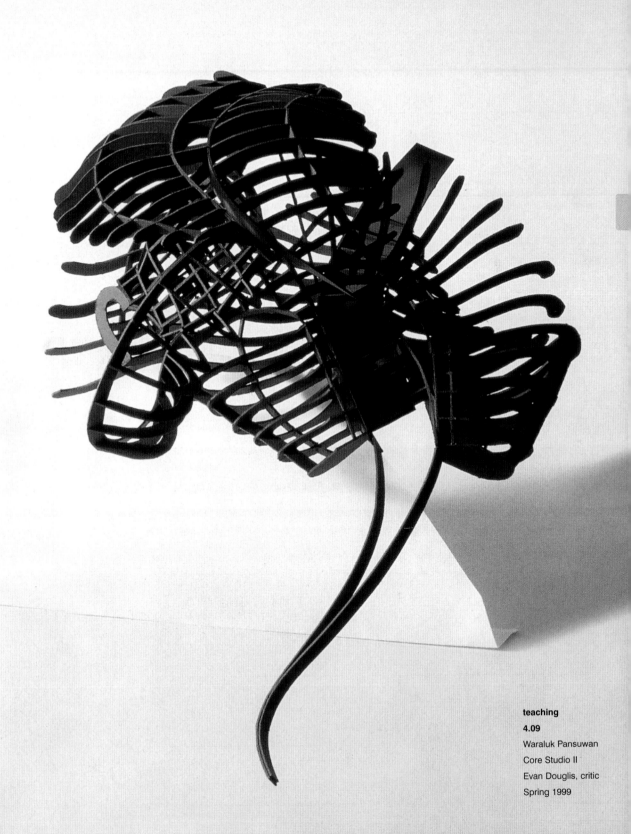

teaching

4.09

Waraluk Pansuwan

Core Studio II

Evan Douglis, critic

Spring 1999

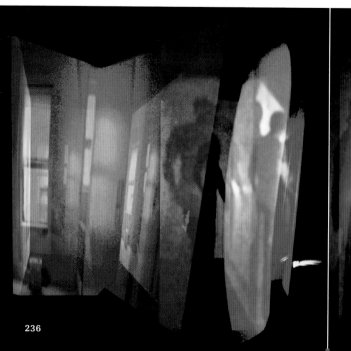

teaching

(left top)
Group Project
Architextures
Advanced Studio V
Hani Rashid, critic
Fall 1995

(left bottom)
Eric Wegerbauer
Kinetic House for a Stationary Bicycle
Advanced Studio
Hani Rashid, critic
Summer 1996

(right)
Asymptote
I-Scape 1.0
(installation)
1999

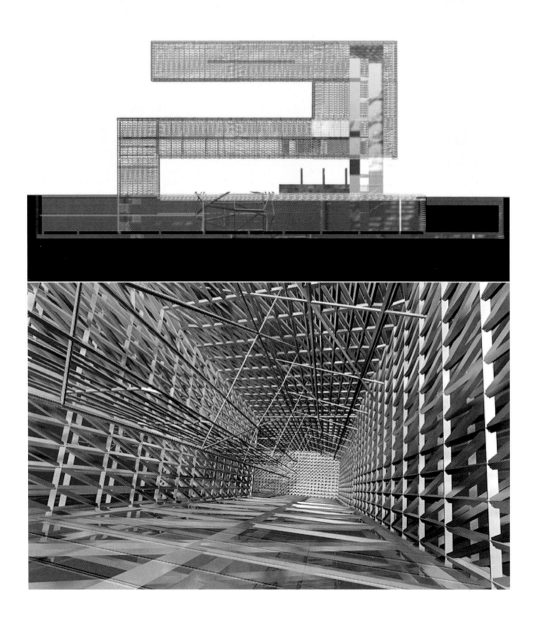

theory

4.15 (left)
Alfio Faro
Zip Manifesto
Advanced Studio VI
Mark Wigley, critic
Spring 2001

4.16 (right)
Jason Lee
Zip Manifesto
Advanced Studio VI
Mark Wigley, critic
Spring 2001

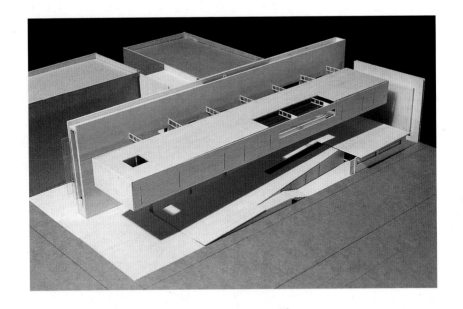

time

4.17 (left)
Hanrahan + Meyers
Inside-Out House
2004

4.18 (right)
Chy-Do Lee
Time: Passage Way
Advanced Studio V
Victoria Meyers,
critic
Fall 1995

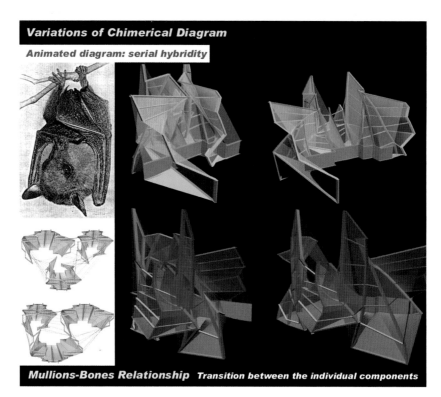

Variations of Chimerical Diagram

Animated diagram: serial hybridity

Mullions-Bones Relationship *Transition between the individual components*

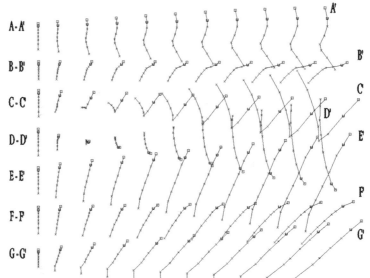

A-A'

B-B'

C-C'

D-D'

E-E'

F-F'

G-G'

A'

B'

C

D'

E'

F

G'

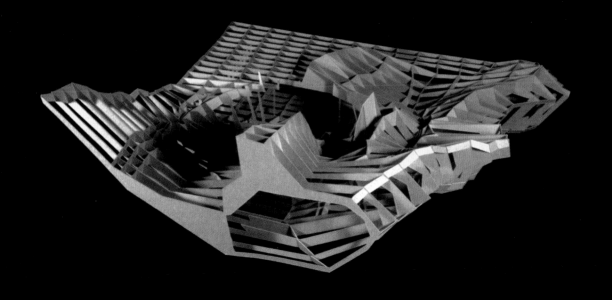

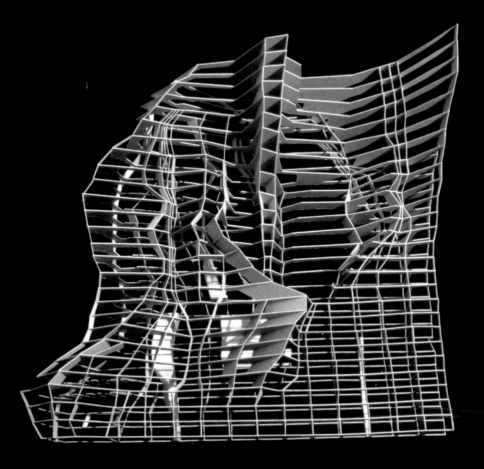

transformation

4.19 (left)

Kyung-San Kim

Serial Hybridity on Park Avenue

Advanced Studio IV

Sulan Kolatan, critic

Spring 1999

4.20 (right)

Kari Anderson

Core Studio I

William MacDonald, critic

Fall 1998

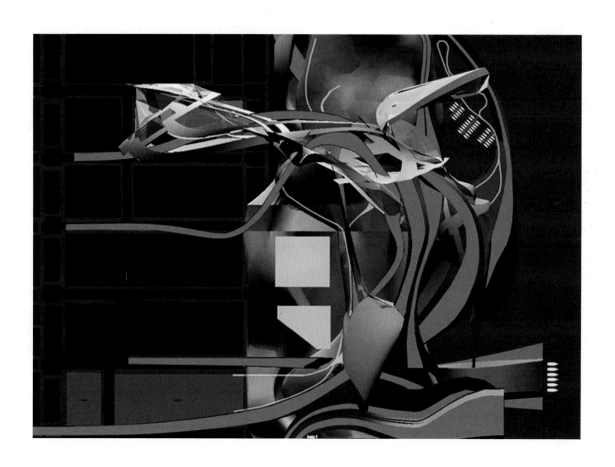

transformation

4.21

Takao Tanaka

Last Site in Manhattan

Advanced Studio VI

Sulan Kolatan, critic

Spring 2000

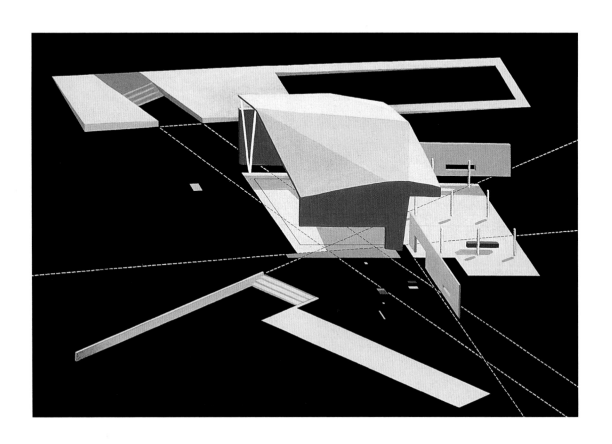

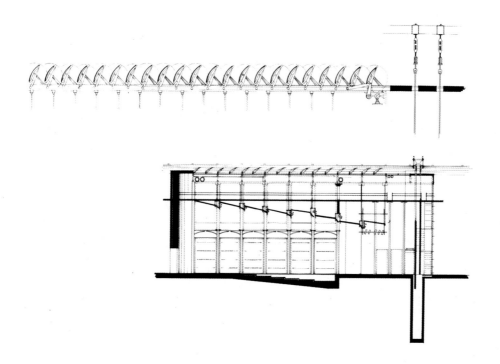

trend

4.22 (left)

Hanrahan + Meyers

*Latimer Gardens
Community Center
"Waveline"*

2002

4.23 (right)

Kimberly Holden

*Lower East Side Public
Works*

Advanced Studio IV

Victoria Meyers, critic

Spring 1993

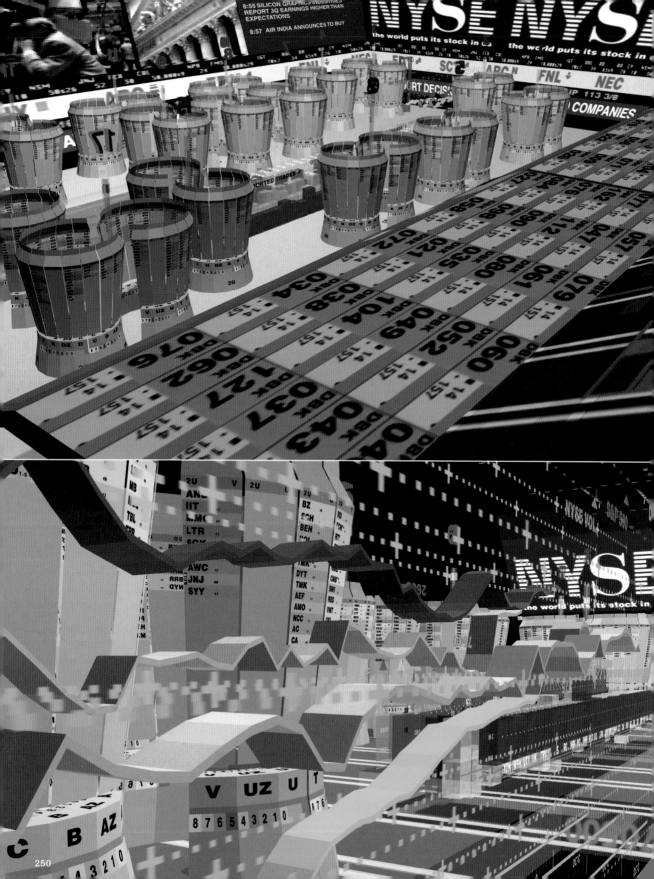

virtual/actual

4.24 (left)

Asymptote

Virtual New York Stock Exchange

1999

4.25 (right)

Asymptote

NYSE Operations Center

New York, New York

1999

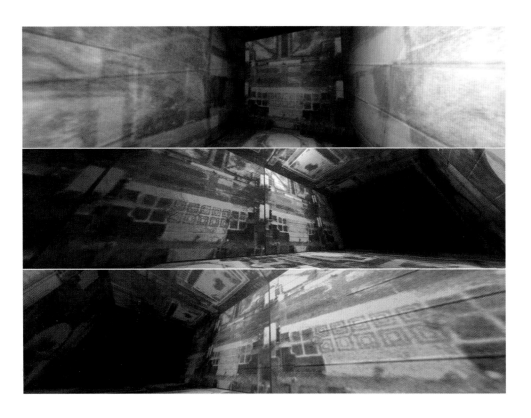

virtual/actual

4.26 (top)

Omar Calderon

Columbia@AlphaWorld

Advanced Studio V

Hani Rashid, critic

Fall 1996

4.27 (bottom)

Jenai Medina

*Informing Interiorities:
Prototypical
Investigations*

Advanced Studio V

Hani Rashid, critic

Fall 1997

JESSE REISER

Nanako Umemoto and I have recently become interested in structural models because in the move toward a more focused notion of architecture as a material science, we have realized that structure and its relationship to force and matter are the most precise delineation of that science. If one wanted to remain within the material realm and work with these forces, then structure is the perfect model to study. We do not claim to be structural engineers, per se, rather structure is a vehicle for architectural inventions.

How much of your research on structure can be traced back to the work of Buckminster Fuller?

JESSE REISER

We are probably taking a path very opposite from Fuller's in that he moved toward maximum lightness as the effect of a reductive methodology. Buckminster Fuller didn't look at aesthetics or effects of architecture, he looked at weight; his ethic was driven by the minimal use of materials as part of the solution to the human problem. In our case, our project is not associated with the myth of solving human problems, and the structural engineer is not interested in employing a minimal or reductive solution to solve a structural problem.

FIG. 115 Reiser + Umemoto, *Cardiff Bay Opera House Competition*, 1994.

structure

Merriam Webster's Dictionary

   1. the action of building
   2. (a) something (as a building) that is constructed; (b) something arranged in a definite pattern of organization
   3. manner of construction
   4. (a) the arrangement of particles or parts in a substance or body; (b) organization of parts as dominated by the general character of the whole
   5. the aggregate of elements of an entity in their relationships to each other

see ARCHITECTONIC; ART/ARTIST; BODY; COLLAGE; COMPLEXITY; COMPUTER; ECOLOGY; GEOMETRY; LANDSCAPE; ORNAMENT; PERFORMANCE; REAL; SPACE FRAME; SURFACE; TEACHING/PEDAGOGY; TIME; TREND

How do you understand the relationship between studio and practice?
Both studio and practice are laboratories that serve as a catalyst for investigation and the continuous testing of emerging concepts and ideologies.

KAREN BAUSMAN

As a means of reference, when in 1982 I opened my first practice with Leslie Gill, it extended the studio experience that we had under the tutelage of John Hejduk at Cooper Union. The firm's projects were rigorous and process-oriented, with no fear of confronting the unimaginable. In 1986, following the completion of a series of commissioned works, I returned to the academy as a studio critic. The move brought me full circle. I have never seen a separation between my endeavors as a student, a practitioner, or an educator.

EVAN DOUGLIS

The question of whether the climate of invention is established by top-down or bottom-up practices is a difficult one to answer. Whether we are discussing the ineffable exchanges found between theory and practice or within the confines of a studio environment, the assumption that there is a privileged direction of influence is obviously suspect. The source of inspiration within the architectural community is constantly in flux. Historically, it is in the very nature of the creative process to react to the established norm. In other words, systems of extreme predictability will always be uprooted if the desired effect is based on originality.

Even within my own studios I am cognizant of the delicate balance necessary to sustain a critical level of work. The assumption that the studio exercise is a kind of infallible construct that arrives as a perfect ready-made is an unrealistic supposition. The students inform the pedagogy to a large extent, and the best studios are wonderful arenas of speculation. I often consider the activity of teaching as improvisation played at various speeds and in both directions. Not only is it important to have at one's disposal a sufficiently pliant pedagogical framework, but teaching is ultimately an act of reciprocity. The broad range of interpretations offer an ideal feedback system, as ideas undergo a perpetual requalification from one semester to the next.

LESLIE GILL

I am very different from other teacher/practitioners because I do not relate my studio methodology directly to the methods that I employ within my office. The premise of my teaching is to provide a framework in which to explore an idea, but I leave the genesis of each project up to the individual student. My studios tend to be very diverse. In other studios, for example, there is a correlation between the work the critics are doing in their office and the work they are doing in the studio.

If I can give a student the tools to do his or her own work, rather than teach that student to think the way I think, I've been a good teacher.

In my practice, we do the reverse of what I do in the studios. The studios start with analytical studies that lead to the formation of conceptual as well as tectonic strategies. In practice, generally because of time constraints, we begin the design process with the programmatic requirements and the design emerges from the set of ideas that we want to explore, usually expanding on ideas from previous projects. We work at such a speed that a lot of what we do is intuitive. Once we go out to bid, we immediately start the analytical work of that project so that we can implement those ideas during construction. We're working at a human scale, so we can make changes during construction. We recently redesigned a townhouse and garden. We're working with the idea of boundary and the interrelationship between the interior and exterior as a kind of blended space. Right now we're doing a lot of residential projects. We try and do five projects at a time, which may be too much.

PLATES 4.04–4.05

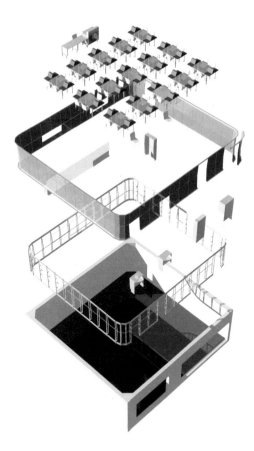

FIG. 116 Leslie Gill, *EdLab: The Edison Schools*, 2000.

In some cases the studio work has a relationship to what I do in practice, but in other cases they're just good projects. I learn from my students and their investigations nourish my practice. It would be a mistake to think that studio work has to have a singular stamp or approach. The School promotes academic freedom and experimentation and although certain formal trends are evident, critics encourage students to think for themselves, which is an important aspect of the American architectural education. People come from all over the world to study at places like Columbia and Pratt because the studio is perceived as a laboratory for discovery as much as it is a place to learn from master critics.

THOMAS HANRAHAN

I always tell my students, if the door is open a little bit, find a way to get in. Look for opportunities to think about a bigger issue. We pursued this, for example, with the canopy that we designed for Continental Airlines. We were designing a new image for Continental—ticket counters, furniture, and carpeting—and we noticed they were building a whole new building at La Guardia. We saw an opportunity to design a canopy that would create another space inside the building for ticketing transactions, so we proposed it to them. They ended up selling the building to US Airways and our ticket counters were never installed, but the canopy was built because the technology to build a repetitive "shell" of carbon fiber ended up being less expensive than anything else they could do there. You look for opportu-

LAURIE HAWKINSON

S

nities. Bernard has shown us what a student center can be. What is a ferry terminal today? The last thing this city saw was something built in 1957 for the Staten Island Ferry. We have recently completed a new ferry terminal at Pier 11. We were involved with writing the program and designing the building for the Department of Transportation/EDC. It is important for the students to engage with the real world in their studio work. For my Governor's Island studio, I took the students to the city planning offices and we discussed specific issues regarding the city's future. The planning department had recently revised the zoning ordinances in downtown Manhattan to establish live/work space. We used our discussions with the city planning office as a motivation to operate downtown and test what that implied. The planning department is trying to propose some difficult changes, but is working within a huge bureaucracy. In the studio we are free agents and we can test the department's ideas in all kinds of ways.

PLATES 4.01–4.03

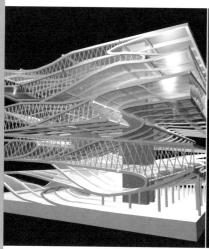 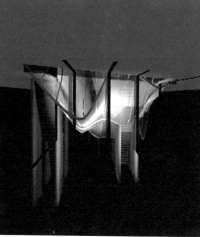

FIG. 117 Yoshonori Sakano, *Digital Domain*, Advanced Studio VI, Laurie Hawkinson, critic, Spring 1996.

FIG. 118 Ingeborg Rocker, *Digital Domain*, Advanced Studio VI, Laurie Hawkinson, critic, Spring 1996.

With some conspicuous exceptions, information tends to flow from the school to the practice, especially as architecture understands itself more as a cultural enterprise than as a service. On the other hand, the perfection of architectural experimentation almost always occurs in professional practice, not in the academy, unlike so many other fields like music, science, and mathematics, where perfection of the field occurs in the academy.

JEFFREY KIPNIS

In architecture and art, ideas first emerge in the schools but reach their most poignant form in practice. There are occasions, as with Herzog & de Meuron, for example, where a body of ideas emerged after school. The first inklings of an architectural idea start to hatch at the academy, but schools do not have the necessary commissions, the time, and the technology to see the ideas through to the end. Generally student work occurs at a very narcissistic level and ideas do not get developed.

Some schools teach design as a series of techniques that will be adhered to in the world of practice; yet, at Columbia this hierarchy between practice and education is collapsed. Here, a student learns about design through critical analysis and research, which assumes that most of our graduates

GREG LYNN

will be making meaningful contributions to architectural design and will occupy leadership positions in design offices. This research agenda does not give the students tested, received, or mainstream design strategies. The School has had the precious arrogance to assume that it will define the new mainstream, so the academy has taken over the leadership role traditionally given to practice. The Columbia studio faculty are also not practicing architecture in the conventional way. Many of the faculty pursue the research they conduct with their students within their offices, often through publications, exhibitions, and alternative forms of practice. We have witnessed the migration of the academic environment into the architectural practices of the faculty and recent graduates. Many of the students begin to emulate the practices of the faculty almost immediately after graduation, often bypassing apprenticeships in offices and moving directly into alternative forms of practice, including exhibitions and publications.

Teaching in this case is in anticipation of a practice that does not yet exist. Students are taught to provoke and instigate rather than how to systematize conventional practice.

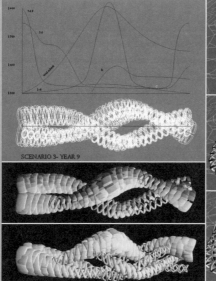 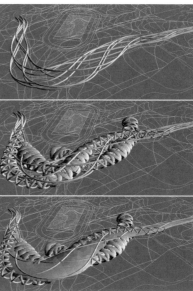

FIG. 119 Avishay Manoach, *Mass Produced Classroom*, Advanced Studio VI, Greg Lynn, critic, Spring 1998.

SCENARIO 3- YEAR 9

Kadambari Baxi and I have been working together since the early nineties. We think of our practice as a laboratory to the same extent that teaching is a laboratory through practice. There is nothing more real than the academy; it is not a peripheral supplement to reality. If you accept that, you have the same structure applying to the different modes of practice. The investigations that are in our book *Entropia* are just as much part of the so-called real world as the commissioned work that we do. We are simply operating under different conditions, rather than specifying that one set of circumstances is more concrete or real or even conventional than the other.

REINHOLD MARTIN

To package oneself as an alternative practice would automatically imply a mainstream, and there is nothing more bizarre than the mainstream of architecture.

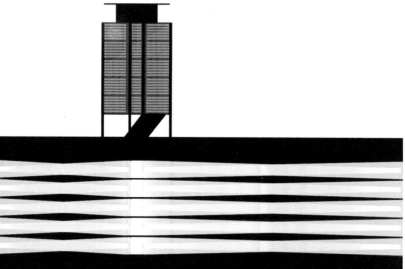

Our work outside of the School found an incredible test bed within the School. We deliberately utilized the opportunity at Columbia to expand and develop ideas that we were already pursuing in our professional work. Aside from the introduction of computer technology, there was a career shift around 1992 in terms of the work we were doing. We began to work on a series of competitions that paralleled the interests of the studio and the studio began to present ideas to us. We were also aided by the other faculty at Columbia. We collaborated with Stan Allen on the Croton Aqueduct study (1992) and the first competition for the Venice Gateway (1991). During that year we shifted from projects that were self-generated to the first small-scale architectural projects, to applying and expanding those ideas through public competitions.

JESSE REISER

The Croton Aqueduct was initially a research project and was our first interest in infrastructure. It began as a mapping problem—a simple recording and collation of information—and became an opportunity to propose interventions along those corridors.

I have always tried to keep the School and my work separate. Yet, in many ways, putting together a school is not unlike putting together a building. You can either look for a unitary aesthetic or aim for fertile dialectics between differentiated parts. I generally attempt the latter.

BERNARD TSCHUMI

Lerner Hall, for example, was unbelievably complex because we dealt with the Columbia community, which is very different from the community within the School of Architecture. The Columbia community included the trustees, the administration, and the neighborhood, all of whom are very architecturally conservative. The historical McKim, Mead & White campus can be interpreted in many ways, but it is often interpreted very rigidly and literally.

I believe, however, that it is better to confront contradictions than to avoid them. It was very successful in certain ways, and in other ways it bears the traces of the complexity of the project.

PLATES 3.20–3.22

In the past, ideas seemed to migrate from the professional practice to the academy. Now because of better technology in academic institutions, it has reversed. How would you characterize this relationship?

This is an incredibly complex layering of relationships because the academy is traditionally set up in opposition to practice. The world of the academy is supposedly the isolated world of theory and the world outside is the world of practice. When you are inside the academy, you live a life that is quite unlike the life you led before and will lead after. But schools of architecture are different from other disciplines because practice and the divide between theory and practice also lives inside the academy. The studio is a form of practice that sets itself up in opposition to theory. From the point of view of a practitioner, the kind of work that goes on at an avant-garde school like Columbia will seem too theoretical and unbuildable. However, many of the proposals made inside the school are more realistic than proposals made outside. Indeed, we look to the academy to help us decide what is real and what is not. Columbia is not just a laboratory for trying avant-garde experiments that may or may not affect the real world; it aggressively tries to define what "real" is.

MARK WIGLEY

see PEDAGOGY, COLUMBIA; TEACHING

studios, advanced

How does your approach in first-year differ from teaching final-year studios, including the AAD?

The AAD is a three-semester program for students who already have a professional degree. It has its own unique dynamics. These students have essentially acquired their foundation in architecture from undergraduate or foreign institutions prior to coming to Columbia. They come already equipped in terms of technical facility and, to a certain degree, possess a greater amount of life experience. In the best of cases, they bring an unsettling "difference," in the form of constructive provocation. Educating the mature student is less about teaching in a classical sense with a rigorous pedagogy set in stone, and more about raising the philosophical stakes in order to intensify the critical nature of the debate.

EVAN DOUGLIS

Third-year students know more about who they are as architects and one would hope they are coming to a particular studio because they are interested in pursuing the ideas that are being investigated in that studio. The critics lay out their issues during the initial presentations, but at the same time, the students are working on their own ideas. In some studios the students are even writing their own programs. I like to set certain parameters, but I always tell students that if they can give me a good reason why they want to break them then they can do it. Anybody can go for a variance, but you have to convince someone why. In the last five years the computer has played an increasingly important role, which is obviously synony-

LAURIE HAWKINSON

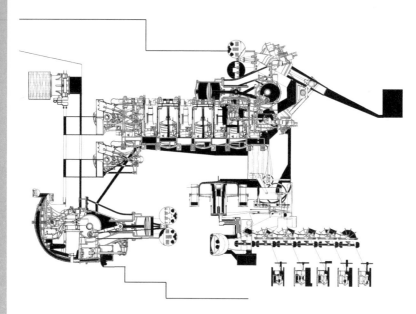

FIG. 121 David Ruy, *E-Z Architecture: Counterfeit Paradigms of Dwelling in the Mail Order House*, Advanced Studio, Evan Douglis, critic, Summer 1996.

FIG. 122 Hernan Alonso, *Liquid Assets: Reassessing Pneumatics as Urban Outfits for the New Millennium*, Advanced Studio, Evan Douglis, critic, Summer 1998.

mous with the way one works today. This train of technology is moving, it is just a question of when you get on it. Everyone at Columbia is using it much the way one works with it in a variety of practices.

Architecture is both a discourse and a discipline and Columbia trains its students to be the leaders of both. I expect that they will be out there in the world operating in a major way. I spend time preparing my students for presentations because they have 20 minutes to present and defend their projects, which is also about the general attention span of any client, so you have to learn how to condense and edit. It is as much about language as representation. I'm very interested in how the students put these two together and how they begin to identify and then build on their own terms.

By their third year at Columbia, students seem to have figured out the code. They have learned how to read the jargon, which enables them to navigate this school. Students in the third year are doing thesis-level work. When Kadambari Baxi and I taught the CNN studio together, students initiated their own combination of the software and hardware that was appropriate to the thesis. We gave them access to the tools, including the three-dimensional modeling machine that had just arrived and we were able to make use of technology as we do in our practice.

REINHOLD MARTIN

It was difficult because most students expect to be taught how to use a certain method, and I don't think that's what graduate education should do, particularly in a university like this.

Unfortunately there is a lot of formula going around and I think the algorithmic approach to computer design has the unfortunate side effect of reproducing or reinforcing the idea of design as formula. One reason that it has been so successful around the world is that it is easily transferred and anybody can perform these steps. It is important for universities to operate critically with respect to anything that is widely accepted and therefore, we need to encourage a self-directed, thesis approach.

see STUDIO/PRACTICE; TEACHING

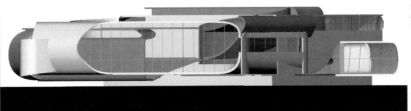

FIG. 123 Martin Zscheigner, *Entropy Lab*, Advanced Studio V, Reinhold Martin, critic, Fall 1999.

studios, core

During the first year, there is an enormous amount of production. Some may feel that the presence of drafting and hand-made models are somewhat antiquated in a culture so thoroughly influenced by digital technologies. On the contrary, I believe the juxtaposition between the two is an ideal scenario to promote in an environment of critical research. As representational systems, both offer unique insights into the mysteries of architecture, utilizing entirely different but complementary techniques, and the inadequacies of one are willingly fulfilled by the other. The real issue no longer concerns the supremacy of one representational system over another, but the means by which a critical discourse can be created that is aimed at the ethical, ideological, and even theological implications of the future practices of digital technology in architecture.

EVAN DOUGLIS

What is your objective as a critic in the core sequence?
As director of the core studio sequence at Columbia, I was responsible for addressing some basic issues, such as the notion that architecture is both contingent on many factors and indeterminate. Architecture does not have to be formally stable in terms of a structural diagram. It can provoke change over time, change with time, or establish a strategy of repeated changes and mutations based on other factors working on it.

THOMAS HANRAHAN

Even though the core program was developed with the rest of the first-year faculty, what was unique about your studio?
There is a calisthenics atmosphere to the first year and the program is set up as a series of exercises. The tone changes quite a bit during the second semester, when the students begin to engage specific sites, which is specifically why the site remains abstract during the first semester.

THOMAS HANRAHAN

It was always interesting to give a theater program in the second semester of the core sequence because it brought up issues of time, movement, and moment—conditions that are not complete or discrete. It was always sited

S

in a city and New York City in particular is a monument to an indeterminate strategy. There is a certain tangibility and concreteness to this block-of-rock, but it is also constantly changing. There was always an effort to understand how students could deal with that on a smaller scale, either through transparency, site fragmentation, change over time, or through building that aggressively starts to change the city itself. We encouraged the move away from an understanding of the city as a stable set of forms or strategies.

Architecture can be an exercise where certain issues are framed independent of others. The studio problems are set up to allow comparisons so that students can look at the other projects within their own studio and in other first-year studios and understand the various approaches. In my studio there was an emphasis on an idea as something that can be explicitly stated in verbal terms either as a paradigm or verbal diagram, or even as a loosely structured narrative.

FIG. 124 Joel Cichowski, Core Studio II, Thomas Hanrahan, critic, Spring 1994.

This enables us to see the gaps between what the students are saying and what their projects are saying. I am interested in how an idea can be understood as a grouping of elements that are related to program or micro

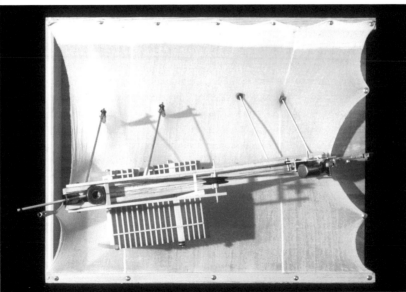

FIG. 125 Brad Bell, Core Studio I, Thomas Hanrahan, critic, Fall 1995.

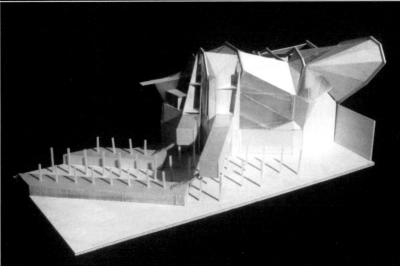

FIG. 126 Tom Chang, Core Studio II, Thomas Hanrahan, critic, Spring 1996.

programs; and, how these elements are analyzed and then put into play as a series of diagrams changing over time or a series of changing sections.

Within many projects is a notion of time that functions as a mechanism to animate an idea once it is understood as a set of architectonic elements, be it a beam, a set of beams, or a series of section frames. Students tested these abstract ideas during the first semester against a literal ground understood in abstract terms as a plan, whereas during the second semester, they began to understand these ideas against the framework of the city.

PLATE 4.06

The first year is very labor-intensive. The students produce so much work and are very energetic. They are interested in understanding the greater discourse within the School and they want to participate. It is a great moment and there is also a tremendous learning curve.

LAURIE HAWKINSON

The students enter the first year enter at different levels because of their various backgrounds. As a critic you want to keep both the intellectual and technical level of the studio high because you want to keep all of the students engaged; you also want to raise the stakes for the entire group. Writing the program for the first-year studio is particularly tricky because it has to be both expansive yet precise and take into account so many different issues. The critics in the first year are a very experienced group of individuals. The program needs to be open enough for each critic to make it his or her own and at the same time accomplish the criteria of the curriculum requirements.

The development and comprehension of a conceptual idea—which is key to any project—is an important issue. We also write the programs to focus on specific technical and conceptual issues that must be developed. The students need to be focused and fearless; they have to take leaps and make mistakes. This is the only way to move forward. By the time the students are in their third year, the critic's hand should not be as heavy.

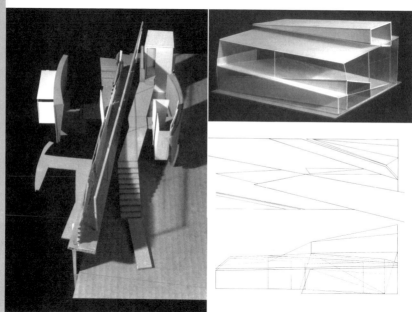

FIG. 127 Stacey Chorches, Core Studio I, Laurie Hawkinson, critic, Fall 1993.

FIG. 128 Irina Verona, Core Studio I, Laurie Hawkinson, critic, Fall 1995.

We have to be very careful and precise about what it is we want to accomplish. The first three semesters, and particularly the first year, is an opportunity to lay the ground work. After the first semester students begin to find their way through the School—in a sense curating their education. They select the critics they want to work with and learn increasingly more about who they are as architects. The first semester, in particular, is key because we set the tone. It's like giving somebody a particular set of glasses to use to move through this environment. We give them tools but we are very careful about how these tools are understood. Much of the burden falls on the student to acquire the basic skills.

For instance, it is very important that they understand that program is an open-ended question, that it is not just about surfaces, materials, and quantity. It's like a script that you rewrite and, like a director, you take the script and you make it into your own vision. They should also understand that a section cut is not just a technical skill but a kind of map through a building, which is very different from a plan. In order to understand what a section is you have to draw one while thinking about it. They learn that each drawing or each piece of information is evidentiary material that is built up and added to support a particular case that they're defending. This is what we do as architects. It's very important that the evidence be very precise and that they take risks, even if they go off the cliff in the end. Each project is like a mini-thesis, a directed question. We're there to help but they have to bring their own ideas and interests to the table. I always tell the students, if they do not believe in the idea, how are they going to convince me or someone else? I am willing to go to the mat for them as long as they believe in their ideas.

When a student (or an architect) is given a program or a site he or she should not take it as a given. When given a program, initially you have to take it apart and deconstruct it before you can put it back together. A specific site might not be necessary, but you might want to know the particular kind of use. The Finnish architect Eliel Saarinen once said, "Always design a thing by considering it in its next larger context—a chair in a room, a room in a house, a house in an environment, an environment in a city plan." You always want to frame the question and the investigation but also be aware of what lies outside the frame.

As a critic in the first-year studios, you are responsible for taking students from varied backgrounds and degrees of architectural proficiency and expertise, and equalizing them in one semester. The role of the first-year critic is pivotal in this respect. Where do you fit in?

Everyone who teaches in the first sequences of core and/or advanced architectural design has decidedly different interests and agendas in his or her work. It is established very early on at Columbia that there are very different ways of looking at the same problems and issues in architecture. For example, all of the core studio critics teach the same program in very different ways while progressing through the project on the same schedule. The mandate is to do what you do well, the idea being that each studio is part of a confederation whose intent is to provide a range of design directions and techniques on a particular topic. Technique and expertise are really addressed through the varieties of scales and format.

In the first semester of the core studio, abstraction is emphasized as a technique for leveling the playing field as it were between architecture and non-architecture majors. For architecture majors it becomes a method through which past educational experiences are tested and questioned. For non-architecture majors, it provides an entry into architecture that is based on concepts rather than experience. The goal, however, even in the first semester, is to produce a building that is conceptually rigorous in its design approach.

WILLIAM MACDONALD

The secret of Columbia is that there is an extremely rigid core curriculum. The school is notorious for the highly experimental studio work, but in the core studios, you do not get to experiment at all. The experimental work at Columbia is premised on the establishment of this rigid core. Experimental does not mean you have to come up with something new, it means you are free to pursue different directions. The School benefits from an array of different directions pursued at the same time that create an environment of diversity and debate.

Columbia's greatest asset is its ability to enable students to keep operating as researchers after they leave the School. It is not the experimental research inside the studios that matters, but the ongoing attitude that architecture, even in its most practical and conservative operations, is a form of research, a way of thinking.

see PEDAGOGY, COLUMBIA; STUDIOS, ADVANCED; TEACHING/PEDAGOGY

MARK WIGLEY

style

I don't know anybody who is concerned with the next style—even Paul Goldberger doesn't talk about it anymore. Around 1950 people realized that modernism, pure modernism from the 1920s and 1930s, was not the answer, but they still sought an answer. Designers began flipping through so many hegemonic styles that by 1975 the modernist possibilities were exhausted. None of them worked as the universal solution so there was a last attempt to return to the stylistic mantle of history. It took 50 years for architects to become comfortable with the notion that the Enlightenment is officially over. During the 1960s and 1970s there were canonical forms that we had to address, and now we see a change every two or three years. We encourage students to exhaust trends and keep experimenting. That is the biggest difference between then and now; there does not need to be a particular answer. There was a strong formal mantle in my architectural education that changed every three or four years. This change brought about a psychological crisis because we thought we had figured it out each time. There was a desire to find a solution. In 1984–85 the profession was a bloated corpse and the academy became increasingly significant as a way out of that disgusting mess.

see PEDAGOGY, COLUMBIA; TREND

THOMAS HANRAHAN

suburb

"Suburban America [is] that region of indiscernible limits whose influences both physical and mental claim city, town, and countryside alike. Oft criticized as a place of unrelenting uniformity and mediocrity, the suburbs, nevertheless, house a major portion of the population and remain a locus of inspiration for most of the rest."[18]

REISER/UMEMOTO
18. *Sub-Urbanity*, Advanced Studio VI, Spring 1995.

surface

"The hope is that all of architecture's surfaces, understood as modulated fields of performance and action, will produce unexpected and spontaneous experiential effects, that the surfaces will engender virtual intensities whose manifestations as actual information or as programmatic activities emerge as a kind of *aprés-coup*."[19]

ASYMPTOTE
19. Introduction to "Analog Space to Digital Field," *Assemblage* 21 (August 1993): 26.

You often talk about complex and blurred relationships between surface and structure. Please explain what you mean.

For example, within the Performance Theater's (1999) enclosing wall assembly is a composite wall section that allows separate systems, or materials in many cases, to perform one or more functions simultaneously and independently. The composite section combines the steel-braced frame required to maintain the curtain wall's structural stability and integrity together with the zinc metal assembly used to enclose the structure. The striated hardwood interior curtain wall has specific acoustical properties. The development of the composite system was the result of analyzing the relationship of surface and structure in an attempt to exhaust the terms of one through the characteristics of the other.

KAREN BAUSMAN

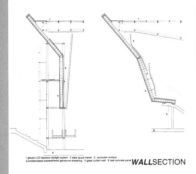 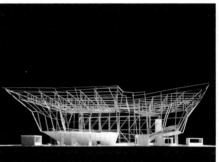

WALLSECTION

FIG. 129 Karen Bausman, *Performance Theater*, 1999.

How do you intuitively understand the literal and figurative aspects of structure and surface that are adaptable to one another?

Generally I ask students to transfer the information they have surveyed, disassembled, and reassembled—usually it is in the form of photographic images of botanical specimens—into material wireframe models. This "re-assembly" allows for newly realized terms of one surface (and, therefore, form) to be juxtaposed with the characteristics of the overall structure.

Form then informs the surface. By rendering the surface through the wireframe, the students create a hybrid relationship between surface and structure.

KAREN BAUSMAN

surface

1. the exterior or upper boundary of an object or body
2. a plane or curved two-dimensional locus of points (as the boundary of a three-dimensional region)
3. (a) the external or superficial aspect of something; (b) an external part or layer

see AESTHETICS/APPEARANCE; BOUNDARY; GEOMETRY; IMAGE; LANDSCAPE; PROGRAM; STRUCTURE

Merriam Webster's Dictionary

symmetry

"In his classic example of the two possible mutations of the thumb, Bateson demonstrated that the monstrosities display higher degrees of symmetry

GREG LYNN
20. "The Renewed Novelty of Symmetry," *Arch Plus* 128 (1995): 82–83.

than do normal hands.... The existence of mutations that exhibit higher degrees of symmetry than the norm led to contradictory explanations. The taxonomic hypothesis locates extra information at the point of mutation in order to explain the increase in symmetry and the decrease in heterogeneity. Bateson proposed an alternative explanation whereby the decrease in asymmetry and the increase in homogeneity was a result of a loss of information. He argued that where information is lost or mutated, growth reverts to simple symmetry. Thus symmetry was not an underlying principle of the essential order of the whole organism, but was, instead, a default value used in cases of minimal information. Organisms are not attributable to any ideal reduced type or any single organization; rather, they are the result of dynamic nonlinear interactions of internal symmetries with the vicissitudes of a disorganized context."[20]

see INFORMATION

system

"Infrastructures organize and manage complex systems of flow, movement, and exchange. Not only do they provide a network of pathways, they also work through systems of locks, gates, and valves—a series of checks that control and regulate flow."[21]

STAN ALLEN
21. *Colossal Urbanism*, Advanced Studio VI, Fall 1993.

"This studio hinged on the idea of expansion through intensive affiliation. Expansion being the ability for a system with seemingly internal orders to proliferate itself within, reorganize, and exploit a seemingly external environment. Affiliations are diagonal alliances across proper categories, where unrelated species, individuals, corporations, or other organizations become integrated not despite but because of their differences. Intensivity is the prerequisite for such a fusional sensibility, where one's internal autonomy is sacrificed so that other forces, influences, and contingencies can be invited in. These contingent forces both reshape the previously autonomous system and become influenced by that same once discrete system.... indeed as an injection into that system, where an alien sensibility might strategically and tactically reconfigure particular aspects of the existing system, transforming it from within."[22]

GREG LYNN
22. *Infesting in New Brunswick through Johnson & Johnson*, Advanced Studio V, Fall 1993.

"The initiative of the studio was to invent a component system of construction that is flexible and variegated in its implementation and construction. Architectonic systems are understood as flexible surfaces that are capable of both local and global differentiation."[23]

23. *Plinth: Options Studio*, Advanced Studio V, Fall 1996.

PLATES 4.07–4.08

"Chaos is the term we use to describe the *apparently* complex behavior of what we consider to be simple, well-behaved systems. Chaotic behavior, when looked at casually, looks erratic and almost random—almost like the behavior of a system strongly influenced by outside, random 'noise' or the complicated behavior of a system with many, many degrees of freedom, each 'doing its own thing.'...[T]his chaotic behavior shows dramatic qualitative and *quantitative* universal features. These universal features are independent of the details of the particular system. This universality means

24. Robert C. Hilborn, *Chaos and Nonlinear Dynamics* (New York: Oxford University Press, 1994), 3,4.

that what we learn about chaotic behavior by studying, for example, a simple electrical circuit or simple mathematical models, can be applied immediately to understand the chaotic behavior of lasers and beating heart cells."[24]

system   *Merriam Webster's Dictionary*

1. a regularly interacting or interdependent group of items forming a unified whole: as (a) (1): a group of interacting bodies under the influence of related forces; (2): an assemblage of substances that is in or tends to equilibrium; (b) (1): a group of body organs that together perform one or more vital functions; (2): the body considered as a functional unit; (c) a group of related natural objects or forces; (d) a group of devices or artificial objects or an organization forming a network especially for distributing something or serving a common purpose; (e) a major division of rocks usually larger than a series and including all formed during a period or era; (f) a form of social, economic, or political organization or practice

2. an organized set of doctrines, ideas, or principles usually intended to explain the arrangement or working of a systematic whole

3. (a) an organized or established procedure; (b) a manner of classifying, symbolizing, or schematizing

4. harmonious arrangement or pattern

5. an organized society or social situation regarded as stultifying

see INFRASTRUCTURE; LOCAL/GLOBAL; NETWORK

T

I do not impose stylistic limits on the studio. My job as a critic is to estab-   STAN ALLEN
lish the intellectual and conceptual limits of the studio work. The images
and forms that the students produce have to be their own. There are times
when that reflects the dominant dynamic of the School and there are times
when it may exist slightly outside. During the late 1990s, there were visible
stylistic shifts, but there are also self-organizing dynamics of the studio
that have very little to do with what any one critic is saying.

*What is the role of the critic within the larger discipline of architectural
education?*

The impact that a critic might have arises from the interplay between three   STAN ALLEN
different factors simultaneously: first, the individual critic's ideas and
directions, and the way in which various studios are structured; second, the
dynamic of architecture as a discipline beyond the boundaries of Columbia
—architects such as Frank Gehry, Peter Eisenman, or Rem Koolhaas (who
are not directly connected to the School) are clearly influential within that
broader architectural discourse; and finally, an individual critic's practice
outside of the academic situation. There is really not a one-to-one relationship between a program brief that a critic sets up and the work that comes
out of the studio.

The flip side, however, of this intensive engagement with the present is
sometimes a lack of awareness of history. So much of what is interesting
and important theoretically and in practice today is the result of the past
20 years of history and it often surprises me how little people know of that
history. When I was in school in 1978–80, Aldo Rossi held the position that
Rem Koolhaas holds now. The world somehow revolved around Rossi, yet
Rossi is seen to be completely irrelevant to students and discussions today.
Perhaps his importance was overstated in 1978, but it is a mistake to lose
sight of what was interesting and important about Rossi's theoretical work
and his architectural production. John Hejduk, for example, is a tremendously important contemporary architect, but he just doesn't enter the
radar screens at Columbia. Students who know Daniel Libeskind's current
work are not aware of the *Micromegas*, the speculative drawing work of
the 1970s. I got a blank look from my seminar a few years ago when
I mentioned Massimo Scolari.

I have always encouraged students to test their ideas through large-scale   HANI RASHID
installations. It gives them a terrific opportunity to build one-to-one architectural works in a short period of time. Also, the experience of testing
something and seeing it through to completion is very enriching. No matter
how much creativity an institution might encourage, there are always
expectations and parameters set by a dominant status quo that tend to be
enforced and inadvertently encouraged by the tenured faculty.

The School has a tenuous relationship with the profession, which often perceives the academy as a place where young practitioners will be trained to contribute to the existing machinery. The better students, however, always understand and pursue paths beyond the confines of current building design. I remember one group of students who was very enthusiastic about computers but who was not interested in the technical approach that was being taught in the computer labs. These students inspired me to rethink this new tool, which eventually led to the implementation of the paperless studios. That caused rumbling from some of the faculty who feared that students would end up as animators in Hollywood, a view which, only five years later, has already been proved incorrect. We currently have very reputable clients seeking our expertise *as architects* in computer-generated environments.

PLATES 4.10–4.12

EVAN DOUGLIS

Each semester I confront an entirely new set of individuals who come from different ethnic backgrounds and geographical regions throughout the world and have their own unique interests. The challenge is to create an environment where we are able to jettison preconceptions and pursue a more conceptually expansive approach to architectural production. The exercises are written to place a certain amount of anxiety, discomfort, and disorientation into the studio. The students' apparent innocence or naiveté is an essential form of strength and, on a strangely perverse level, it empowers them to take risks.

I am inspired by Friedrich Froebel, the nineteenth-century child educator who developed a brilliant series of exercises for teaching small children. Froebel's exercises, which he called "gifts," translated highly complex organizational logics into accessible and uniform vehicles for learning. It is believed that Froebel may have indirectly influenced early modernist academic institutions such as the Bauhaus.

What impressed me most about Froebel's work was his visionary belief that the capacity for learning has no limits, and that the essential challenge is to develop techniques to liberate the imagination. Similar to Froebel, I

FIG. 130 Seungki Min, Core Studio II, Evan Douglis, critic, Spring 1999.

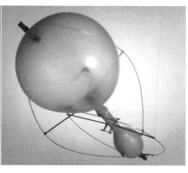

FIG. 131 Evan Douglis, *Theater of Operations: Building in Reverse*, 1995.

FIG. 132 Hize Maing, Core Studio I, Evan Douglis, critic, Fall 1997.

FIG. 133 Anthony Tumminello, Core Studio I, Evan Douglis, critic, Fall 1997.

have always considered the exercise a valuable and opportune vehicle for the acquisition of knowledge.

If, as you say, the critic's responsibility is to inform, to impart to the students new information, new ideas, new concepts, and new constructs, what would the message be?

EVAN DOUGLIS

First, there are fundamental issues that need to be addressed within any studio concerning the operative strategies necessary to develop abstraction within the production of architecture. I am speaking less about the actual content of the "message," than about the means by which it is delivered. It is essential to encourage students to relinquish preconceptions and accepted methodologies of working, and to be fully responsive to the "unknown"— to arenas of speculation that simply cannot be predicted. The pedagogical exercises I have developed over the years are conceived to liberate the student through some form of conceptual disorientation or "involution of thought." Moments of instability offer passage to a more radicalized conception of architectural practices.

Pedagogical approaches must be updated to reflect the way that computers dramatically altered the conventions of architectural representation at the end of the twentieth century. New softwares make readily available highly complex form-finding and time-based modeling techniques that, up until ten years ago, would have been considered futuristic. But the accepted practice throughout most architecture schools at the beginning of the 21st century is still the traditional approach of actualizing a three-dimensional architectural object that excludes the pressures of time and growth capabilities. In other words, no provision has been made in the protocols of physical modeling to keep apace with the virtual experiments presently under development.

PLATE 4.09

STEVEN HOLL

I cherish individual students' ideas. If they start with something that looks like what I would do, I push them to do their own work. I don't allow them to start making forms if they cannot articulate their ideas and I try to encourage them to bring their deepest thoughts to whatever is being investigated in the studio. On one hand, I find critics who try to operate their own work through the students problematic. It's a violation of the student's autonomy and it's a corruption of the critic's work. On the other hand, I respect certain people's ability to catalyze students around a single project. Together, they produce a project that is basically the instructor's work, but it becomes larger than life and therefore assumes another role. One of the more successful experiments was Hani Rashid's 220-Minute Museum, where all the students built Hani's piece but had their own fragments inside it. On a pedagogical level, however, I do not believe that the instructor should use the studio to explore the issues they want to explore in practice or outside of the studio. The students should be thinking for themselves; that is when they really learn. If you are given a direction, you are really not thinking, you are just following—you might as well go work in an office. When my students put all of their work up on the wall at the end of the term, it looks different.

You have said that you find it offensive when critics operate their own work through the studio. In 1993, your studio program was a museum of science and you were simultaneously working on the Cranbrook Institute of Science. What is the difference?

Although we had the commission, we had not begun the Cranbrook Institute of Science at that point. I read the science section of the *New York Times* every Tuesday front-to-back because science is a field that is really accelerating. I am trying to explore some of the scientific properties that have architectural implications. Science as a general topic is inspirational and I could easily do another museum of science. I have known critics to take the site and the brief that they are working on, and give it as a studio problem. That used to be a way of teaching, but it's problematic. It's really important to get practitioners in the studio because if ideas have no possibility of ever being concretized in real material and space, they do not have the same implications. I like to see people who struggle to make things out of physical materials and it's important for the younger teachers to build. Those wonderful ideas reach a kind of catharsis and that moment is excit-

STEVEN HOLL

FIG. 134 Steven Holl, *Cranbrook Institute of Science*, Bloomfield Hills, Michigan, 1998.

FIG. 135 Jason Sandy, *Eclipse*, Advanced Studio V, Steven Holl, critic, Fall 1999.

ing. I encourage my studio to make physical models because then they have to deal with the resistance, translucency, and transparency of material.

PLATES 4.13–4.14

How do you teach students?

It takes two steps. For example, if you are teaching film students, first you teach them how to see a film like a critic, then you teach them to see a film like a filmmaker. For architecture students, first you look at buildings from the point of view of making the architecture that you want. If you are interested in making a topological architecture, you look at buildings for their latent topologies and their performance as topological buildings. Then if you are a good teacher, you turn them into filmmakers or producers of architecture.

There are several models of teaching. The model preferred by students and academic institutions is for the faculty to act as a critic because it causes the least tension between the students and the faculty. The student pursues a particular interest and the faculty member then evaluates the project. That is an ineffective model. I am in favor of the "I tell you" model where students do what I say. The history of architectural education supports that kind of teaching. It requires more time on the part of the teacher, and demands suppression of the student's own self-interest, sense of self-importance, and narcissistic impulses. It is difficult to charge students high tuition and then ask them to set aside their own interests, but if you look at the history of great teaching in architecture, it is this form of teaching that has the best record.

A school must decide whether to expose the student to a large number of competing arguments or compel the student to become an expert in one argument, like Cooper does. The current studio environment at Columbia produces the most sophisticated architectural students as members of an audience, but it is often superficial and not functional. They know a little bit about a lot of stuff.

Does that mean that you have either a strong pedagogy or creative freedom?

If Columbia's education were merely a studio program, these would be opposed. However, through a body of seminars and coursework that teaches both the historical and intellectual foundations of becoming an independent critical thinker, you get the tools necessary to make judgments.

In music education, there are two kinds of teaching. The first entirely subordinates the student to the grueling processes of the teacher. The second happens long after students have graduated and have demonstrated the capacity to perform with an independent voice. This is a form of coaching where somebody listens to them and responds to them as a critic. Coaching is important in architecture too, but the supposition is that there is no inadequacy or defective knowledge that has to be supplemented. You are essentially entering into a discussion at the critical level. The problem with studios that use critical techniques is that they have to do two things that are mutually exclusive: supplement deficient knowledge and at the same time treat the student as a colleague and peer. I think it's corrupt.

Is it an either/or condition or an additive condition?
To find out, I studied what I thought was another really great successful
pedagogy that had the institution in mind, i.e. method acting, which is
incredible because it is a pedagogy that is also a theory of acting. It is successful, not because all the actors come out well-trained and the same, but
because they all come out different. There are seventeen exercises that
enable each actor to find his or her own expressive personality through a
set of techniques.

JEFFREY KIPNIS

Does teaching contribute to the evolution of your research and thinking?
I actually like to teach this year's material, not last year's material and not
next year's material. I like the idea of teaching as a way to both deepen and
refine whatever my present thinking is. It gives me more focus both academically and professionally and allows for a broader kind of experiment
where I can roster the different characters of the school, my office, publications, and exhibitions. I will take either active projects or active research
and use them as the subject matter for the studios and seminars.

GREG LYNN

FIG. 136 Greg Lynn, *Predator*,
1999.

The teaching of architecture is the teaching of a way to critically think
about the process of making. For us, what we discuss is not necessarily the
best or the most efficient way to do something or even the way that yields
the most, but we are interested in the cultural consequences of a particular
design research and its production. Teaching architecture gives you the
great luxury of continually being asked, "Why?"

WILLIAM MACDONALD

I am not interested in academically based intellectual investigations that
have no translation in the real world. Columbia brings people together to
collaborate, produce a product, and then return to their own realms. We all
have our own individual lives. The product of that collaboration is very
rich. There is a very mature recognition at the School that although everyone will do their own thing, everybody has a valid place within the system.

VICTORIA MEYERS

Part of the unconscious ideology of the School, if you look carefully at what
is happening, is that the students perceive an "either/or" condition, which is
unfortunate because the greatest potential exists in the in-between.
see COMPETITION; METHODOLOGY; PEDAGOGY, COLUMBIA; REAL; RESISTANCE;
STUDIO/PRACTICE

JESSE REISER

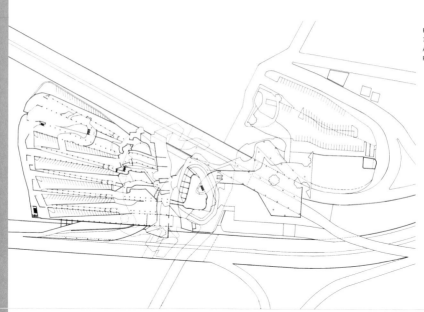

FIG. 137 Rhett Russo,
Television Programs Mall,
Advanced Studio V, Jesse
Reiser, critic, Fall 1994.

technique

see PROCESS

technology

"[A]rchitects should be encouraged to discriminate between science-fiction maximization of high technology as an end in itself and the deployment of an appropriate technology as a means to a liberative and poetic end. In my view, one cannot make claims for the total independence of function from form (and hence from formalization) without risking the loss of our capacity to articulate and enrich the 'micro-space' that is so essential to the liberation of the species in a corporeal sense. That we will be able to achieve all this in the future through the push-button activation of electronic servo-mechanisms (Henry Miller's air-conditioned nightmare) is neither technologically convincing nor experientially reassuring. The maximization of air conditioning (sealed windows) is just like all the other technological excesses of our time, like the overuse of insecticides and nitrates in agriculture and the gratuitous use of antibiotics in medicine. Surely high-tech may occasionally be the appropriate technique, but we should always keep above our desks the Loosian motto: There is no point in inventing anything unless it is an improvement."[1]

KENNETH FRAMPTON
1. Sara Hart, "Technology, Place, and Architecture" (interview), *Architecture* 88, no. 7 (July 1999): 116.

"At the end of the century it seems that the teaching of technology may be best approached through two strategies; (i) the teaching of current technique through analytical case-studies of contemporary building culture and (ii) the teaching of technology through simplified comprehensive design projects in order to expose the student to the task of synthesising different techniques."[2]

2. "Seven Points for the Millennium: An Untimely Manifesto," *Journal of Architecture* 5, no. 1 (Spring 2000): 23.

"[A]rchitecture offers the hope of returning to us all those experiential qualities; light, material, smell, texture, that we have been deprived of by the increasingly synthetic environment of images on video screens. Architecture is an antidote to an existence which is synthesized in the space of TV and

STEVEN HOLL
3. Alejandro Zaera Polo, "A Conversation with Steven Holl" (interview), *El Croquis* 78 (1996): 28–29.

lived out in sheetrock apartment buildings with low ceilings and synthetic carpets. As soon as you turn the machine off and call for your Chinese takeout, you are sitting in a mean environment which doesn't go away just because you can plug yourself into a completely synthesized environment. The challenge is to raise architecture back up to its role of framing our daily lives. I doubt that complete simulation of the environment could ever take precedence over concrete experiential space. I think architecture still has an essential role to play within these emerging technologies."[3]

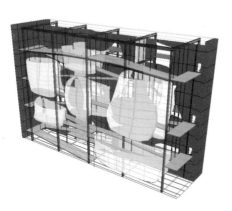 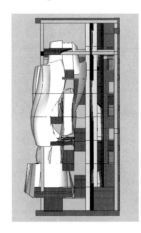

FIG. 138 Elissaret Chryssochoides, *Laboratory/Museum of Water, New Haven, Connecticut*, Advanced Studio V, Steven Holl, critic, Fall 1998.

For the dormitory project at MIT, the rooms are located around a social space that acts as an interior street. We were also trying to make this a solar-stacked building that would absorb heat in the winter and draw it out in the summer. There is an array of solar cells hidden on the roof that operate small high-tech fans to pull the air out. It is a low-tech green building, which is going to be more important as we get further into the 21st century. Paul Virilio talks about this other kind of ecology in a new book called *Open Sky*. He outlines a polemic regarding a gray ecology; things gradually disappear and you find yourself missing an entire dimension of existence. The questions he raises need to be grappled with as a kind of weathered call to thought. There is a neurosis about the unknown, but anything that questions what is going on or instigates critical thought should be part of the academic world.

STEVEN HOLL

Architecture is hard. It is a sacrifice, a struggle, and a commitment, but it has an amazing power to change the way we live our daily lives. Maybe I am a skeptic, but I am interested in peculiar events like the crash of the central file server at Columbia where the students lost all of their digital files and only those with physical models had projects. The more society connects to one electronic circuitry, the more vulnerable we are, so it is a strange moment now where everybody has their tongues hanging out just dripping with enthusiasm without understanding the consequences. I like the way Frank Gehry works with the CATIA system by building a physical model first, measuring it, and then digitizing it. The process begins with the mind, the hand, and the heart and then gets input into a very sophisticated system in order to build. I begin with a watercolor and the mind—an important argument that counters the likes of William Gibson.

You speak about "the spatial and instrumental use of technology" repeatedly in your programs. The instrumental aspects are clear. What are the spatial implications?

In the Angelika Project, which we did with Kryzstof Wodizcko, we were interested in participating simultaneously with five different protocols—the theater, the "lobby," the Web, the home, the workplace—and we used them both spatially and instrumentally in terms of a "feedback network system"; we called it a "lobbyingforbitparts": a "cineplay." We installed experimental robotic cameras with remote controls and high-quality zoom lenses in the projection booths of the cinemas. The cameras were operational twenty-four hours a day for an eight-week period. The cameras and their lenses were set so that they could scan the entire surface of the screen but only a portion of the screen was allowed to be viewed. The controls for the cameras were directed from "loungebits" that we had built and installed in the lobby.

WILLIAM MACDONALD

FIG. 139 Kolatan/MacDonald Studio, *'lobbyingforbits,'* 1995.

The "loungebit," a kind of chaise longue, was derived from bits of the cinema (i.e., seats, backs of seats, arms of seats, supports, etc.). These groupings of elements were coevolved/transformed with their respective sites, in this case, the columns with counter "collars" located in the lobby of the cinema. The "loungebits" outfitted with a 4 x 6 LCD monitor and remote controls acted as invitations to the "lobbyists"—cinema customers waiting for their film in the lobby—to play our game. As the "lobbyist" scanned the screen, he or she was unknowingly capturing film sequences that were then loaded into a Web site that allowed access to these images from the home or work-place. The Web site also afforded the possibility of reediting the sequence or uploading your own film sequences or personal minutiae into the site. The Web site allowed a text- and image-based multi-user-dimensional space to be simultaneously linked on the screen. In turn, the text of these conversations (as subtitles) and reconstituted images were collected and then projected in the cinema during the time usually allotted for previews. The multi-user-dimensional space is and always has been a "public" condition—all kinds of people lurking and discussing—but the minute it was projected into the theater, it became another kind of public space—a gradational public space.

How does that differ from the panopticon, or the perception of surveillance versus the act of surveying?

It is an interesting comparison. What appears to be crucial here is not so much one mode over another, but the intersection of various modes.

SULAN KOLATAN

It is a feedback system, so it is not just about that singular moment of two systems intersecting but rather it declares an organizational relationship between multiple systems and their connections. In terms of your question, the difference might be that "lobbyingforbits" proposes a nonhierarchical evolving field condition.

see ARCHITECTURE CULTURE; BOUNDARY; ELECTRO-SPHERE; FRONTIER/EDGE/MARGIN; LOCAL/GLOBAL; PEDAGOGY, COLUMBIA; PERFORMANCE; SERIALITY/MASS PRODUCTION; STUDIO/PRACTICE; STUDIOS, ADVANCED; VIRTUAL/ACTUAL

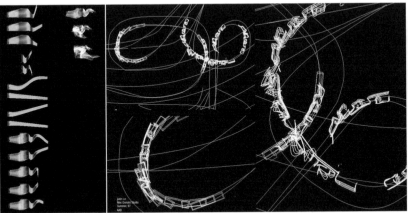

FIG. 140 Roger Hom, *Composited Architectures for the Port Authority Bus Terminal*, Advanced Studio, William MacDonald, critic, Summer 1997.

FIG. 141 Jia Lin Le, *Composited Architectures for the Port Authority Bus Terminal*, Advanced Studio, William MacDonald, critic, Summer 1997.

tectonic see DRAWING; MATERIAL/MATERIALITY; TRACE

theory *You object to the tendency to derive architecture from philosophy, yet you talk about many similar ideas. How do you avoid pulling from those areas?*
Going to the original source is imperative. Architects use linguistic models and theories taken from other disciplines because they have already been legitimized, but those observations and reflections are often of existing conditions.

LISE ANNE COUTURE

Lise Anne and I object to the habitual quoting and citing of other people's ideas simply to substantiate one's own argument. We are more compelled by a pursuit for some form of originality, so when Lise Anne says we go to the source she recognizes that there is a moment when research and analysis compels us to think and create.

HANI RASHID

We always resist compartmentalization and the belief that we have to theorize and legitimize everything before we produce work. There has been a tendency in the past 10 to 20 years toward a preeminence of theory over the built artifact. The ability to see architecture without a theoretical road map is lost. The construction of architecture is the making of theory, as far as we are concerned, and not the filling of a prescription.

LISE ANNE COUTURE

The gates separating Columbia from the outside world are mirrored within the School itself. The relation between the theory sequence and the design

MARK WIGLEY

T

studio is akin to the divide between Columbia and the outside world. Traditionally, in architecture schools, theory is discussed in the morning while design is executed in the afternoon. In the morning, you pause, withdraw, and reflect, and then in the afternoon, you put those ideas into practice. Ironically, however, what is produced in the afternoon is still regarded by the outside world as very theoretical.

PLATES 4.15–4.16

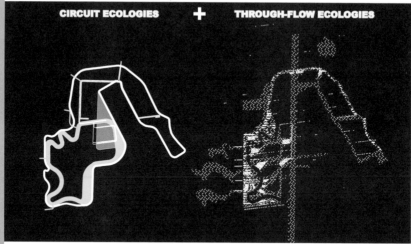

CIRCUIT ECOLOGIES   +   THROUGH-FLOW ECOLOGIES

FIG. 142 Field Operations, Stan Allen and James Corner, *Downsview Park Competition,* 2000.

"Procedures are not merely the objects of a theory. They organize the very construction of theory itself. Far from being external to theory, or from staying on its doorstep, [these] procedures provide *a field of operations within which theory is itself produced.*"[4]

SEE ARCHITECTURE CULTURE; DIAGRAM; INTERDISCIPLINARY; PEDAGOGY, COLUMBIA; PROCESS; REAL; TEACHING

4. Michel de Certeau, *Heterologies: Discourse on the Other,* trans. Brian Massumi (Minneapolis: University of Minnesota Press, 1986), 192.

time

I want to react against a concept of the continuum. I am most interested in forestalling a "conclusion" that a continuum provides. I am concerned with expanding the present, what I term the *thickened present,* as a means to subvert reaching any one conclusion or definite end.

KAREN BAUSMAN

"Proust's *Remembrance of Things Past* is one of the first works of literature to offer a modern reading of time and space. Proust is concerned with what is transient and what is permanent in his desire to render time eternal. Joseph Frank asserts, 'To experience the passage of time, Proust had learned, it was necessary to rise above it and grasp both the past and present simultaneously in a moment of what he called 'pure time.' But 'pure time,' obviously, is not time at all—it is space. And, by the discontinuous presentation of character Proust forces the reader to juxtapose disparate images spatially, in a moment of time, so that the experience of time's passage is communicated directly to his sensibility.' By giving architectural form to Proust's ideas of memory, we will cross his threshold of 'pure time' and reinterpret shelter for the late 20th century."[5]

LESLIE GILL
5. *Memory: Transience and Permanence of Dwelling,* Advanced Studio VI, Spring 1993.

*Sanford Kwinter has said that architects, not architecture, have a stopping
problem. How do you work with your students or in practice to reevaluate
this time-related stopping problem through the medium of architecture?*

Time is related to practice; clients, cities, and real people frequently have
bigger stopping problems than do architects. Architecture is trying to
understand the dynamic forces that have been at play for 200 years of capitalist regimes. Walter Benjamin, for one, addressed the remnants of an ideology that attempted to frame art in a stable format, or at least frame our
understanding of art in stable terms. In the 19th century, artistic responses
(in Benjamin's terms) masked this dynamism in a nostalgic art, while modern architects argued that modern society should strive for some fixed form
of relations based on modern ideals. In the early part of the 20th century,
the new art form of the cinema created an art more congruent with "reality,"
hence a potential relation with architecture as it is experienced in a dis-
tracted mode, that is, architecture as experienced "on the street." Benjamin
poses a radical challenge to art and architecture in this analysis, suggest-

THOMAS HANRAHAN

T

ing that our mode of perception is different in the modern world and that modes of artistic production should change in order to keep up. In a very idiosyncratic and elliptical way his writings challenge those artists who claim to have found the "real" answer to contemporary artistic expression. He seems to say that the very notion is absurd, as contemporary capitalism constantly destabilizes society.

Architecture that is nostalgic tends to disguise this instability, while modernism hoped for a perfection and stability in society (often in authoritarian fantasies) that would allow modernism to "fix" itself as the legitimate and stable expression of the society. One idea is based on anxiety, the other on an Enlightenment delusion. Architects finally abandoned that effort, which was a last gasp of that Enlightenment need to perfect everything.

If architecture is to have any meaning or role in society, it has to have a stopping problem. Sanford is addressing architecture's contentious proposition with respect to capitalism—at a certain point you have to stop and make it visible and concrete, and it has to last beyond a couple of minutes in order to turn a profit. Architects play an antagonistic, critical, contentious, and interesting role in society today. There is a constant rebuilding and reevaluation, but even then it is not completely stable in the conventional sense. Architecture can be an investigation on paper or in a model and it will be subject to transformations in time.

At Columbia, I designed my studio exercises to introduce a plan/section relationship to the students. In my studios, we tried to understand the plan as a diagram activated by the body, a route, and the section as an active or dynamic element, even if it's literally a series of frames transforming in time. We tried to emphasize programs like theater, music, cinema, and the

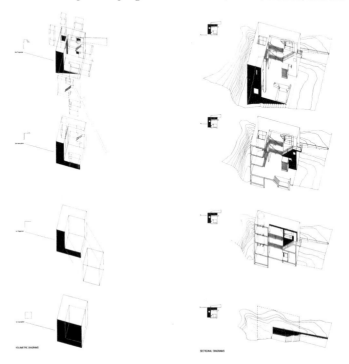

FIG. 144 Hanrahan + Meyers, *Inside-Out House*, anticipated completion 2004.

notion that architecture is both activated by the time in which a body occupies it, and subject to transformations similar to those within machines, organic elements, and cities.

"The studio addressed the issue of time-based structures and motion-based organizations in architectural design.... Building forms and organizations were evolved through the interaction of disparate forces and gradients of influence in time-based environments within which the designer guides their often undecidable growth, transformation, and mutation. This shift from determinism to directed indeterminacy is central to the development of a dynamic design method and will present a new role for design direction and authorship."[6]

GREG LYNN
6. *Tate Gallery Competition*, Advanced Studio V, Fall 1995.

"Time in architecture is directly related to the structural bays of a building. A structural grid, for example, can demarcate a specifically timed rhythm when calibrated by the human footstep. This rhythm establishes one's perceptual sense of the time it takes to move through space in a manner similar to the pulse in music, or the human heartbeat, or fleeting image in a mirror or daguerreotype.... Science and the technologies that accompany it continue to change our understanding of time as it is experienced in architectural space, as the liberating potential of reductive form and endless space creates a series of fleeting perceptions and momentary experiences. The idea of temporality is a central, but very elusive idea in our work. It is found at unusual points in space, or moments of tangency where one visual world collapses as another momentarily appears."[7]

VICTORIA MEYERS
7. "Space and the Perception of Time," *Journal of Architectural Education* 53, no. 2 (November 1999): 91.

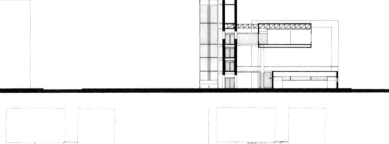

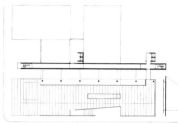 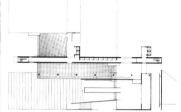

FIG. 145 Chy-Do Lee, *Time: Passage Way*, Advanced Studio V, Victoria Meyers, critic, Fall 1995.

Architecture can make time stand still or speed up, and that is one of the things I try to do in my work. I also try to push my students to build a means of registering and knowing about time into their architecture. There are many different ways of doing it. It has to do with different architectural devices that create various windows that either push the space out or freeze-frame it.

VICTORIA MEYERS

PLATES 4.17–4.18

SEE DIAGRAM; IDEA/CONCEPT; PHENOMENON/PHENOMENOLOGY; PRESSURE; SERIALITY/ MASS PRODUCTION; SITE; SLICE; SPACE; STUDIOS, CORE; TREND

trace

"In architecture the trace is produced out of the movement of process and the heterogeneity of its procedures. Translation is always already at work within the discontinuity of architecture's operations. Buildings do not simply embody the abstract concepts that enable them but erase those concepts—incompletely—in the assertive physicality of construction. The trace, if it remains, persists as an excess unaccountable according to the simple logic of the tectonic."[8]

STAN ALLEN
8. "Tracks, Trace, Tricks," *ANY* 0 (May/June 1993): 10.

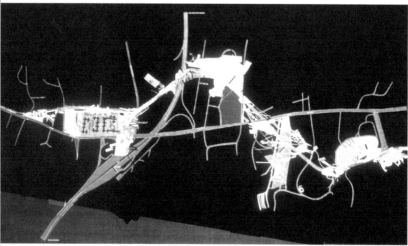

FIG. 146 RAAUm, *Croton Aqueduct*, 1992.

"This studio developed architecture by following a path divined from the traces within a specific literature. We assimilate knowledge through the dissemination of signs or clues. Though those signs exist with or without our interaction, it is our imaginative interpretation that breathes life into the indexical sign. Traces of architecture exist already within the ruined fragments strewn throughout rural and urban landscape—they are simply waiting to be decoded. This studio posits to track the traces of a particular site, mimicking the cathartic journey from city to country found within selected novels and films."[9]

LESLIE GILL
9. *Without Resting: The Tracking of Home Within the Mystery/Spy Genre*, Advanced Studio, Summer 1993.

trace

Merriam Webster's Dictionary

1. (a) a mark or line left by something that has passed; (b) a path, trail, or road made by the passage of animals, people, or vehicles
2. a sign or evidence of some past thing
3. something traced or drawn: as (a) the marking made by a recording; (b) the ground plan of a military installation or position either on a map or on the ground
4. (a) the intersection of a line or plane with a plane; (b) the usually bright line or spot that moves across the screen of a cathode-ray tube; the path taken by such a line or spot
5. (a) a minute and often barely detectable amount or indication; (b) an amount of a chemical constituent not always quantitatively determinable because of minuteness

see EXCAVATION; MAP/MAPPING; PROCESS

tradition

"I agree with Hans Georg Gadamer's contention that there is no innovation without tradition and no tradition without innovation. Tradition has to be culturally renewed, but you cannot create significantly without tradition. Certain modern ideologies are absolutely obsessed with rupture, where tradition is to be discarded, but it seems to me that a constant reinterpretation of tradition is what culture is ultimately about."[10]

KENNETH FRAMPTON
10. "An Interview with Kenneth Frampton," *Oz* 20 (1998): 79.

transformation

"Together with this hyperaccelerated growth/multiplication there is a proliferation of transportation/information technologies. In which specific ways are these two tendencies interrelated? What are the transformative effects of transportation/information technologies on the city? How and where can these effects be manipulated and controlled? Where does the interruption of movement occur and how can the gap be spatially as well as programmatically appropriated beyond the obvious 'architecture' of transition or an 'architecture of waiting' (stops/terminals/piers)? It is here that existing practices will play a formative/informative role in suggesting 'augmentary' programs and spaces."[11]

SULAN KOLATAN
11. *Chiasmati-city (Case 1, Istanbul)*, Advanced Studio V, Fall 1993.

PLATES 4.19–4.21

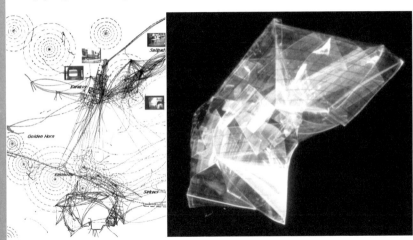

FIG. 147 Group Project, *Chiasmati-city (Case 1, Istanbul)*, Advanced Studio V, Sulan Kolatan, critic, Fall 1993.

FIG. 148 Jose Herrasti, *Malltown Manhattan*, Advanced Studio, Sulan Kolatan and William MacDonald, critics, Summer 1996.

"This studio addressed an array of constructions too large to be mere objects yet too small to constitute even a small work of architecture. It is a domain formerly closed within the category of 'interior.' Yet even this label is inadequate because it upholds the dualism that this studio attempts to derail. The process involves the constituents of the interior: furniture, fittings, coverings, etc., in a transformational matrix that might fundamentally alter formal and social space."[12]

REISER/UMEMOTO
12. Architecture "One to One," Advanced Studio, Summer 1996.

"It was the intention of this studio to address aspects of domesticity through strictly architectural means, that is, to leave the expository mode to the critic or social scientist and instead engage in the transformative project(ion) that is peculiar to architecture itself. A positive reading of Walter Benjamin's statement suggest that new and unforeseen modalities of dwelling might be produced in this way."[13]

13. *Sub-Urbanity*, Advanced Studio VI, Spring 1996.

On the one hand, Columbia sets trends, yet on the other, many trends are accepted without question by the students. Is that a concern?
I am a big fan of trends. People coalesce around certain strategies and ideas for a period of time, and they spread very rapidly throughout the School. You can exhaust an entire topic and move on, whereas professional practice moves slower.

THOMAS HANRAHAN

It cannot be underestimated how fashionable Columbia is as a school, and how important it is that it remains a fashionable school. Oscar Wilde's dictum that if fashion were not so terrible we would not have to change it four times a year holds true for architecture right now. I am interested in the ability of architecture to think through changeability as a conceptual design provocation rather than as an obstacle to timelessness and good taste. You can either try to change yourself and your teaching every year, or you can just build a machine that changes it for you while keeping the work fashionable. Most other design fields have found ways to build variation and change into their discourse. They think, conceptualize, and theorize change and evolution in a way that architects have yet to do. Being in such a fashionable place forced me start to thinking about branding, variation, and all of these market issues. The fact that it is a fashionable, global school, located in New York City, forces the issue even more. You cannot underestimate the culture of the School and the need for it to stay fresh. It is a very particular school in a particular place with a culture of novelty just swarming around it.

GREG LYNN

There is a tendency within architecture to want to codify one's work as one is making it, to justify it, to make it a bigger event.
There is a conversation that goes on at Columbia that can be trendy. I do not often participate in it because I think architecture only comes from individuals who lead lives that revolve around a meditation about space; if your work does not spring from that source, it can be thin. I have a desire to communicate with the world on my own terms and therefore I want to set out what those terms are. I am interested in Tadao Ando's and Alvaro Siza's work and in work that expresses unique positions in the world.

There is a tendency in the United States to create stars and to follow trends, and every ten years there is a whole group of buildings that are constructed to represent those fashions. Curves, for example, are very fashionable right now; yet, in a few years that group of buildings will most likely look dated. They are usually built by contractors who do not quite know why they are doing what they are doing, but they are doing their best to simulate the architect's design. We designed a gym for the New York City Housing Authority called "Wave Line," in which we designed a slightly curved roof. It took months for us to calibrate the alignments of the various pieces so that we could get roofing contractors to bid on it.

I met with a client recently who, after talking to me and reviewing my work said, "It seems what you are really interested in is to create things that are timeless, undatable." I responded, "You are absolutely correct." I feel incredible angst over anything that has a time frame associated with

VICTORIA MEYERS

it. The trendiness that flies through architecture can be very datable. I prefer to exist outside of it. I am much more interested in the way that an artist exists in the world in relation to the history of the human race. I am less interested in whether or not the thing that I do is the most current thing that would make the cover of a glossy publication.

I also try to bring that out in my students. If I see someone producing something that mimics what is around them or is fashionable, I push them to investigate their own unique thoughts and rethink what they are doing. That is the only way that you can really be in the world as an artist, and that is what I have always looked for in my students.

see PEDAGOGY, COLUMBIA

PLATES 4.22–4.23

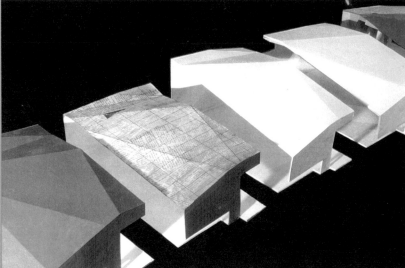

FIG. 149 Hanrahan + Meyers, *Latimer Gardens Community Center: "Wave-Line," 2002.*

type

"The studio attempted a different apprehension of type by multiplying its conventional limits; or, put another way, by encouraging a fundamental shift from type understood as the essential, static geometric lineament underlying building to type as a performative condition. A convergence of flows; of graduated scales and limits—to which an inscription of type in the conventional sense represents but an artifact in a field of flux. Complexity theory provides a compelling model and term for this shift. We will use the theoretical physicist Murray Gell-Mann's theories on complex adaptive systems and his concept of the 'schema' as a structure that exceeds type."[14]

REISER/UMEMOTO
14. *From Type to Schema: Westchester County Center,* Advanced Studio V, Fall 1995

type
1. (a) a person or thing believed to foreshadow another; (b) one having qualities of a higher category; (c) a lower taxonomic category selected as a standard of reference for a higher category; also: a specimen or series of specimens on which a taxonomic species or subspecies is actually based
2. a distinctive mark or sign

Merriam Webster's Dictionary

3. a rectangular block usually of metal bearing a relief character from which an inked print can be made

4. (a) qualities common to a number of individuals that distinguish them as an identifiable class: as (1): the morphological, physiological, or ecological characters by which relationship between organisms may be recognized; (2): the form common to all instances of a linguistic element; (b) a typical and often superior specimen; (c) a member of an indicated class or variety of people; (d) a particular kind, class, or group; (e) something distinguishable as a variety

see PROGRAM

typology

"Typology originated with the formation of civic institutions during the Enlightenment. As the social, political, and technical roles of those institutions were called into question, the corresponding typologies lost their special capacity to order and represent the space of these institutions."[15]

STAN ALLEN
15. *Logistics of Context: A Library for Columbia University*, Advanced Studio V, Fall 1996.

typology

1. a doctrine of theological types; especially: one holding that things in Christian belief are prefigured or symbolized by things in the Old Testament

2. study of or analysis or classification based on types or categories

see FRAME; PROGRAM

Merriam Webster's Dictionary

U

urban

"The various mechanisms of deployment and dissemination of information globally have created auspiciously powerful structures both within and outside the public realm. News on demand, Home Shopping Networks, the Internet, cellular communications, video conferencing, have all created vast arrays of virtual economies and communities. Media itself has reached the status of being a self-sustaining culture, with efficient and eloquent management of images, concepts, lifestyles, demographics, and politics. Shrouded within these vectors are the new spaces that we will inhabit. The studio utilized digital technologies and techniques to unravel certain aspects of media culture and by extension, created new architectures for a yet to be understood media urbanism."[1]

HANI RASHID
1. *Media City: Architecture at the Interval*, Advanced Studio V, Fall 1994.

"Considering the site of Manhattan's waterfront edge as an event of urban fray, the research critically highlighted the ideological battle latent in a territory of heterogeneous pressures. Paradoxical in its nature, the program is simultaneously in a state of being and in pursuit of somewhere, and thereby personifies the cultural crisis that confounds contemporary architecture."[2]

EVAN DOUGLIS
2. *An Architecture of Waiting*, Core Studio II, Spring 1997.

"The wilderness is no longer the natural environment. Instead, it is the abandoned and decaying centers of our urban fabric."[3]

LESLIE GILL
3. *Prototype of a Post-Industrial Resource, Newburgh, NY*, Advanced Studio VI, Spring 1996.

"The late-20th-century urban site occupies a vertical interstice between a quasi-perpetual mobility on the one hand, and the dislocation experienced through the powers of a ubiquitous technology on the other. This 'dis-place' of shifting boundaries and unlimited thresholds defies traditional definitions. Its constituent elements consist of aggregate linkages within a global and local scene of the transportation/information metropolis."[4]

SULAN KOLATAN
4. *Urban Penumbra: Public Space in the New American City – Atlanta 1996*, Advanced Studio IV, Spring 1994.

"The proliferation of tract housing, commercial strips, spec office buildings, and shopping malls along webs of ever-expanding technological infrastructure has displaced the distinct urban center with its attendant suburbs; so much so that the dependency on the urban implied in the word *suburban* begs for a redefinition both in terminology and more importantly at the level of implementation."[5]

REISER/UMEMOTO
5. *Sub-Urbanity*, Advanced Studio VI, Spring 1995.

Columbia is in New York City. The School cannot but take advantage of this condition. It has led to overcrowding and congestion in the studios, but it also has meant intense daily interaction and inventiveness. The School as it has become could exist nowhere but in a major metropolis; you would not get the same quality and quantity of young teachers and critics elsewhere.

BERNARD TSCHUMI

U

"The Graduate School of Architecture, Planning, and Preservation offers a series of distinctive programs. The educational objectives of these programs deal in different ways with one open-ended field: urban society and its future. The presence of several areas of study within a single school enables a critical understanding of the forces that affect the building of spaces and the making of cities, so as to encourage appropriate formulation of original concepts, designs, and policies."[6]

see CITY; FIELD; HYBRID; PEDAGOGY, COLUMBIA; SCALE

BERNARD TSCHUMI

6. *Columbia University Bulletin 2000–2002, Graduate School of Architecture, Planning and Preservation* 34, no. 3 (2000), 5.

V

"Architects today have at their disposal the tool of Virtual Reality Mark-up Language (VRML). Its significance, however, is not its potential for representation of built space nor for entertainment. Instead, what might intrigue us as architects is the revisiting of the problematic of perception, formation of meaning, perspectival certainty, plasticity, and form coupled with the procedures of dislocation, disembodiment, illusion, and distraction. VRML experiments now found throughout the Web seem to be conspicuously devoid of architectural 'content' and, for the most part, are essentially disembodied presences. How then does the 'architect' engage this tool? Can the production of simultaneously 'occupied' and transformational space reveal a new spatiality? Does the aspect of record, memory, and mutation afford any spatial possibilities for architecture? Is the transmission of spatiality a form of information exchange particular to our time?"[1]

HANI RASHID
1. *Informing Interiorities: Prototypical Investigations in VRML*, Advanced Studio V, Fall 1997.

FIG. 150 Asymptote, *NYSE Operations Center*, New York, New York,1999.

We are interested in investigating the realm of the digital, in terms of building this reality. For example, we built a virtual environment for the New York Stock Exchange that allows people to map and correlate a myriad of different types of information and construct meaning in a three-dimensional environment. Given a different set of constraints in the virtual realm, there are certain opportunities that one can begin to exploit in terms of architecture. By inhabiting that realm, our clients question the environment in which they perform. The project we did for the Stock Exchange is a very robust, pragmatic, and large virtual reality environment. There was no room for style but rather the design had to be extremely logical and efficient. This may sound like a throwback to a functionalist model, but we needed

LISE ANNE COUTURE

to rely on a longer history of architecture, and discover ways in which perception, reasoning, and movement would facilitate experience. What was interesting about working on both the Virtual Exchange and the actual intervention on the trading floor was that on one side of the studio I would hear people on the phone talking to structural engineers and general contractors, and on the other side of the room, we were e-mailing our programming engineers in Israel with concerns about wireframe efficiency, data streaming, and pixel real estate. That reverberated into our reinterpretation of program and site by taking into account the idea of being in two places at the same time. It collapses the distance and time by virtue of technology.

PLATES 4.24–4.27

Through projects such as the Virtual Stock Exchange and the Virtual Guggenheim, we have become very aware of our role as architects, but more important, as spatialists. I have become very interested in the streaming phenomenon as it pertains to data and information and we are exploring its potential as a spatial entity. My students are working with VRML, and I encourage them to make virtual environments that have been implicated by streaming data with the hope that they can propose innovative and inspired architectural environments.

HANI RASHID

  We are looking at streaming data and virtual reality with the intent of building a "smart building"—not the Bill Gates clapping-hands-and-music-plays idea of smart building—to see how these new technologies are changing the experience of space and how architecture might be transformed on many levels by the integration of new technologies that enable movement and mutation.

FIG. 151 Martin/Baxi Architects, *Timeline: A Retroactive Master Plan for Silicon Valley*, 2001.

When computers first arrived in the design studios there was less of a focus on reality than there is now. Why do you think this shift occurred?
I suppose you could call them the early days of digital architecture, even though we are really about three decades into it. This time however, begins

REINHOLD MARTIN

with a fantasy about what architecture is. A computer is a very adaptable device that can be configured in different ways and architects have used these particular configurations to manifest certain kinds of fantasies about architecture.

We are exploring this interpenetration of the real and the virtual, although these categories are very provisional. Among the architects who have identified themselves with digital media, the logic has taken the form of an ideology that is effective in closing down alternative ways of thinking about the way technology, architecture, and culture work together.

see E-GORA; FRONTIER/EDGE/MARGIN; INDEX; MATERIAL/MATERIALITY; PERFORMANCE; REAL; SPACE, SURFACE; TEACHING; URBAN

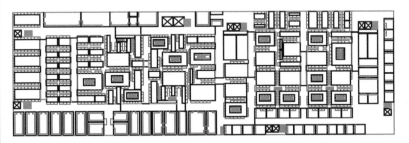

FIG. 152 Mike Latham, *Entropy Lab*, Advanced Studio V, Reinhold Martin, critic, Fall 1999.

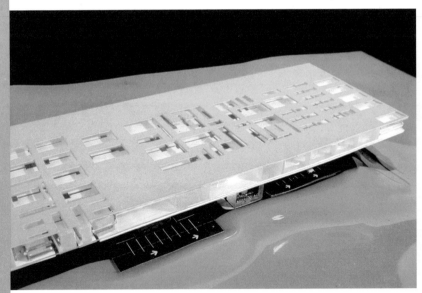

W

waiting

"The provisional ebb and flow of crowds associated with 'waiting' raises the possibility of problematizing the notion of logistics. The need for a speedy movement of large numbers of persons, vehicles, etc., is not dissimilar from the pressures in the arenas of war or circus."[1]

SULAN KOLATAN
1. *Logics and Logistics of Waiting*, Advanced Studio IV, Spring 1995.

water

see PHENOMENON/PHENOMENOLOGY

watercolor

"Watercolor allows you to make bodies of light, to go from the bright to the dark. When I am making a series of perspectival views through a series of spaces and thinking about light, watercolor is a better medium than line drawing."[2]

see TECHNOLOGY

STEVEN HOLL
2. Alejandro Zaera Polo, "A Conversation with Steven Holl" (interview), *El Croquis* 78 (1996): 19.

FIG. 153 Steven Holl, *MIT Residence*, Cambridge, Massachusetts, 1999.

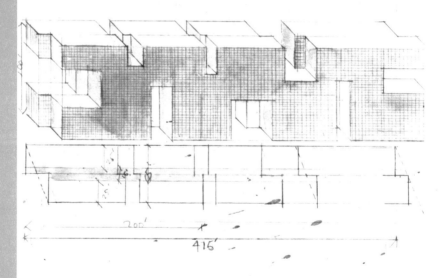

window

"[A window] is part of the building where an attitude toward space and materials is most clearly stated. Mies's minimalist use of material was clearly captured in his bronze window wall detail. Le Corbusier reinvented the window and 'cleaned-up' its messiness, clarifying the window's programmatic readings. He separated 'window' into component parts determined by function: opaque aerators juxtaposed fixed windows with glass for viewing and the 'brise-soleil' as a sun shade. The window necessarily deals with light. It can focus light into a formal element or fracture it, revealing its component colors. At the Bauhaus Johannes Itten used light

VICTORIA MEYERS
3. *Visibility/Invisibility*, Advanced Studio V, Fall 1994.

and color theory as a means of injecting a modern vision of spirituality into the building. As a receptor for sunlight, the window is also an instrument for measuring the seasons. In that sense it also can be used to measure time. Finally, the window deals with notions of visibility and invisibility. It is that part of the building where the interior can be exposed or not. By overtly choosing invisibility the building becomes enigmatic. Two antipodes are proposed for investigation: the clarity of glass versus the instability of the mask."[3]

writing

see EPIPHANY; GEOMETRY

W

Z

zero

"Zero Degree Architecture.... Equally an urban environment and an electronic machine, the City of Architecture is wary of aesthetic tendencies as well as of humanist theories directed toward formal morality. It is, instead, through the rigorous amplification of its programmatic logic that the school develops the conditions required for inquiry into the new century's architectural conditions."[1]

see LANGUAGE

BERNARD TSCHUMI
1. *Event Cities 2* (Cambridge, Mass.: MIT Press, 2000), 515, 521.

zip manifesto

"Manifesto: Each student wrote a short manifesto saying what architecture should stand for today.

Program: Each student was randomly assigned a program.

Site: Each student was randomly assigned a Manhattan zip code (10001–10044) as his or her site—any part of which was used.

Task: To develop a design that exemplified the attitude of the student's manifesto—as if this one commission (program/site) was the student's best chance to make his or her point.

Schedule: The first version of each student's manifesto was prepared before thinking about program or site. Discussions about which architects or projects the student admired or disliked and the state of architectural discourse today were used to identify each student's particular issues of concern. After each review, both the manifesto and project were revised to establish the strongest possible resonance between the final manifesto and the final design.

Goal: To produce stunning projects that have something polemical to say about the state of things today."[2]

MARK WIGLEY
2. *Zip Manifesto*, Advanced Studio VI, Spring 2001.

Contributors

Allen, Stan

Stan Allen is principal of Field Operations. He became Dean of the Princeton School of Architecture in 2002. At Columbia University's Graduate School of Architecture, Planning and Preservation he held the position of Associate Professor of Architecture, serving as Director of the Advanced Design Program from 1991 to 2002. After working with Richard Meier and Partners in New York and Rafael Moneo in Spain, he established his own practice in 1991. His urban projects have been published in *Points and Lines: Diagrams and Projects for the City* (1999) and his theoretical essays in *Practice: Architecture, Technique and Representation* (2000).

Asymptote
Lise Anne Couture and
Hani Rashid

Lise Anne Couture co-founded Asymptote in New York in 1988 with Hani Rashid. She received her Master of Architecture degree from Yale University in 1986. Couture has been a professor in the Department of Architecture at Parsons School of Design in New York since 1990. Hani Rashid received a Master of Architecture degree from the Cranbrook Academy of Art in 1985. He has been a professor at Columbia University since 1989, leading architectural design research and experimentation with respect to digital technologies since the inception of the School's Advanced Digital Design program. Recent projects by Asymptote include the Guggenheim Virtual Museum and the virtual trading floor of the New York Stock Exchange.

Bausman, Karen

Karen Bausman is principal of Karen Bausman + Associates, founded in 1995. Her recent work has focused on medium-scaled cultural institutions in urban and ex-urban areas and on the spatial and social implications of site and structure. She has taught at Columbia University since 1990. She received her professional degree in architecture from The Cooper Union for the Advancement of Science and Art in 1982.

Berman, Matthew

Matthew Berman is co-founder with partner Andrew Kotchen of workshop/apd, an architecture, planning, and design firm in New York City and Nantucket, Massachusetts. He received his Master of Architecture degree from Columbia University, and a Bachelor of Arts in Architecture and Spanish from Lehigh University in Pennsylvania. Prior to graduating from Columbia, he served as Assistant Director of the Institute for Tropical Architecture in San José, Costa Rica, and as Associate Editor of *ANY* magazine.

Couture, Lise Anne

see ASYMPTOTE

Dean, Kathryn

Kathryn Dean has taught design studios at Columbia University since 1991, and has been a Visiting Distinguished Professor at the University of Florida, Gainesville, and a Visiting Assistant Professor at Harvard University's

Graduate School of Design. She established her practice in New York City in 1991 with partner Charles Wolf. The firm's project Urban Interface Loft won a 1999 National AIA Honor Award. Dean was the 1987 Rome Prize Fellow of the American Academy in Rome.

Douglis, Evan

Evan Douglis studied at the Architectural Association in London prior to receiving a Bachelor of Architecture degree from The Cooper Union for the Advancement of Art and Science in New York and a Master of Architecture degree from Harvard University's Graduate School of Design. An adjunct professor at Columbia University for the last 12 years, he is also the Director of the Architecture Galleries there. A catalogue of his exhibition installations is forthcoming.

Frampton, Kenneth

Kenneth Frampton trained as an architect at the Architectural Association in London. He has worked as an architect and as an architectural historian and critic in England, Israel, and the United States. He is currently the Ware Professor of Architecture at Columbia University. He is the author of *Modern Architecture and the Critical Present* (1993), *Studies in Tectonic Culture* (1995), *American Masterworks* (1995), *Le Corbusier* (2001), and *Labor, Work and Architecture* (2002). His book *Modern Architecture: A Critical History* (1980) has been translated into 10 languages.

Gill, Leslie

Leslie Gill presently serves as a Trustee at The Cooper Union for the Advancement of Art and Science, where she was educated. She is an Adjunct Associate Professor at Columbia University and at Parsons School of Design, and a Visiting Critic at Harvard University's Graduate School of Design. She is Vice Chair of the Van Alen Institute: Projects in Public Architecture, and is actively involved in the New York State Council of the Arts and the Architectural League of New York. After 12 years as a founding partner of Bausman Gill Associates, she initiated her own practice, Leslie Gill Architect, in 1995.

Hanrahan, Thomas

see HANRAHAN + MEYERS

Hanrahan + Meyers
Thomas Hanrahan and
Victoria Meyers

Thomas Hanrahan and Victoria Meyers have practiced in Manhattan since 1985. Their work has focused on the fine arts and residential design, and includes galleries and performance spaces and houses for private clients. Thomas Hanrahan received his Bachelor of Architecture degree from the University of Illinois at Urbana-Champaign and his Master of Architecture degree from Harvard University's Graduate School of Design. He has taught at Columbia, Harvard, and Yale Universities, and is currently Dean of the Pratt Institute School of Architecture. Victoria Meyers received a Master of Architecture degree from Harvard's Graduate School of Design and a Bachelor's degree in Art History and Civil Engineering from Lafayette College in Pennsylvania. She has taught architecture at Columbia University since 1993.

Hawkinson, Laurie	Laurie Hawkinson is an architect and principal in the office of Smith-Miller + Hawkinson. She received her Master of Fine Arts degree from the University of California at Berkeley and her Bachelor of Architecture degree from The Cooper Union for the Advancement of Art and Science. She is currently an Assistant Professor of Architecture at Columbia University. Recent projects by Smith-Miller + Hawkinson include the Corning Museum of Glass in Corning, New York and the North Carolina Museum of Art in Raleigh, North Carolina (in collaboration with artist Barbara Kruger and landscape architect Nicholas Quennell).
Holl, Steven	Steven Holl established Steven Holl Architects in New York in 1976. A graduate of the University of Washington, Holl studied architecture in Rome, Italy in 1970 and did post-graduate work at the Architectural Association in London in 1976. Among his most recent honors are Progressive Architecture Awards (2000) for the Nelson-Atkins Museum of Art and the MIT Undergraduate Residence, the New York AIA Design Award (1999) for the Cranbrook Institute of Science in Bloomfield Hills, Michigan, and the National AIA Design Award (1999) for Kiasma, the Museum of Contemporary Art in Helsinki, Finland. Holl has taught at Columbia University since 1981.
Kipnis, Jeffrey	Jeffrey Kipnis is the Curator of Architecture and Design at the Wexner Center for the Arts in Columbus, Ohio, a Professor of Architecture at Ohio State University, and a Visiting Professor of Architecture at Columbia University. He is also the founder and former director of the Graduate Design Program of the Architectural Association of London. His publications include *In the Manor of Nietzsche* (1990), *Philip Johnson: the Glass House* (1993), *Chora L Works: Jacques Derrida and Peter Eisenman* (1997) (co-edited with Thomas Leeser), and *Perfect Acts of Architecture* (2001).
Kolatan, Sulan	see KOLATAN/MACDONALD
Kolatan/MacDonald Sulan Kolatan and William MacDonald	Born in Istanbul, Turkey, Sulan Kolatan received a Diplom Ingenieur degree from Rhenisch-Wesfalische Technische Hochschule in Aachen, Germany, and a Master of Science in Architecture and Building Design from Columbia University. She has taught at Columbia University since 1990. William MacDonald studied at the Architectural Association in London and received a Bachelor of Architecture degree from Syracuse University before obtaining a Master of Science degree in Architecture and Urban Design from Columbia University. He has taught at Columbia University since 1985. In 1988, Kolatan and MacDonald founded Kolatan/MacDonald Studio.
Lynn, Greg	Greg Lynn has taught throughout the United States and Europe and is presently a studio professor at the University of California at Los Angeles. Along with Hani Rashid and students from Columbia University, he and his UCLA students represented the United States American Pavilion in the 7th International Exhibition of Architecture at the Venice Biennale,

where his own work was also featured in the Italian and Austrian pavilions. He is the author of several books, including: *Folds, Bodies and Blobs: Collected Essays* (1998), *Animate FORM* (1999), and the forthcoming *Embryological House*. He graduated cum laude from Miami University of Ohio in 1986 with a Bachelor's degree in Philosophy and Environmental Design. He received a Master of Architecture degree from Princeton University in 1988.

MacDonald, William	see KOLATAN/MACDONALD
Martin, Reinhold	Reinhold Martin has been an Assistant Professor of Architecture at Columbia University since 1997. He is also a partner in the firm of Martin/Baxi Architects and an editor of the journal *Grey Room*. His writings have appeared in a variety of publications and he is the coauthor, with Kadambari Baxi, of *Entropia*, a book documenting their collaborative theoretical projects, which have been exhibited internationally. He is also the author of *Architecture and the Organizational Complex*, a forthcoming book on organizational systems in corporate architecture during the postwar period, to be published by The MIT Press.
McLeod, Mary	Mary McLeod is an Associate Professor of Architecture at Columbia University, where she teaches architecture history and theory, and occasionally design studios. Her research and publications have focused on the history of the modern movement and on contemporary architecture theory, examining issues concerning the connections between architecture and ideology. Her articles have appeared in *Assemblage*, *Oppositions*, *Art Journal*, *AA Files*, and *JSAH*, as well as numerous anthologies. She has recently completed editing a book on the French designer Charlotte Perriand.
Meyers, Victoria	see HANRAHAN + MEYERS
Rashid, Hani	see ASYMPTOTE
Reiser, Jesse	see REISER + UMEMOTO
Reiser + Umemoto Jesse Reiser and Nanako Umemoto	Jesse Reiser and Nanako Umemoto have practiced in New York City as Reiser + Umemoto RUR Architecture P.C. since 1986. An internationally recognized architectural firm, Reiser + Umemoto has built projects at a wide range of scales, from furniture design to residential and commercial structures to landscape design. The firm was awarded the Chrysler Award for Excellence in Design in 1999. Jesse Reiser currently teaches at Princeton University. He received his Bachelor of Architecture degree from The Cooper Union for the Advancement of Art and Science and completed his Master of Architecture degree at the Cranbrook Academy of Art. He was a fellow of the American Academy in Rome in 1985. Architect and landscape architect Nanako Umemoto graduated from Cooper Union following studies at the School of Urban Design of the Osaka University of Art.

Tschumi, Bernard

Bernard Tschumi has been Dean of the Graduate School of Architecture, Planning and Preservation at Columbia University since 1988. First known as a theorist, he exhibited and published *The Manhattan Transcripts* (1981) and wrote *Architecture and Disjunction* (1994), a series of theoretical essays. In 1983, he won the prestigious competition to design the Parc de la Villette in Paris, France. He established his Paris office in 1983, followed by his New York office in 1988. Recent projects in the United States include Lerner Hall Student Center at Columbia University and the Museum for African Art in New York City, currently in design.

Umemoto, Nanako

see REISER + UMEMOTO

Wigley, Mark

Mark Wigley is a Professor of Architecture and the Director of Advanced Studios at Columbia University. From 1987 to 1999 he taught at Princeton University. He received his professional and doctoral education in architecture at the University of Auckland, New Zealand. Mark Wigley is the author of numerous books and articles on modern architecture and contemporary theory, including *The Architecture of Deconstruction: Derrida's Haunt* (1993), *White Walls, Designer Dresses: The Fashioning of Modern Architecture* (1995), and *Constant's New Babylon: The Hyper-Architecture of Desire* (1998). He recently co-edited *The Activist Drawing: Retracing Situationist Architectures from Constant's New Babylon to Beyond* (2001).

Photograph Credits